THE

CRIMINAL

JUSTICE

CLUB

———

A Career Prosecutor
Takes on the Media—and More

WALT LEWIS

Walbar Books – Montrose, California

Published by Walbar Books, 2029 Verdugo Blvd. #726, Montrose, California 91020.
Visit Walbar Books at www.walbarbooks.com and www.criminaljusticeclub.net

Publisher's Cataloging-in-Publication
(Provided by Quality Books, Inc.)

Lewis, Walt, 1936-
    The criminal justice club : a career prosecutor takes
    on the media--and more / by Walt Lewis. -- 1st ed.
    p. cm.
    Includes bibliographical references and index.
    Library of Congress Control Number: 2007925499
    ISBN-13: 978-0-9787870-0-4
    ISBN-10: 0-9787870-0-5
    1. Lewis, Walt, 1936- 2. Public prosecutors--
California--Los Angeles County--Biography. 3. Criminal
justice, Administration of--California. 4. Mass media
and criminal justice--California.   I. Title.
II. Title: Career prosecutor takes on the media--and more.

KF373.L47A3 2006   345.794'93'092

                          QBI06-600294

First Edition

Printed on acid-free paper
Manufactured in the United States of America

Book interior by www.KarenRoss.com

To the memory of Lois Haro, who was murdered

October 18, 1988 in Pasadena, California;

to Lois' husband Tony, Lois' father, Professor Herb Purnell;

and to the memory of Lois' mother, Elsie Purnell.

CONTENTS

ABOUT THE AUTHOR

In my youth and throughout law school, and even as a young prosecutor, I was the typical, predictable liberal. I was raised by my mother to believe in the essential goodness of mankind. I later came to learn that this idea of basic goodness was a core belief of the liberal community of which I grew up to be a proud member and advocate. If mankind is basically good, the reasoning goes, it is just a matter of learning how to rehabilitate criminals who repeatedly hurt people so they can be restored to be the good people they naturally are.

In law school, I was one of the most politically liberal students in my 1964 graduating class. In the 1960s, my heroes were Jack and Bobby Kennedy and Martin Luther King Jr. I participated in a civil rights demonstration in the street in front of Los Angeles City Hall while holding hands singing "We Shall Overcome." I joined the ACLU. My favorite United States Supreme Court justices were such outstanding liberals as Earl Warren, Hugo Black, William Brennan, and William O. Douglas. Reading the opinions of these legal giants in law school was really exciting—especially their First Amendment decisions. Although my political philosophy has changed a good deal, with regard to First Amendment issues and my commitment to civil rights, my views have not changed.

I was taught to believe that criminals were mostly sick people with low self-esteem. After passing the bar exam, I decided I wanted to defend minorities, the poor, and the disadvantaged. Not only was I vehemently against the death penalty, I was also against locking people up. I could not understand why any fair-minded, reasonable person would want to put someone in prison for years instead of rehabilitating him and enabling him to live in society as a good citizen. After all, we were dealing with people who were all fundamentally good. No matter that they had murdered, raped, robbed, and beaten innocent people—often repeatedly. It was, I thought, simply a matter of rehabilitating them.

My liberalism was so deeply rooted, it took me a long time to accept the fact that a great many of the violent and career criminals I prosecuted were not "sick," did not suffer from low self-esteem, enjoyed committing their crimes and inflicting pain upon their victims, and felt no remorse for the pain they inflicted. Still, while on the road to that acceptance, I continued to make excuses for them. For example, I would assert the often-heard psychiatric-sounding line that "The outward bravado of these violent criminals was just a cover for a frightened, immature person who suffered mightily from low self-esteem." Those whom I was taught to respect kept saying this, so I thought it must be true. It was difficult for me to accept that there were people out there, and not just a few, who would constitute a continuing threat to others and who were beyond help. I know, it sounds presumptuous to proclaim any person is beyond help, but after 32 years as a deputy district attorney, I have no reluctance in saying it.

I thought the best way to learn the tricks of police and prosecutors was to become a prosecutor for a couple of years. Then I would take this knowledge into my private law practice to help the "real victims" of society, the poor and minorities and, yes, the criminals. So, in 1965, I joined the Los Angeles City Attorney's Office.

After a few months, my deeply entrenched, preconceived ideas about the supposedly evil, racist criminal justice system slowly began to change. My experiences as a deputy city attorney were not what I had expected. Could it be, I wondered, that nearly everything I had seen on my favorite television shows in the 1950s and '60s, *Perry Mason* with Raymond Burr, and *The Defenders*, with E.G. Marshall, was false or misleading? Every week for nine years in the 1950s and '60s, the viewing public saw criminal defense attorney Perry Mason brilliantly defend an innocent man or woman wrongfully charged with murder. The prosecutor was always the villain trying to obstruct justice. The real murderer (never the defendant) always blurted out a confession from the witness stand or from the spectator section of the courtroom.

As a deputy city attorney, I prosecuted hundreds of drunk driving (DUI) cases and other misdemeanors. I began to understand that I was on the right side—if being on the side of the truth is being on the right side. I discovered that I liked being on the side of the truth. But as a deputy city attorney I could only prosecute misdemeanors. I wanted a bigger challenge—to prosecute felony cases. So, in 1968, I joined the Los Angeles County District Attorney's Office and became a deputy district attorney.

Although my parental and media-influenced liberal resolve continued to crumble, I had such an emotional attachment to my liberal philosophy that I remained a Democrat and voted consistently for Democrats for another twenty-seven years—to the mid-1990s. One of the reasons for finally changing my party registration was the pervasive bias of the media, which I was able to recognize mainly because of my experiences as a deputy DA.

For a more extensive autobiography, see "More About the Author" at the end of the book.

INTRODUCTION

This is a story I was waiting for someone else to write. It is a story about the criminal justice system from the perspective of a career prosecutor. It is a story that needs to be told because the media does a poor job of giving the public accurate information about how the system works. And for most people, the media is the only source of knowledge about the criminal justice system. This book reveals how the system really works. It is also a critique of a media driven by such a pervasive liberal bias that the public is often misinformed.

Otherwise well-educated people, including television anchors, lack basic knowledge of the criminal justice system. I point out many examples, over the years, of instances in which the media has misled the public, causing many to believe the criminal justice system is unfair, unreasonable, racist, and unduly harsh. *The Criminal Justice Club* is a rebuttal to this media misinformation, and also seeks to educate the reader about the criminal justice system and the roles of the players within the system. Some of these players comprise what I call the "Criminal Justice Club," because only these Club members know how the system *really* works. As a result of this shared knowledge, there often exists a camaraderie between prosecutors and criminal defense attorneys even though we are on opposite sides of a case.

It is also my personal story, an unlikely story of a kid growing up in Hollywood, California, the only child of divorced parents in the entertainment industry, a high school dropout who once worked the night shift on an automobile assembly line, delivered liquor on the Sunset Strip in Hollywood, became a civil rights demonstrator, ACLU member, a lawyer and finally a career prosecutor in the Los Angeles County District Attorney's Office. It is also the story of my conversion from a young liberal, who always sympathized with the criminal, into an advocate for crime victims and for longer sentences for violent and career criminals. This conversion was partly the result of my witnessing the suffering of crime victims and their families throughout my career as a deputy district attorney.

I include several of my cases and experiences as a deputy DA: some humorous, some gratifying, some heartbreaking, some frustrating. One of the realities of the system is that relatively few crimes are ever solved by the police. Of the crimes that are "solved" by an arrest of a suspect, DAs in L.A. County refuse to file charges in about 30% to 40% of these cases. Thus, prosecutors in Los Angeles County charge suspects with only a small fraction of the crimes committed.

The Criminal Justice Club:

- Exposes the lack of truth in sentencing and reveals the large differences between the sentences pronounced by the judge and reported in the media, on the one hand, and the actual time criminals *really* serve in jails and prisons.

- Reveals that from 1965 through 1978, the state of California paid its counties $4,000 for each convicted felon who was *not* sentenced to prison, thus avoiding for many years the necessity of having to spend hundreds of millions of dollars building new prisons. Under this plan, called "The Probation Subsidy Act," many thousands of violent and career criminals were repeatedly released back to the streets after each felony conviction.

- Commends women's groups for demanding and achieving significant reforms in the areas of sexual assault, child molestation, domestic violence, and drunk driving in the 1970s and 1980s.

- Shows how California's criminal justice system has undergone dramatic reform since 1978. Most of the credit goes to California's initiative process, an exercise in direct democracy

1

THE CRIMINAL
JUSTICE CLUB-AND
THE POLICE

Much of the information in this book cannot be learned from reading newspapers or watching television—with rare exceptions.

The truth is, the courtroom part of the criminal justice system, the part that starts when the DA files criminal charges, is only understood by the members of a very exclusive group which I call the Criminal Justice Club.

The members of this Club are the deputy district attorneys, deputy public defenders, private criminal defense attorneys, criminal court judges, and the career criminals who have been through the system many times. Many of these career criminals are quite sophisticated about how the system works.

I do not include police officers in this exclusive Club for two reasons: The most obvious reason is that the role of the police officer in the system precedes, for the most part, the filing of charges by the DA. The other reason is that police officers receive very little training about court proceedings and the roles of the judge, jury, prosecutor, and defense attorney. Consequently, most police officers, other than the most seasoned detectives, have little understanding of what deputy DAs and criminal defense attorneys do for a living or what criminal trials are really all about—except for what they, like everyone else, see on television and read in the newspapers.

Relatively few police officers have ever sat through an entire felony jury trial. Therefore, few police officers have ever heard a prosecutor make an opening statement to the jury. Most have not

seen a defense attorney cross examine a victim or witnesses in front
of a jury. They have never heard the prosecutor and defense
attorney make their final arguments to the jury at the end of the
trial. Nor have they heard the judge instruct the jury on the law.
Police officers are largely unaware how little prison or jail time
convicted criminals actually serve. Members of the Criminal Justice
Club, including the career criminals who have sat through their
own jury trials, understand the courtroom part of the system far
better than the average police officer. And the Club member knows
that the sentence pronounced by the judge in court and reported in
the media is far greater than the amount of jail or prison time the
defendant will actually serve.

One reason for the typical police officer's comparative lack of
knowledge in these areas is that police departments will not pay
their officers to watch a jury trial when the officers are not waiting
to testify. Court proceedings are only a small part of police training.
Police department brass may not realize how important such training can be because they themselves have never had such training.
One reason such training is important, especially for detectives, is
that watching how defense attorneys attack police investigations in
nearly every case would help both officers and detectives conduct
better investigations. Also, watching even a few jury trials would
help police officers see the trial from the perspective of a juror.
It might also help them, as investigators, to anticipate the defense
attorney's best defense, i.e., the defense story most likely to create a
reasonable doubt of the suspect's guilt. Observing some jury trials
would help detectives become better investigators by highlighting
the weaknesses in the cases they investigate.

In California, police officers are exempted from jury service.
If watching a jury trial is never made a part of police training, police
officers will likely *never* see a jury trial—at least not until they retire.
I've had more than one investigating officer (I/O to Club members)
who sat with me at the counsel table (which is the practice in felony

trials) throughout a murder trial tell me how much he learned, and that he wished he had had this experience years before.

When you finish reading this book, you will know far more about the workings of the criminal justice system than the vast majority of the general public, including most police officers.

2

ROLES OF THE PLAYERS IN THE CRIMINAL JUSTICE SYSTEM

You will have a much easier time understanding this book if you have a basic understanding of the roles the police, the judge, the jury, the prosecutor, and the defense attorney each play in the system. Many of you may think you already know how the system works. After all, you have been watching courtroom drama shows on television for years, perhaps even the O.J. Simpson trial. But, after reading this book, you will see there is much you did not know—unless, of course, you are already a Club member.

THE POLICE

The role of the police in the criminal justice system is to maintain order, respond to crime scenes, collect and preserve evidence, interview witnesses, make arrests, interrogate suspects, write reports, and present the cases to the District Attorney for the filing of criminal charges. Prosecutors depend on police detectives to investigate felony crimes and build cases sufficiently strong for a DA to determine there is enough evidence to convince twelve reasonable jurors that the person arrested is guilty. But police power is limited. In California, the police can hold a felony suspect in jail for only 48 hours. If the DA has not filed charges within this 48-hour period, the suspect must be released. After the DA files criminal charges, the "suspect" is then referred to as the "defendant." The important thing to remember is that the police cannot officially charge anyone with a felony crime. I mention this because the media often report that the police "charged" the suspect with murder, robbery, etc. This is not true. Only prosecutors, who, of course, are all attorneys, can charge someone with a felony.

THE JUDGE

Judges have complete control over criminal proceedings. In a jury trial, the role of the judge is to make sure the jury only hears legally admissible evidence. The judge, applying the laws of evidence, rules on objections made by the attorneys throughout the trial. For example, an attorney may object to what he believes is a legally improper question asked of a witness by the opposing attorney. The judge instructs the jury on the law applicable to that case. In short, the judge's role in the system is to make sure everyone plays by the rules. The judge also sentences the defendant if the jury (or the judge in a "court" trial) finds the defendant guilty. In a jury trial, the judge has no power to determine which witnesses are telling the truth, or which witnesses are lying or mistaken, or what the facts are. That is the function of the jury.

Sometimes the defendant does not want to plead guilty, but also does not want a jury trial. In that case, the defendant can give up his right to a jury trial and permit a judge to hear the evidence from both sides. In such cases, the judge determines whether the defendant is guilty or not guilty. This is called a "court" or "bench" trial.

THE JURY

The jury's role is to carefully listen to and consider the *evidence* in the case. *Evidence* consists of testimony under oath from the witness stand and physical exhibits, i.e., any tangible thing, such as a gun, a letter or a tape recording that the judge *admits* into evidence. An agreement between attorneys as to certain facts, called a *stipulation*, if accepted by the judge, is also *evidence* in the case. It is important for jurors to understand that nothing the attorneys say in the courtroom, other than a stipulation, is *evidence*. Stipulations are commonly entered into between attorneys. For example, if the expected testimony of a defense witness is not in dispute, rather than force that witness to come to court, the defense attorney might ask the DA to stipulate to his testimony, that is, to agree to what the witness would say on the witness stand. The exact terms of the stipulation are read into the record in front of the jury. I always agreed to a stipulation offered by the defense attorney regarding the testimony of a defense witness, unless I felt the need to cross examine that witness. Defense attorneys would most often accommodate me when I asked them to enter into a stipulation. Of course, there would not be a stipulation if the witness was crucial.

In California, the jury is obligated to follow the judge's instructions on the law whether or not they agree with the law. When the jurors begin their deliberations, they will have with them in the jury room the instructions on the law the judge read to them in the courtroom.

The jury is instructed that in arriving at their verdict, they must not be influenced by pity or sympathy for the defendant, nor by prejudice or bias against the defendant because he has been arrested or charged with a crime. The jury is instructed to conscientiously consider and weigh the evidence, apply the law, and reach a just verdict regardless of the consequences. That means jurors are prohibited from considering punishment or penalty in arriving at their verdict—except, of course, in the penalty phase of a death-penalty case. A juror can be removed from the case if, on his own, he visits the scene of the crime, consults with outside experts or law books, or refuses to follow the law or deliberate with his fellow jurors. The judge also instructs the jury not to discuss the case with any person other than a fellow juror, and not even with a fellow juror until the start of deliberations when all jurors are present in the jury room.

THE PROSECUTOR

The prosecutor, whether he is called state's attorney, deputy district attorney, or deputy city attorney, represents the People of the state. As a deputy DA, I represented the "People of the State of California." In court we refer to the DA's side as "The People," as in, "Your honor, the People call John Jones," meaning the DA is asking John Jones to take the witness stand. The prosecutor's initial role is to make the decision whether to file charges or to reject the filing of charges.

I believe few people outside the Criminal Justice Club know that deputy district attorneys in Los Angeles County reject 30% to 40% of all cases presented to the DA by the police. That means we tell the police to release from jail 30% to 40% of all felony suspects they have arrested, including suspects arrested for murder, robbery, rape, kidnapping, burglary, forgery, child molestation, narcotics, theft, and fraud crimes.

It is not uncommon for the DA and the police to have an adversarial relationship at the time the police investigator presents the case to the DA for the purpose of filing charges. After all, the police investigator assigned to the case has often worked hard investigating the case, and he does not want to hear a DA tell him his case is being rejected and to release the suspect—especially when the police officer believes strongly that the suspect is guilty of the crime.

Why do DAs reject so many cases that the police believe are good, solid cases? The police would not have arrested the suspect if they had not believed they had a case strong enough to be filed by the DA. In fact, DAs agree with the police that of the 30% to 40% of the cases they reject, the great majority of these suspects are guilty of the crimes for which they were arrested.

The reason DAs reject so many cases for the filing of criminal charges is not that DAs sympathize with criminals or are too lazy to prosecute them. It is because DAs are bound by many legal and ethical rules, and one of these ethical rules says a DA cannot file criminal charges against a suspect just because she believes the suspect is guilty. (Again, today most L.A. County DAs are women.)

Before a DA can ethically charge a suspect with a crime, she must believe, based on her training and experience, that with the available, *admissible* evidence, and after anticipating the most likely defense, she will be able to convince all twelve people on the jury that the defendant is guilty of the crime charged beyond a reasonable doubt.

This ethical rule dictates that only the cases with the strongest evidence of a defendant's guilt are filed. This is a powerful safeguard against prosecuting an innocent person. As a result of this high standard for filing criminal charges, with which I agree, many suspects who are guilty of very serious crimes are permitted to go free.

If I had to sum up in just a few words what the criminal justice system is all about, I would give this answer: "We need 12, they need only one." That is, the defense attorney only needs to persuade *one* juror to vote "not guilty" to prevent a conviction. The DA needs to convince *all twelve* jurors to vote "guilty" to get a conviction. That is it in a nutshell. For both the DA and the defense attorney, everything else revolves around this central fact. Any jury vote that is less than unanimous is called a "hung jury." When a jury "hangs," the case is usually reset for a new trial—unless only one or two jurors voted for conviction. Most of those cases where the jury hangs 11-1 or 10-2 in favor of acquittal are dismissed. Juries which hang 11 to 1 or 10 to 2 in favor of conviction are not uncommon in Los Angeles County. These cases will likely be retried. Of the hung-jury cases that are retried, about 75% of these defendants are found guilty by the second jury.

I have no doubt, after having dealt with police officers from many different police departments on a daily basis for my entire career as a prosecutor, that most police officers don't think about the fact that twelve ordinary people, the jurors, hold the real power in the criminal justice system. But the DAs, the defense attorneys, and the career-criminal defendants certainly understand this.

The lesson here for police officers is that it would be very helpful to the DA, and the system, if, while they are conducting their investigations, they keep in mind that twelve people from the community may be critiquing them and second-guessing what they did during their investigation, and the defense attorney will be trying to attack just about everything the police did. Many people witnessed an attack on the police in the O.J. Simpson case. Attacking the police investigation by the defense attorney, i.e., putting the police on trial, is a favorite defense tactic used in just about every criminal jury trial.

Inasmuch as the DA, (i.e., the prosecutor) must convince all twelve jurors of the defendant's guilt beyond a reasonable doubt, it follows that the most important job of the DA in any trial is to select a good jury. The DA and the defense attorney are looking for very different types of people to serve on the jury. As a DA, I always wanted intelligent, well-balanced, successful people who would be able to follow the law and the evidence and return a verdict according to the evidence.

Defense attorneys normally want jurors who would feel sympathetic towards the defendant, or who might identify with the defendant. They look for those who may not be able to handle the responsibility of voting to find a person guilty, regardless of the evidence presented, or who may see the defendant as a victim simply because he is in jail charged with a crime.

As a DA, I liked homeowners and people with children—people who have something to protect. The problem is that many intelligent, well-balanced, successful homeowners with children have been able to get excused from jury service. The late comedian, Henny Youngman, asked his audience, "How would you like to be a defendant and be judged by twelve people who were too dumb to get out of jury duty?" As a DA, I looked at it from another perspective: how would you like to be the prosecutor and know that many of the most intelligent, successful people have been able to get themselves excused from jury duty?

The law allows the DA and the defense attorney the opportunity to question the prospective jurors and to excuse a certain number of them if it is believed they would not be good jurors for their side. This process of jury selection is called "voir dire," meaning, "to speak the truth"—commonly pronounced "vor dyer," but more accurately "vwar deer."

The DA and the defense attorney have no idea of the hidden biases and prejudices of the prospective jurors. Some may not like prosecutors, or police, or anyone they see as an authority figure. Of course, they are not likely to admit their biases in court. Remember, the defense attorney only needs to pick one juror who, for whatever reason, cannot or will not vote to convict, regardless of the evidence.

There are jurors who, for a number of reasons, find it very difficult to convict anyone of a crime. I know of many cases where jurors said they could not vote to find the defendant guilty for reasons not based upon the evidence such as:

- "I just cannot vote to convict a brother" (racial) or,

- "I just don't think it is our place to sit in judgment on another human being" (religious) or,

- "I'm afraid, what if his gang comes after me" (fear) or,

- "I don't like that law and cannot follow that law" (non-compliance with the judge's instructions) or,

- "I just cannot vote guilty. What will happen to the defendant's wife and children if we convict him?"(sympathy) or,

- After an 11-1 hung jury in which the lone holdout juror said, "He [the defendant] seems too nice to have done what the witnesses say he did."

I remember an 11-1 hung jury in favor of a guilty verdict in which the lone holdout juror refused to deliberate, sat apart from his fellow jurors and read the Bible throughout the jury deliberations. We were not made aware of this until too late, that is, until after the judge declared a mistrial. The deputy DA had to try the case again, resulting in a guilty verdict.

In the mid-1990s, there was a movement in California to amend the state Constitution to permit convictions and acquittals in criminal cases, other than capital cases, with a 10-2 jury verdict. A Field poll at the time found that convictions based on non-unanimous juries were supported by 71% of Californians. If the movement had been successful, we would have joined Oregon and Louisiana, which, for many years, have permitted nonunanimous jury verdicts, except in death penalty cases. England has permitted 10-2 jury verdicts in criminal cases since 1967. The proponents of this measure did not have sufficient funds to finance the collection of the signatures required to place the issue on the ballot and the effort collapsed. The U.S. Supreme Court has held that nonunanimous jury verdicts in criminal cases do not violate the Constitution.

My own experience with 11-1 hung juries, that is, where 11 voted for guilt, has been that the lone holdout was basing his "not guilty" vote on something other than the evidence. Many lone-holdout jurors find themselves the center of attention and in a position of power they have rarely, if ever, experienced. Society pays a big price to give the lone holdout this feeling of power. Harold J. Rothwax, author of *Guilty: The Collapse of Criminal Justice* (1996), stated that in his experience, "In every instance…where the jury was split ten to two or eleven to one, the holdout was not being rational."

Jonathan Turley is a criminal defense attorney and a professor at George Washington University Law School. In an op-ed piece published in the *L.A. Times* on March 31, 2004, Professor Turley said, "The fact is that in the nearly 8,000 instances of hung juries each year in this country, single holdouts are often not inspired but irrational; not catalysts of justice but obstacles to it." A California jury study found that 12.2% of jury trials in criminal cases result in hung juries. It is very expensive to retry that many cases following a hung jury. What often happens is, rather than retry the case, the DA will allow the defendant to plead guilty to a less serious charge. That is why a hung jury is considered a victory for the defense.

The *Los Angeles Times* reported in August 2004 that Derrick Todd Lee, a serial killer in Louisiana, was found guilty of murdering a 21-year-old woman.[1] Lee had been linked to the murders of seven women by DNA. The defense attorney never refuted the DNA evidence. Nevertheless, one juror voted "not guilty." But because Louisiana has a 10-2 jury verdict law in criminal cases (except for death penalty cases), the 11-1 jury verdict was sufficient to convict Lee of second-degree murder. In California, we would have had to either retry the case or permit Lee to plead guilty to a lesser charge.

If the deputy DA makes a mistake and chooses one juror who is not able to return a guilty verdict, regardless of the evidence, and we are unable to discover this before the jury hangs, the judge will declare a mistrial; perhaps several weeks or even months of trial will have been lost, and we must start all over again. Sometimes other jurors will report to the judge that one of the jurors refuses to discuss the case with his fellow jurors or follow the law.

In such a case, the DA will request that the judge excuse that juror and replace him with an alternate juror. The role of the alternate juror is to take the place of a juror should he or she become ill, or, for whatever reason, can no longer serve as a juror.

The most obvious role of the prosecutor is to present evidence to the jury by calling witnesses to the witness stand and asking them questions, introducing physical exhibits into evidence, such as the murder weapon, fingerprint evidence, DNA analysis, etc. One of the deputy DA's most important jobs is to cross-examine defense witnesses and the defendant, if he chooses to testify. Finally, the DA argues the case to the jury in an attempt to persuade them that the evidence they have heard and seen is sufficient to find the defendant guilty beyond a reasonable doubt. The deputy DA's role is to help the jury ascertain the true facts surrounding the crime. The DA is required by legal ethics to present to the jury only what she believes to be the truth.

THE DEFENSE ATTORNEY

The role of the defense attorney in the criminal justice system is very different than the role of the prosecutor. The public will not likely be made aware of the defense attorney's role in the criminal justice system from watching television or reading newspapers. The defense attorney's job is to get the best possible deal (plea bargain) for his client. The fact that the defense attorney believes, or even knows, his client is guilty of committing the crime is irrelevant. Many years ago, the role of the criminal defense attorney was discussed in a case decided by the U.S. Supreme Court. The message of this case is so instructive that I have included here the relevant excerpt from the 1966 Supreme Court case of *United States v Wade*:[2]

Law enforcement officers have the obligation to convict the guilty and to make sure they do not convict the innocent. They must be dedicated to making the criminal trial a procedure for the ascertainment of the true facts surrounding the commission of the crime. To this extent, our so-called adversary system is not adversary at all; nor should it be. But defense counsel has no comparable obligation to ascertain or present the truth. Our system assigns him a different mission. He must be and is interested in preventing the conviction of the innocent, but, absent a voluntary plea of guilty, we also insist that he defend his client whether he is innocent or guilty. The State has the obligation to present the evidence. Defense counsel need present nothing, even if he knows what the truth is. He need not furnish any witnesses to the police, or reveal any confidences of his client, or furnish any other information to help the prosecution's case. If he can confuse a witness, even a truthful one, or make him appear at a disadvantage, unsure or indecisive, that will be his normal course.

Our interest in not convicting the innocent permits [defense] counsel to put the State to its proof, to put the State's case in the worst possible light, regardless of what he thinks or knows to be the truth. Undoubtedly there are some limits which defense counsel must observe but more often than not, defense counsel will cross-examine a prosecution witness and impeach him if he can, even if he thinks the witness is telling the truth, just as he will attempt to destroy a witness who he thinks is lying. In this respect, as part of our modified adversary system and as part of the duty imposed on the most honorable defense counsel, we countenance or

require conduct which in many instances has little, if
any, relation to the search for truth.

So, when I say the role of the defense attorney in a criminal
case is not to seek the truth, this is not just my opinion. This
concept, as you have just read, is deeply rooted in our criminal law.

The *California Business and Professions Code*, which sets forth
the rules regulating attorneys, provides, as follows:

Section 6068. Duties of Attorney

It is the duty of an attorney:

(a) To support the Constitution and laws of the United
States and of this State.

(b) To maintain the respect due to the courts of justice and
judicial officers.

(c) To counsel or maintain such actions, proceedings or
defenses only as appear to him or her legal or just, *except
the defense of a person charged with a public offense.* (empha-
sis added)

Thus, even the *California Business and Professions Code* states
that the defense used in a criminal case does not have to appear to
the defense attorney to be "just" when defending someone charged
with a crime. To put it bluntly, whatever defense theory or story
which has the best chance of convincing at least one juror that there
is reasonable doubt of the defendant's guilt is the defense that I, as
a deputy DA, would anticipate in a criminal case. And the *California
Business and Professions Code* clearly says the defense attorney is
breaking no rules in using a defense that does not appear to be just.

The only newspaper article I have ever read that accurately
reveals the role of the defense attorney in a criminal trial was written by USC law professor Susan Estrich. In 1988, Professor Estrich
served as a campaign manager for the Democrat candidate

for president, Michael Dukakis. She also served as a spokesperson for Senator John Kerry's bid for president in 2004. Professor Estrich's article was published in the *Los Angeles Times* in 1994 and was titled "Defense Lawyers and Truth: Just Where Do They Meet?"[3] Because Professor Estrich's article so accurately describes the criminal defense attorney's role in a criminal trial, I have included here relevant excerpts:

> Look around the courtroom in a criminal trial and almost everyone is bound by one oath or another to tell the truth: the witnesses, of course; the jury and the judge, bound to find the truth; the prosecutor, whose lying can lead to reversal in the appeals court and at the polls; even members of the press, who can be sued for libel. The one person not pledged to tell the truth, seek the truth, let alone be bound by it, is the defense attorney. For me, the only question that matters in the O.J. Simpson case is whether he did it. Everything turns on that. For Robert L. Shapiro and Johnnie L.Cochran Jr., Simpson's lawyers, nothing turns on it. Their job is to get Simpson off, innocent or guilty. If he's innocent, that means advocating the truth. If he's guilty, it means attacking it.

> Criminal defense lawyers are not supposed to put witnesses on the stand who they know will commit perjury; of course many criminal defense lawyers claim they're incapable of ever really knowing anything. They can't hide the murder weapon in their desk drawers, though they're not obligated to pick it up. Other than that, they're pretty free to obstruct the search for truth in any way they can, within the rules of evidence.

Witnesses are fair game—even if they're telling the truth. So is every piece of evidence, and every scientific test, even if it was accurately performed. You can impeach the person who found the evidence, question whether it was securely maintained, debate the accuracy of the test, undermine the reliability of the lab—even if you know, all the time, that the witness is telling the truth about where he found the evidence, it is your client's hat and the test turned up the right answer. You have an absolute right to libel anyone in the courtroom. The explanation academics offer for the "different mission" [from *United States vs Wade*, above] of criminal lawyers that allows them such latitude with the truth is the adversary system of justice.

The way we find truth, and protect the innocent, in an adversary system of justice is by putting the government to its proof, by arguing each point, each fact.

Certainly, no one questions the right of an attorney to attack the credibility of witnesses who are lying or attack the validity of tests he believes are inaccurate.

No one doubts his right to argue to the jury that lies are lies or that facts are true. No one, in short, is seeking to limit the advocacy of an attorney attacking a prosecution case that is untrue and defending an innocent man.

The harder question is why he is allowed to do these things when their purpose is to obfuscate the truth, to create doubt—and he knows that, or he would if he allowed himself to "know" anything.

Does every man deserve a defense, even if the only ones available are false defenses? How does it make truth-finding better when a lawyer undermines a truthful witness? If the rape victim is telling the truth, do you get to destroy her anyway? How does it help the jury do its job if you tell them that in is out or up is down or lies are truth.

These are not just questions for lawyers to resolve in codes of ethics. More is at stake than just the relationship between a lawyer and his client. This is also about how the criminal justice system works.

I have never seen another article like this outside of law books. Kudos to Professor Estrich for having the courage to write and publish the truth about the role of the defense attorney. Reluctantly, I also give credit to the *Los Angeles Times* for publishing these truths known by few outside the Criminal Justice Club. I say reluctantly, because the *Los Angeles Times* has consistently editorialized against nearly every meaningful reform of the criminal justice system. As I will explain more fully in the following chapters, the *Times* is no friend of crime victims or law enforcement.

What do you think would happen if a defense attorney who believed his client was guilty conceded his client's guilt in front of the jury? This actually happened in a 1991 bank robbery case, *United States of America v Swanson*.[4] The defense lawyer told the jury in closing argument that "The evidence [against my client] was overwhelming and I'm not going to sit here and insult your intelligence." The defense attorney told the federal jury that he did not believe there was a reasonable doubt of his client's guilt of the crime of bank robbery. Not surprisingly, the defendant was convicted. But he appealed, alleging that his attorney abandoned him when he conceded his guilt to the jury.

The federal Ninth Circuit Court of Appeal reversed the defendant's bank robbery conviction and reported the defense attorney to the State Bar of Arizona for the purpose of considering the appropriate discipline for abandoning his client. The lesson from this case is that it does not matter if the defense attorney is convinced of his client's guilt. An attorney is not permitted to tell the jury he believes the evidence is so strong against his client that there is no reasonable doubt of his guilt. If he does concede his client's guilt to the jury, unless it is for a tactical reason, for example, saving him from the death penalty, the conviction will be reversed and the attorney will likely face discipline by the state bar.

This may surprise the reader, but I agree with this decision. A criminal defense attorney should not be permitted to tell the jury that his client, whom he is supposed to be defending, is guilty. As stated previously, our criminal justice system operates under the adversary system. This means the defense attorney is legally obligated to give his client the best possible defense and to argue for his client's acquittal, or perhaps for a reduced charge, or at least hope to hang the jury, even though he believes or knows his client is guilty. Those of us in the Criminal Justice Club understand and accept that this is how our adversary system works. But the media perpetuates the lie that the honorable defense attorney must believe in his client's innocence, thus leaving the implication that if he vigorously defends a client he believes is guilty, he is less than honorable. As you have learned, nothing could be further from the truth.

In July 2004, the *Los Angeles Times* published a story about a rape trial which ended with a hung jury. The three defendants had videotaped the alleged rape of the unconscious victim. In the article, the *Times* stated that "When defense attorneys believe a false rape accusation has been made, their job is to expose that by whatever means necessary—within the boundaries set by the trial judge."[5] Of course, this is a true statement—as far as it goes. But a more forthright statement would have said that when a defense attorney is representing a defendant charged with rape, *or any crime*, the attorney's duty, if he cannot settle the case, is to try to get an acquittal or a hung jury—whether the defendant is innocent or guilty. After all, this is the law. Why do the media continue to mislead the people about the role of the criminal defense attorney?

It would be a mistake for the readers of this book to doubt the personal honor and character of the individual defense attorney simply because his legal and ethical obligations require conduct which, as was stated by the U.S. Supreme Court in *U.S. v Wade*, "has little, if any, relation to the search for truth."

Because the DAs and PDs (deputy public defenders) are both members of the Criminal Justice Club, and we each know and accept our roles in the system, we can be friends. However, I learned from personal experience that non-Club members often do not understand this relationship. In a murder case I was trying, the parents of the murdered woman who saw me in court being friendly with the defense attorney were very hurt. They told me they did not understand how I could be so friendly with the defense attorney who was trying his best to defend their daughter's killer by attacking the People's witnesses on cross-examination and trying to make them appear to be liars. I tried to explain that this is what defense attorneys are supposed to do and that he was a good lawyer.

When I told the parents the defense attorney was really a nice guy, and tried to explain that he was just doing his job, the parents would have none of it. All they saw was the attorney defending one of the men who had kidnapped, robbed, raped, and murdered their beautiful daughter. Frankly, I had not been aware of my own insensitivity. I had been acting friendly with defense attorneys in all my cases, including murder cases, for my entire career. I had not thought how it would affect the close relatives of the victim until they expressed their feelings to me in this case.

When I say a defense attorney is a nice guy, don't misunderstand me. They will try to obliterate my case in front of a jury, but I do not recall being personally attacked verbally by a defense attorney during a jury trial.

How would it work if our adversary system of criminal justice were radically changed to require a criminal defense attorney to join with the deputy DA in the search for truth? Under such a system, the defense attorney would not be permitted to attack witnesses he believed were telling the truth and he, like the DA, could only argue to the jury what he believed was the truth. And if after considering all the evidence in the case, the defense attorney agreed with the prosecutor that his client was guilty, he would be required to tell the jury to find his client guilty—just as in the bank robbery case discussed earlier.

In my judgment, such a system would not be a satisfactory alternative to our present system which, in reality, permits the defense attorney to present the most plausible story, true or not, pointing towards the defendant's innocence or the finding of reasonable doubt. It is then left to the jury to determine whether the defense story leaves them with a reasonable doubt of the defendant's guilt.

I have faith in the current system, having tried jury trials since becoming a deputy city attorney in 1965. I believe most jurors are sophisticated enough to detect sham defenses. However, I must admit that it was not uncommon to see defendants, who we believed were clearly guilty, acquitted by juries. But the fact that guilty defendants are sometimes acquitted is insufficient reason to abandon the adversary system and require criminal defense attorneys to join the DA in the search for truth, although I concede, the idea has plenty of superficial appeal. I have no doubt, however, that such a system would not work in the real world of criminal trials. Consider a scenario in which the defendant tells his attorney he wants a jury trial—and his attorney responds, "OK, but if you have a jury trial, I will tell the jury I believe you are guilty." Winston Churchill said that "Democracy is the worst form of government except for all those others that have been tried." The same might be said of our criminal justice system.

So, what does all this mean? It means just what was said in the Supreme Court case of *U.S. v Wade*: that in a criminal prosecution, the role "of the most honorable defense attorney has little, if any, relation to the search for truth," because seeking the truth is not the "mission" of the defense attorney. As Professor Estrich said, "Their job is to get [their client] off, innocent or guilty."

I would guess that the most common question non-Club members ask defense attorneys is: "How can you defend a person if you believe he is guilty?" The defense attorney's truthful answer to that question would go something like this: "It is not my responsibility to determine whether the defendant committed the crime. That is up to the jury to determine. The laws and ethical rules that regulate the conduct of criminal defense attorneys require us to defend our clients whether they are innocent or guilty. My job, as a defense attorney, is to defend my client to the best of my ability, and if the DA and I are unable to arrive at a satisfactory settlement, then my duty is to provide my client with the best defense available and to use my legal and persuasive skills to get my client off, or at least a hung jury, regardless of whether he is innocent or guilty. This is how our criminal justice system works. This is how our system has always worked in this country. This is the law. I have never known a criminal defense attorney who would represent a defendant only if he thought his client was innocent."

3

MEDIA MISINFORMATION

"*How* can you defend a person if you believe he is guilty?" This question continues to be asked of criminal defense attorneys by otherwise well-informed, educated people. It is one of the reasons I felt compelled to write this book. In these times, when we are all subject to a constant information overload, I have often wondered how it can be true that well-informed people are so naive about the criminal justice system that they believe a good percentage of the defendants charged with crimes are innocent. The answer, of course, is that movies, television, liberal politicians, and the print media continue to perpetuate this myth—which casts doubt on the integrity of the criminal justice system. The criminal justice system is a matter of great public interest and should be presented fairly and accurately in the media—which is certainly not the case. Our tax dollars pay for the system, and those who pay the taxes are entitled to be told the truth. There is no good reason to continue the myth that the prisons are filled with innocent people.

Media misinformation about the criminal justice system is common. Sometimes it is subtle. Sometimes it is flagrant. In August 2003, I was watching the *Bill Maher Show*—a liberal comedian and television talk-show host. One of his guests was Willie Brown, then Mayor of San Francisco. Next to the governor, Willie Brown was the most powerful politician in California during his fifteen-year reign (1980-1995) as Assembly Speaker. Also on the show was former Georgia Republican congressman, Bob Barr. Bill Maher raised the issue of black crime. He cited a rather startling statistic that 12% of all black men between the ages of twenty and thirty-four were currently in prison as compared to 1.2% of white men. Bob Barr responded, "It tells you that we have a very serious problem with a lot of young black men in this country." Willie Brown, a black man, immediately countered, "No, it tells you that you have a very serious problem with the criminal justice system." The audience applauded enthusiastically. Bob Barr said, "Blaming it on the criminal justice system doesn't address the problem. Why are they there in the first place?" Willie Brown responded, "They are there because the laws are all screwed up. They are there because those who administer the laws are screwed up even more." Bob Barr responded, "They are not there because they are innocent." Willie Brown proclaimed loudly, "They *are* there because they are innocent. They are victims—absolute cold-blooded victims."

This flagrant example of demagoguery does a great disservice to the public. After all, Willie Brown, an attorney, knows better. He is, or at least was, a role model for many young people, especially young black children and adolescents. They should not be fed this awful lie that most black men in prison are innocent—and worse yet—victims. The media is irresponsible for going along with this lie. Sure, Willie Brown has a First Amendment right to say just about anything he pleases. But why should he not be held accountable by the media for disseminating such ludicrous untruths?

What if a white mayor of a major U.S. city said of the executives of Enron, WorldCom and other white, corporate crooks who have been convicted in huge corporate scandals that *they* are all innocent? Does anyone believe the media would let him get away with that? Of course not! There would be a media frenzy and a public outcry. And rightly so. Why does Willie Brown get a pass? Is it simply because Willie Brown is black? If so, why isn't this racism? And if it is racism, why aren't we condemning it?

Willie Brown's claim that all or a substantial number of the black men in prison are innocent, and are themselves victims, does a great injustice to those who have devoted their professional lives to achieving justice in the criminal justice system.

But Willie Brown should not be singled out as the sole example of racial demagoguery. According to a *Washington Times* story published July 14, 2004, Senator John Kerry, in a speech about education to a predominantly black audience, said there are more blacks in prison than in college. "That's unacceptable, but it's not their fault," he said. This is the liberal line: "It's not their fault." The liberals look upon blacks as helpless to determine their own destiny without the assistance of government preferences and programs. I sense an increasing number of blacks are feeling insulted by the historic patronization by the Left. In commenting on Kerry's, "It's not their fault" quote, conservative black columnist Walter E. Williams wrote (Townhall.com, August 4, 2004), "...his [Kerry's] vision differs little from one that holds that blacks are a rudderless, victimized people who cannot control their destiny and whose best hope depends upon the benevolence of white people."

Another flagrant example of media misinformation was aired on the *Larry King Show* December 21, 2005. Bob Costas was the guest host. The show featured four men who were wrongly convicted but later exonerated by DNA evidence. Also on the show were criminal defense attorney Mark Geragos and Mary Fulginiti, introduced as a former federal prosecutor. It appeared to the viewing audience that this was a match up between the points of view of a prosecutor and defense attorney. What was omitted from Ms. Fulginiti's introduction was that she, like Geragos, is also a criminal defense attorney, according to a February 5, 2005 article in the *New York Times*. Bob Costas should have told his audience that they were to hear from two criminal defense attorneys—and that one, Ms.Fulginiti, *had been* a federal prosecutor. Or, better yet, he should have invited a career prosecutor to counter Mark Geragos.

Geragos, after saying our criminal justice system was the best in the world, claimed that "In every courtroom, in every state in the union, there are terrible injustices that are taking place." Geragos said, "There are people being wrongly convicted on a daily, if not weekly, basis— and it's awful." He said that judges, whom he referred to as "DAs in a robe," often do the bidding of the DAs. He claimed that California judges, because they have to run for election every six years, are intimidated by DAs. Geragos claimed to have seen studies that say up to 20% of defendants are wrongly convicted in this country. He said that [statistic] would not surprise him in the least. Geragos said that prosecutors take an oath to seek truth and justice, but that "prosecutors ultimately don't care about justice."

Although the other criminal defense attorney (former federal prosecutor Fulginiti) was shaking her head in disbelief during much of Geragos' diatribe, she offered very little rebuttal to his irresponsible and outrageous charges. As I was listening to Geragos' preposterous claims, I reflected that in my youth, I would have readily believed such drivel. I wanted to believe it. I have no doubt that thousands, perhaps millions, of Larry King's audience, many of whom are prospective jurors, will accept it as truth. Perhaps this was Geragos' objective. I challenge Mr. Geragos to produce a study from a reputable organization (other than an organization of criminal defense attorneys) that says "up to 20% of defendants are wrongly convicted in this country." Geragos' reckless statements regarding California prosecutors and judges are terribly insulting to judges and also to prosecutors who, throughout their careers, have abided by their ethical duties to seek the truth, follow the law and do justice.

When I first met my wife, we told each other what we did for a living. She was a registered nurse. When I told her I was a deputy DA, it was not long before she asked me how many defendants I had prosecuted who I thought might be innocent. I asked her how she could think that I would prosecute a person I thought might be innocent. She responded, "Surely they are not all guilty." I explained to her that the DA's office rejects a large number of cases presented to us by the police and that we only file criminal charges in those cases where the evidence is so strong that we believe we could convince any twelve reasonable people of the defendant's guilt beyond a reasonable doubt. That explanation did not seem to satisfy her. I decided I liked her, and I did not want to poison a potential relationship before it had a chance to bloom. So, I took the easy way out. I changed the subject. But I did not forget her concern about pairing up with a guy who might be prosecuting innocent people for a living.

Several months later, Barbara and I were on a skiing trip in Mammoth, California. I spotted a deputy public defender and a private criminal defense attorney, both of whom I had known for many years. I told Barbara I wanted her to meet a couple of people, and we skied over to where they were standing. After the introductions, I told my PD friend that I wanted him to settle an issue I had with Barbara. I asked the deputy public defender, who at that time had been a PD for over twenty years, how many defendants charged with serious felonies he had represented. He replied that he had no idea but it was in the thousands. I then asked my PD friend, who happens to be an excellent defense attorney, to tell Barbara how many of these thousands of defendants he thought could possibly have been innocent. He smiled at his friend, then looked at Barbara and held up one hand and said, "Less than the fingers on this hand." She was amazed. She had watched the same television shows and movies and read the same newspapers as I had. How could this be true? But now the information was coming not from the prosecutor but from the defense attorney. She looked at me and I felt I had established instant credibility—which, for a prosecutor, is everything.

There is no greater injustice than when an innocent person is convicted and imprisoned. Even though our Constitution and state laws afford defendants many rights, the system is not perfect. Any system depending on people to make it work, by definition, cannot work perfectly all the time. But miscarriages of justice in Los

Angeles County, that is, where twelve jurors vote to convict an innocent defendant, are rare. When a miscarriage does occur and is discovered, the story hits the front page, and it should.

A University of Michigan Law School study released in April 2004,[6] stated that nationwide, in the fourteen-year period between 1989 and 2003, 328 people who had been convicted of criminal offenses in this country were later found to be innocent—about 23 people per year. This is 23 people per year too many. But it is a tiny fraction of the number of criminals who had been convicted in this country during that period. In 2002 alone, according to the Bureau of Justice Statistics, over one million adults were convicted of felonies in state courts. Many thousands more were convicted of felonies in federal courts.

Deputy district attorneys have a great deal of power to do the right thing. For a person who wants to be a lawyer, but who also needs to believe he or she is on the side which represents the truth, a career as a prosecutor is a great career choice. If a deputy DA has any doubt about a defendant's guilt, she can reinvestigate the case, she can reduce the charges, or she can dismiss the charges.

4

A CASE OF INNOCENCE—
THE LAKE TAHOE BASEBALL ALIBI

I can remember only one case I had where I felt uncomfortable about the defendant's guilt. The defendant was charged with cutting the throat of a homeowner in the city of South Pasadena. The victim's injuries were serious, but he recovered. The victim homeowner positively identified the defendant at the preliminary hearing (see Chapter 5 for a discussion of the preliminary hearing), and testified that several years before the crime occurred he had had a money dispute with the defendant over the charges for a yard clean-up job the defendant had done for the homeowner.

The homeowner testified that on the day of the assault, the defendant came to his door and asked for a glass of water. When the homeowner went to get the water, the defendant entered his house and attacked him, cutting his throat. The case would never have been filed except for the fact that, according to the victim, this was not the first time he had had dealings with the defendant. That is, it was not a case where the crime victim, who had never before seen the defendant, picked the defendant's photo out of a photo line-up—which police and prosecutors call a "six-pack." Such a "one-on-one" ID case, without any corroboration, is invariably rejected by the DA's office. In fact, the victim did pick the defendant's photo from a six-pack, but there was more. The victim told the police that he had had plenty of time to observe the defendant years earlier when he cleaned up the victim's yard. And when the defendant appeared at the victim's door asking for a glass of water, the victim said he immediately recognized him.

When the defendant was arrested in the area a few weeks later, he told the police they had the wrong man, because on the date of the crime he had been in Lake Tahoe, California playing baseball. The police never checked out the defendant's Lake Tahoe alibi, and the filing deputy DA was so impressed by the victim's "positive" ID from a six-pack of photos, and that he recognized defendant from having had dealings with him, he filed the case. From the time I first read the police report, I felt the police should have attempted to verify the defendant's Lake Tahoe alibi before bringing the case to the DA's office for a filing. But remember, the police only have 48 hours to investigate a case after the suspect is arrested. If the DA does not file charges within that 48-hour time limit, the suspect must be released—and Lake Tahoe is a long way from Los Angeles.

I assigned a DA investigator (all of whom are former police officers) to the case. He went to Lake Tahoe to check out the defendant's baseball alibi. My investigator established a solid alibi for the defendant. He interviewed several baseball players on both teams, all of whom said the defendant played the night of the assault. This was corroborated by the inning-by-inning scorecard which was dated and included the defendant's name and showed each at bat. It so happened that in the late innings the game was stopped because of rain. We even corroborated that with the weather bureau. My investigator called me at home from Lake Tahoe and told me we had the wrong guy. The following morning I asked the judge to dismiss the case and the defendant was released.

The ugly part of this story is that the young defense attorney had checked out his client's Lake Tahoe baseball-alibi defense before I did, but rather than tell me, he decided he would wait and surprise me in trial. Meanwhile, his innocent client was sitting in jail. The defense attorney should have told me about his client's alibi defense at his earliest opportunity so I could check it out, dismiss the case, and get his client released from custody.

5

DEFENDANT'S RIGHTS

Our Constitution and state laws make it very difficult to convict a person of a crime, and it should be difficult. Our system goes to great lengths to try to avoid convicting the innocent. To this end, our system of criminal justice affords a defendant many constitutional rights to make sure that a defendant is fully armed to defend against unfounded criminal charges:

- A defendant in a criminal case has a right to a jury trial.

- A defendant has the right to insist that the prosecutor prove his guilt beyond a reasonable doubt to all 12 jurors. As stated earlier, if any one juror is not convinced of the defendant's guilt beyond a reasonable doubt, the defendant cannot be convicted. And don't take the phrase "beyond a reasonable doubt" lightly. Many DAs and defense attorneys who speak to jurors outside the courtroom after they return a "not guilty" verdict have been told by the jurors, "Oh, we believed he was guilty. But we had a reasonable doubt." This may seem contradictory, but it is not. The jury was just following the judge's instructions which say, in effect, that it is not enough for a jury simply to believe the defendant probably committed the crime. If the juror is left with a reasonable doubt about the defendant's guilt, the juror *must* find the defendant "not guilty" even if that juror really believes the defendant is most likely guilty.

- A defendant has the right to a trial which shall be open to the public and the press.

- A defendant is presumed to be innocent. He is not obligated to prove his innocence.

- A defendant charged with a crime has the right to an attorney, and if he cannot afford an attorney, he gets an attorney paid for by the taxpayers—who also pay the DA's salary. In Los Angeles, both the DAs and PDs are county employees. The great majority of defendants charged with felonies in Los Angeles County claim poverty and are represented by public defenders who have limited resources to check out claims by defendants that they cannot afford to hire a private attorney.

- As we have all seen on television innumerable times, a suspect has the right to remain silent. He need not talk to the police or testify at his trial.

- A defendant represented by a PD also has a right to have the tax-payers pay for any expert the PD believes he needs to help his case. For example, if the defense attorney has any question about the accuracy of the results obtained by crime lab technicians, whether it be drug analysis, fingerprints, shoeprints, handwriting analysis or DNA analysis, the defense attorney will ask the judge to appoint an independent expert who will conduct his own tests and report his opinion in confidence to the defense attorney. If the PD is considering a psychiatric defense, he will ask the judge to appoint one or two psychiatrists to examine the defendant at no cost to the defendant.

- A defendant has a right to confront and cross-examine the People's witnesses.

- A defendant has a right to get up on the witness stand and tell his side of the story—but nobody can make him "take the stand" to tell his side of the story or say anything at all. Remember O.J. Simpson? His attorney wisely thought it would be smarter to keep O.J. off the stand so he could not be cross-examined by the DA.

- A defendant has the right to "discovery." That means he can demand from the prosecutor copies of all police reports and lab reports as well as a list of all the witnesses who will be testifying against him, and he has a right to see all the physical evidence that will be used against him in the trial.

- A defendant, of course, has a right to call his own witnesses to testify for him.

- Except for defendants eligible for the death penalty, and cases in which the DA proves to the judge that the defendant would constitute a danger to the public, or to a specific person if released, a defendant has the right to be released from jail on reasonable bail.

The defendant's first court appearance, which must take place within 48 hours after he is arrested, is called the arraignment. It usually takes just a few minutes. At the arraignment, the defendant is handed a copy of the "complaint" filed by the DA which informs him of the charges. At the arraignment, in the great majority of cases, a public defender is appointed to represent the defendant. The defendant then enters a plea of "not guilty," and a date is set for the preliminary hearing (called the "prelim" by Club members) within ten days, unless the defense attorney requests more time to prepare.

A defendant is entitled to a preliminary hearing in every felony case, other than those commenced by a grand jury indictment. The DA's burden of proof at the prelim is only to present enough evidence to cause the judge to have a "strong suspicion" that the defendant committed the charged offenses. Some prelims take as little as a half hour. Typically, they take about 45 minutes to an hour. However, I had a prelim that lasted about five months in which I called 99 witnesses. If the "strong suspicion" threshold is satisfied, the judge "holds the defendant to answer" for trial on the charges.

After the defendant is held to answer, an "information" (similar to the complaint) is filed by the DA within 15 days, typically listing the charges for which the defendant was held to answer at the prelim. He is then arraigned again on the information and invariably again pleads not guilty to the charges in the information. At this second arraignment, he is given a copy of the transcript of the testimony taken at the preliminary hearing. In the typical felony case in Los Angeles County, the judge, at this point, sets a date for a pretrial hearing about two to three weeks hence. At the "pretrial," the defendant has a number of options. If he chooses to have a jury trial or court trial, a trial date will be set, again within two or three weeks. If he chooses to plead guilty or "no contest," he will typically do so at the pretrial hearing. A defendant who pleads "no contest" is saying, in effect, that he will not contest the charges. A plea of no contest, from the Latin, "nolo contendere" ("nolo" to

Club members), has all the same consequences as a guilty plea, but for some defendants, it is easier to say "no contest" than "guilty."

- A defendant has the right to a speedy trial. In California, he has a right to have his trial start no later than sixty days after he is arraigned on the information. In the great majority of cases which are tried before a jury, the defendant will give up his right to a speedy trial, and his attorney will ask the judge for more time to prepare his defense.

I have read many times in the media about a defendant who "had to sit in jail" for many months or even years before "being brought" to trial. What the media fail to tell us is that in almost every case it was the defendant's attorney who asked for all the continuances which resulted in the long pretrial delay. Again, except in very rare circumstances, defendants charged with felonies have a right to be brought to trial no later than sixty days from the arraignment on the information. As all defense attorneys know, a delayed trial almost always benefits the defendant. With the passage of time, witnesses disappear; their memories fade. There is an old saying, "Justice delayed is justice denied." This is often the case.

Although, in felony cases, virtually all defendants plead "not guilty" at the arraignment, about 90% of these defendants, at some point, change their plea to guilty. This approximate 90% figure remained the same my entire career, no matter whether the current district attorney was a Democrat or Republican, liberal or conservative.

That leaves only about 10% of the defendants who ask for a trial. Some of these trials are jury trials. The remainder are court trials. In 2005, only about two percent of the defendants charged with a felony by the DA in Los Angeles County had a jury trial.

So when district attorneys running for re-election tell the voters they have over a 90% conviction rate, the whole truth would seem to require them to tell the voters that about 90% of all the defendants pled guilty. That is, there was *no trial* for about 90% of the defendants.

6

PLEA BARGAINING

The fact that about 90% of defendants charged with felonies in L.A. County plead guilty raises the issue of plea bargaining—a practice, or at least the phrase, that seems to be unpopular with the public. A candid candidate for district attorney should tell the voters that in a county the size of Los Angeles, there has always been plea bargaining, and there will always be plea bargaining. Don't believe any candidate for district attorney of any highly populated county who tells the voters that if he is elected he will end plea bargaining. He will not—because in a highly populated county it is not possible.

A plea bargain occurs when the DA (or the judge) tells the defense attorney that if the defendant pleads guilty to a particular crime or crimes, a specified sentence will be imposed. If the defendant accepts the DA's (or the judge's) offer, the defendant pleads guilty, the judge orders a probation report, and the case is continued for sentencing, usually for about three weeks. On the date of sentencing, the defendant is sentenced as promised unless the judge, after reading the probation report, decides not to approve the plea bargain. This rarely occurs, but if the judge refuses to sentence the defendant as promised, the defendant will be permitted to withdraw his guilty plea and demand a trial. That is the procedure followed by DAs and defense attorneys in the cases of about 90% of all felony defendants in Los Angeles County. In the federal courts in Los Angeles, about 97% of the defendants plead guilty, leaving just three percent who go to trial.[7]

The reason that about 90% of all defendants charged with felonies in Los Angeles County plead guilty is a result, primarily, of the district attorney's strict filing policy, discussed earlier. Deputy DAs only file charges in cases where the evidence is very strong. In most cases it is the defense attorney who persuades the defendant that, considering the strength of the People's case and the DA's plea offer, it would be in his best interest to accept the DA's offer and plead guilty. The defense attorney explains to his client that if he chooses to go to trial and is convicted, the judge could give him a longer sentence than offered by the DA.

Sometimes defendants don't take kindly to their attorneys' attempts to persuade them to plead guilty. A good friend, JoAnn Glidden, is a retired deputy district attorney. Prior to becoming a DA, she had been a deputy public defender. I once asked her why she transferred over to the DA's office. She told me she had been representing a defendant charged with a felony. She was in the lock-up, a jail cell which adjoins the courtroom, discussing a plea bargain offered by the DA. She was explaining to her client why she believed the DA's offer was a good deal and why he should accept the offer. After she finished, the defendant spit in her face. She told me that as his saliva ran down across her lips, she decided she didn't want to be a PD any longer. Soon thereafter, she joined the DA's office.

Some defendants refer to PDs as "dump trucks" meaning that because DAs and PDs have the same employer, Los Angeles County, they assume the PDs are insufficiently independent and are not interested in giving them good representation and are too eager to persuade them to plead guilty. In my experience, nothing could be further from the truth. Some of the best defense attorneys are deputy public defenders. After all, criminal law is all they do. Also,

PDs don't get paid by the case. PDs don't make any more money if the defendant pleads guilty or has a full jury trial. They, therefore, have no monetary incentive to take the case to trial rather than to attempt to get the best possible plea bargain for the defendant, which will usually result in less jail or prison time than if the client is convicted by a jury.

Consider what would happen if, instead of 90% of defendants pleading guilty, only 80% pled guilty. That is a 100% increase in trials—from 10% to 20%. A DA can take a guilty plea from a defendant in about ten or fifteen minutes. A jury trial may take several days or weeks or even months. If the Los Angeles courts had a 100% increase in trials, the courts would be deluged. It would be chaotic.

But suppose plea bargaining were eliminated. Very few defendants would plead guilty if they had no idea what their sentence was going to be. They would think they had nothing to lose by going to trial. If this should occur, it is not an exaggeration to say that the criminal justice system would collapse very quickly in Los Angeles County. There would not be nearly enough courtrooms, judges, DAs, PDs, bailiffs, clerks, and court reporters to handle all the trials. That is why we will always have plea bargaining in Los Angeles County and other large cities.

In law school, students learn very little about our criminal justice system. Even experienced civil attorneys (who represent clients in divorces, auto accidents, medical malpractice, wills, trusts, business, tax, and corporate law) often have no clue how the criminal justice system actually works. Only members of the "Criminal Justice Club" really know what is happening in a criminal court room.

7

THE CLASSY HOOKER— JURY "PARDONS"

When I was a fairly new deputy DA, the big boss, District Attorney Joe Busch, would often speak to small gatherings of deputy DAs and give us valuable tips and share his experiences. In my long career, I served under six district attorneys, Evelle Younger, Joe Busch, John Van de Kamp, Bob Philabosian, Ira Reiner, and Gil Garcetti. Some of these men were great administrators, but only one, Joe Busch, had the reputation as a top trial attorney. During one of his talks, he said that sometimes jurors don't convict or acquit, they pardon. I understood what he meant because a few years earlier, as a deputy city attorney, I had tried a case where the jury, by their "not guilty" verdict, had given the defendant a pardon. The defendant had been charged with prostitution.

The defendant was a very attractive young lady—not a street prostitute by any means. She was dressed in a business suit, and she had her little girl in court being cared for by her nanny. My witnesses were two LAPD vice officers. They testified they first met the defendant at an upscale restaurant/bar. They were working undercover pretending to be businessmen from out of town. For a negotiated price, the vice officers agreed with the defendant to meet her the next day in a hotel room on the Sunset Strip in West Hollywood. The vice officers testified that according to plan they met the defendant in the hotel room, paid her the agreed upon price for the specified sexual acts and then arrested her. The officers searched the hotel room and found what they described as the defendant's "trick book," an alphabetical listing of all of her prostitution clients using code names.

This is what prosecutors refer to as a "dead-bang" case. I could not imagine what the defense could be. The defense attorney called three witnesses. The first witness testified that he was the defendant's supervisor at the Los Angeles Department of Water and Power. He testified that the defendant was a conscientious, hardworking employee who had never missed a day of work. The second defense witness, a very large, unattractive man, testified that he was the defendant's fiancé and the so-called trick book found in the hotel room was his. He testified he was in the garment business and his customers' names were written in the book in code because if the book was lost, and found by the wrong person, he did not want them to have his customer list.

On cross-examination I asked him if he knew the defendant's phone number. He said he could not remember phone numbers very well. I asked him if he had his fiancé's phone number in his wallet. He said he did not. I asked him if he wanted to call his fiancé on the telephone, how he would do it. He said he would call information. I asked him to tell the jury where the defendant lived. He said he had not lived in the area very long and he really didn't know the name of her street. I asked him what city she lived in. He wasn't sure. I asked him how he would drive to her apartment. He said he wasn't sure. The defense attorney called his third witness, the defendant.

Just before the defendant took the witness stand, she leaned over the railing into the spectator section and kissed her little girl being held by her nanny. You could almost hear the jury say, "Aahh." The defendant was very pretty and sat straight in the witness chair. I felt certain she had been to charm school. She denied much of the two vice officers' testimony. Her reason for being in the hotel room with these two vice officers seemed to me to be ludicrous. It had something to do with her alleged fiancé's garment business and that her fiancé and a customer were supposed to join her at the hotel for a business meeting. It made no sense. I figured my biggest challenge in my cross-examination was to make sure she didn't start to cry. If this attractive, well-dressed, sweet-looking, soft-spoken, mother started to cry on the witness stand, my instincts told me my case, which I had thought earlier was dead-bang, would, instead, be just plain dead. I asked her, in the nicest way I knew how, to explain certain facts, like how her alleged fiancé didn't know her phone number or where she lived. Why was it that she had her fiancé's customer book in the hotel room? Why didn't she meet with her fiancé and his customer at her apartment or her fiancé's apartment or his office instead of paying for a hotel room just to have a business meeting? Why were two police officers in her hotel room?

But I guess I was not soft-spoken enough because it happened. I saw the tear well up in the corner of her eye–on the jury side of her nose. The tear was growing bigger and bigger. I tried to change the subject, but it was too late. The tear broke like a dam break and cascaded down her face, around her nose, over her mouth, and dripped onto her blouse. The jury looked distraught. They looked at me as if they wanted to find *me* guilty. I thought I had better stop before it got even worse. "No more questions your honor." The jury deliberated about a half hour before they returned with a "not guilty" verdict.

It is customary, in nearly every criminal case, after a jury is excused by the judge, for the DA and defense attorney to speak to the jurors in the hallway outside the courtroom. This case was no exception.

I asked the jurors if they thought the big, unattractive guy who didn't know his alleged fiancé's phone number or where she lived was really her fiancé. The jurors said they didn't believe a word of his testimony and certainly didn't believe he was the defendant's fiancé. I then asked, "What do you think that little book was that the two vice officers found?" The jurors stated almost in unison, "That was her trick book just like the officers testified." Now I was really confused. "If you all didn't believe the big guy was her fiancé, and you believe the little book was her trick book, then why did you find her *not guilty*?" The jury foreman looked me straight in the eye and said, "Here's a woman who's trying to support her little girl. She works full time at the Department of Water and Power. She has never missed a day of work. So she moonlights a little. Big deal!"

This was what District Attorney Joe Busch meant when he told us that sometimes juries don't acquit—they pardon. These jurors all knew that this attractive, hard-working mother was guilty of prostitution. But by their verdict they simply said, "So what."

That was my first (and last) experience with "jury nullification"—where jurors really believe the defendant is guilty as charged, but refuse to convict. Instead, they gave the defendant a pardon in the form of a "not guilty" verdict. These jurors simply saw a higher kind of justice to be served. I would discourage this kind of jury misbehavior, but in this case I understood it.

8

THE BUSY REAL ESTATE LADY

My first murder case was in 1969. I had been a deputy DA for only one year. The case did not result in a trial. The defendant was a wife and mother of a teenage daughter. She was a successful real estate agent. She had had an argument with her husband. After the argument, and while the husband was sleeping, she fired several rounds from a 38-caliber revolver into his back, killing him instantly. The couple's daughter called the police, and the mother was arrested.

At her arraignment on the murder charge, she pled "not guilty." The judge set bail and shortly thereafter she was released. There were numerous additional court appearances. The defendant never claimed her dead husband had ever physically abused her. Her defense was going to be that after their verbal argument she started drinking, and when she shot him she was not in her right mind. I had received letters from the victim's co-workers saying what a great guy he was. Family members had also said he had been a good husband and father.

In every court appearance the defendant was dressed elegantly, always wearing business suits. While in court, she occasionally looked at her watch and then at me as if telling me to hurry up as she didn't have time for all this nonsense. After all, she was a busy real estate lady and had important things to do and people to see. After many court appearances, she finally entered a plea of not guilty by reason of insanity. The judge appointed two psychiatrists to evaluate her, as is required by California law.

After several months and many more court appearances, necessitated by the fact that the defendant failed to keep her appointments with the psychiatrists (she was a very busy lady), both psychiatrists finally interviewed her and filed their reports with the court. Both concluded that this successful real estate agent was insane when she murdered her husband.

The defendant chose to give up her right to a jury trial and have a court trial with the judge. The judge found her guilty of second-degree murder. Based on the two psychiatric reports, the judge then found her to be "not guilty by reason of insanity." The judge, following the required legal procedure, then appointed two additional psychiatrists to examine the defendant to determine if her sanity had been restored and if she constituted a danger to others. Both of these newly-appointed psychiatrists opined that she was now sane and not a danger to others.

In 1969, no additional incarceration time was required under these circumstances and the defendant was simply permitted to go on her way. Today, a defendant would be required to remain in custody for 180 days while he or she is being evaluated by the doctors. I doubt that this real estate agent missed any real estate appointments as a result of her little problem with the law.

I must say I was impressed. I had always thought, even after graduating from law school, that something unpleasant happened to people who are convicted of killing other people—like prison or, at the very least, if found insane, hospitalization. Although this case occurred early in my DA career, I continued to learn that many of my preconceived, media-influenced ideas about the criminal justice system were wrong.

9

THE HIT MAN THE JURY LOVED TO HUG

Early in my career, I witnessed a trial that moved me and influenced me greatly. A famous attorney, who was regarded as one of the best criminal defense attorneys in Los Angeles, was defending a hit man. This was not my case, but the trial took place in my assigned courtroom.

The defendant was on trial for an execution-type murder. He had a prior murder conviction as a juvenile, but the jury was not allowed to learn about his prior murder conviction. The case against the defendant was strong. The excellent woman defense attorney had the hit man dressed up to resemble a studious-looking college student. He wore black, horn-rimmed glasses, a pale yellow, pullover, sleeveless sweater over a high-collared, white shirt that hid from the jury the gang tattoos on his neck and arms. He wore brown and white Pat Boone-type saddle shoes. His hands were folded on the counsel table and he looked forlorn. He had obviously been given humility lessons. The defense attorney had done an excellent job. The defendant looked like anything but a gang hit man. In this case, the evidence was that he and his gang crime partners had tied the victim to a chair. Then the defendant shot him in the head after admonishing him about being disloyal to his gang. The defendant did not testify.

The murder victim's mother and sister were sitting in the first row of the spectator section. When the jury returned with its verdict of "not guilty," the victim's mother and sister began to cry. They were aware of the defendant's prior murder conviction. But what made this scene indelible for me was that after the judge excused the jury, several jurors lined up to give hugs to both the female attorney and the gang hit man who had just gotten away with murder. All the while this hugging was going on, the murder victim's mother and sister continued to sob quietly. I knew at the time, this scene would be with me forever.

10

MORE MEDIA MISINFORMATION

The media misleads us in both major and minor ways, sometimes for their own convenience, sometimes for their own legal protection, sometimes because of their liberal bias, sometimes from ignorance, and sometimes just from carelessness.

With respect to carelessness, my own experience is that when the media reported on my cases, the stories were almost never 100% accurate. It is a running joke among some deputy DAs how often the media misstates the facts. In this category of media misinformation, there is no reason to believe their mistakes are intentional. It may be a matter of reporters working under deadlines and having to get the story written and not having the time, or perhaps the inclination, to verify facts with the people involved.

Robbed vs Burglarized

We have often read in the newspaper about somebody's house being "robbed." And it has caught on. Just about every lay person I know uses the word "rob" to describe a break-in of a house. The fact is, no house has ever been "robbed" in this country. It is legally impossible to rob a house. Someone who enters a house to commit theft or any felony commits the crime of burglary. Only a *person* can be "robbed." The crime of "robbery" occurs when money or other personal property is taken from a person or from his immediate presence by "force or fear." The word "burglary" has eight letters. The word "burglarized" has eleven letters. The word "rob" has three letters. I am speculating that for their own convenience, to save space and newsprint, newspapers use the word "rob" or "robbed" to describe burglaries. Pointing out this error may seem like quibbling. However, it requires so little effort and expense to give us accurate information that I suggest the media try a little harder.

First-Degree Murder

The media frequently tell us that a defendant has been charged with "first-degree murder." No defendant in Los Angeles County is charged with "first-degree" murder. The defendant is simply charged with the crime of murder. Depending on the state of the evidence after both sides have rested their cases, the judge may or may not instruct the jury on first- or second-degree murder. Only if the judge instructs the jury on a particular degree of murder does the jury have the option of returning a guilty verdict on that degree of murder. But the phrase, "first-degree murder" or "murder one" sounds more dramatic than simply "murder" and so the former is preferable to the media for its entertainment effect.

Probation vs Parole

The media often use the term "parole" when they mean "probation" and vice versa. In California, a judge does not sentence a defendant to "parole." A prison inmate is released on parole *after* he serves a prison sentence. A judge may sentence a defendant convicted of a felony to "probation" with certain conditions attached, for example, that he serve a period of time, up to a year, in the county jail, or perform a number of hours of community service, or attend a drug rehab program or anger-management therapy. Defendants placed on probation are also ordered to obey all laws and are commonly ordered to pay a fine or restitution to the victim. If the defendant fails to abide by all the conditions of probation (the DA must prove this to the judge), his probation can be revoked and he can then be sentenced to state prison.

Jail vs Prison

The media often use the terms "jail" and "prison" interchangeably. In fact, a convicted felon who receives a sentence to a county jail as a condition of probation is much better off than if he had been sentenced directly to state prison—also known as the penitentiary. A prison sentence is almost always longer than a county jail sentence. There are two main categories of crimes: felonies and misdemeanors. A defendant convicted of a misdemeanor may be fined or sentenced to the county jail, or both. He cannot be sentenced to prison. However, a defendant convicted of a felony, in most cases, may be sentenced to either probation or to prison. If he is placed on probation, usually for three years, he is commonly ordered to serve a few days, weeks, weekends or months in the county jail as a condition of his probation.

Probation with some county jail time is the most common type of sentence for convicted felons in Los Angeles County. After he completes his jail sentence, he remains on probation. As mentioned, if the convicted felon is sentenced to prison, after he is released from prison he remains on parole—usually from one to three years.

Innocent vs Not Guilty

The media will tell you the defendant pleaded "innocent" to the charges or was found "innocent" by the jury. This is not true. Defendants do not plead "innocent." They plead "not guilty." Jurors may find a defendant "not guilty," but jurors *never* find defendants "innocent." But the media is afraid of a typo which omits the word "not" from "not guilty" which might result in a lawsuit against them. So they simply tell their readers the defendant pleaded "innocent" or was found "innocent."[8] This would not be a big deal except there is an important, substantive difference between "innocent" and "not guilty."

As mentioned earlier, prosecutors and defense attorneys frequently speak with jurors after they return with a verdict or were unable to reach a verdict. It is an enlightening experience for the inexperienced DA or defense attorney. Jurors will frequently tell the DA that all the jurors thought the defendant committed the crime, but they found him "not guilty" because they believed there was insufficient evidence to convict. In other words, jurors often tell DAs and defense attorneys that they don't really believe the defendant is "innocent" but they found him "not guilty" because they had a reasonable doubt of his guilt. This demonstrates that jurors take the judge's instructions on the law seriously. Jurors thus learn that there is an important distinction between "innocent," which means the defendant did not commit the crime, and a verdict of "not guilty," which often does not mean the defendant is "innocent," but only that there is insufficient evidence to prove the defendant's guilt beyond a reasonable doubt.

Circumstantial vs Direct Evidence

Another example of the media misleading the public is when they report that the case is weak because it is based *"only* on circumstantial evidence." In fact, I don't recall ever seeing a media report using the phrase "circumstantial evidence" without it being preceded by the word "only." It has become a cliché—repeated more often, it seems, than the phrase, "winter wonderland." What other category of evidence is there other than circumstantial? The media never tell us. I believe this is because the media talking heads do not understand what they are saying when they keep repeating that the case is weak because it is *"only* circumstantial."

Experienced prosecutors and defense attorneys (Club members) know that a circumstantial evidence case is the best case a DA can have. When the defendant's DNA, or his fingerprints, or his unique shoeprint is found at the crime scene, this is circumstantial evidence that the defendant was at the crime scene. When the defendant's handwriting is identified on the forged check, this is circumstantial evidence that the defendant wrote the forged check.

The other category of evidence is called "direct" evidence, which is eyewitness evidence, not always the most reliable evidence. The Los Angeles County DA's office will not file a case, no matter how serious the crime, based solely on the identification of a suspect by a single witness, during a brief encounter—no matter how positive the eyewitness—in the absence of other corroborating evidence.

For example, suppose a robber robs a convenience store clerk at gunpoint and escapes with all the day's cash. The next day an anonymous caller tells the police that John Jones, who lives at 123 6th Street, is the person who robbed the clerk. The police put a six-pack of photos together, including John Jones' photo, and show them to the store clerk who was the victim of the robbery. The clerk immediately points to the photo of John Jones and says, "That is the man who robbed me, I'm positive." Unless there is something very unusual about John Jones' photo, such as a distinctive tattoo or scar or some other evidence to corroborate the victim's identification, this case will be rejected by the L.A. County DA's office. The reason is that a study was done in the early 1970s that found that the DA cannot win a purely "one-on-one" ID case, that is, where only one witness identifies one suspect based on a brief encounter, with no other corroborating evidence, and there is nothing physically distinctive about the suspect.

The reason the DA cannot win such a case is that several of John Jones' friends or family members, or both, will surely testify that John Jones was with them at the time the robbery occurred. Club members call this the *SODDI* defense—"Some Other Dude Did It." However, only a bit more corroborating evidence would tip the scales in this example to justify charging John Jones with robbery. For example, the DA is more likely to file a robbery charge if the clerk had placed the money he gave to the robber in his own distinctively marked bank-deposit bag that the clerk can identify, and the bag is recovered from John Jones' house or car, or if John Jones had a distinctive scar or tattoo which the clerk had mentioned to the police when the initial robbery report was taken.

The truth is that circumstantial evidence is the strongest kind of evidence a DA can present to a jury. At the end of the trial the judge instructs the jury on the applicable law. He will tell the jury that neither direct evidence nor circumstantial evidence is entitled to any greater weight than the other.

An especially heinous example of the media misleading the public occurred in the spring of 2004. Eleven-year-old Carlie Brucia was kidnapped and murdered in Sarasota, Florida. The entire nation saw the abduction which was caught on videotape. A few days later, the police arrested Joseph P. Smith for the girl's murder. It was revealed that Smith was on probation at the time. Smith was a chronic drug user who had had numerous drug arrests, as well as a conviction in 1993 for hitting his girlfriend with a motorcycle helmet—not a serious record compared to what I was accustomed to seeing. It was also revealed that about two months prior to the murder, Smith's probation officer had recommended to Judge Harry Rapkin, who was handling Smith's probation case, that Smith's probation should be revoked because the often-unemployed Smith was about $400 behind in making payments on his court-imposed fine.

The media were acting like a school of piranha fish. The anchors on almost every network news show, including CNN and Fox, were asking, "Why was this man out of jail?" "Why was he on the street?" The talking heads attacked Judge Rapkin who had refused to rule that the defendant had violated his probation by falling behind in making the payments on his fine. How disingenuous! How ugly! In my thirty-two years as a deputy DA, I have never seen *any* defendant's probation revoked and the defendant jailed for failing to keep current in paying a fine or restitution to the crime victim. The reason is that the prosecutor must prove to the court [the judge is referred to as "the court"] that the defendant had the ability to pay *and* that he willfully refused to pay.

In a busy prosecution office, there is simply no time to send out a DA investigator to try to determine if the defendant has the money to pay his fine. I have never seen this done. And here is the really ugly part. Each of these TV networks has a large legal department. It is difficult to believe that all of these lawyers in all of these legal departments failed to realize that Judge Rapkin could not have legally revoked Smith's probation and put him in jail. Even the Florida Attorney General was interviewed on several television shows. The same question was put to him: "Why was Smith out on the street?" Not once did he ever say that Judge Rapkin could not have legally revoked Smith's probation. Is it possible that the Attorney General was ignorant of the law? Not likely. The media and the Attorney General just allowed Judge Rapkin to dangle in the wind. Fox anchor Bill O'Reilly repeatedly called for the defeat of Judge Rapkin at the next election.

But suppose the DA in Sarasota, Florida had the evidence to prove that Smith had the $400 to pay the fine *and* that he willfully refused to pay, and the judge revoked probation and jailed the defendant for failing to keep current on paying his fine. The jail time would have been for a few days—not months or years. This is a good example of the media ganging up and pummeling a totally innocent man, in this case a judge, for their own benefit—to create some drama and controversy by finding someone else to blame for little Carlie's murder in addition to Joseph P. Smith.

This incident shows how the media takes advantage of the lack of legal knowledge of the American people. As a result of these false stories, Judge Rapkin reported receiving death threats. If the networks sincerely desired to avoid such mistakes in the future, it would require only one phone call to the DA or to their own legal departments to seek advice before destroying someone's reputation without justification. But I do not expect any changes in this regard, because it is very difficult for a public figure, such as Judge Rapkin, to defend himself or to prove libel or slander against the TV networks. In other words, the networks will most likely continue doing what they are doing *because they can*—without fear of any sanctions. As we teach our kids, it's a tough world out there—and not always fair.

Opening Statement vs Opening Argument

Another media-created confusion in criminal justice terminology is that they persist in calling the prosecutor's "opening statement" the "opening argument." In a criminal trial each side has the right to make an "opening statement." The opening statement is made first by the prosecutor after the jury is chosen and before any witnesses are called. The opening statement by the prosecutor is simply a statement to the jury of what she believes the evidence will prove. It is the story of the case the DA expects the People's witnesses to tell the jury from the witness stand. The prosecutor is careful to tell the jury that the opening statement is not evidence in the case. It is made simply to help the jury follow the evidence as it unfolds from the witness stand. The "argument" made by each side comes at the end of the trial after all witnesses have testified.

The defense attorney in a criminal case is also entitled to make an opening statement, but experienced defense attorneys often do not. The reason is that the defense attorney does not want to lock himself into a particular story because, if weaknesses develop in the People's case, another defense story might make more sense. Another reason the defense attorney often does not make an opening statement is that he does not want to fall into the trap of promising the jury more than he will be able to deliver. So, when the DA finishes her opening statement and the judge asks the defense attorney, "Would the defense like to make an opening statement?" the defense attorney often says, "Your honor, the defense will reserve our opening statement." What this means is that the defense attorney has no intention of making an opening statement—at least not until the People "rest"—which means the People have finished calling witnesses and introducing evidence.

I remember a case in which an inexperienced defense attorney made an opening statement and told the jury that his client, the defendant, would testify. He told the jury what his client would tell them. After the People rested their case, the defense attorney decided it would not be wise to put the defendant on the witness stand. But, he had already told the jury what the defendant would tell them when he took the stand. And now the defendant is not taking the stand. What is the jury to think? This is just one example of what can happen when a defense attorney makes an opening statement, thereby giving up his advantage of "flexibility."

A good defense attorney does not want to lock himself into any particular story if it should develop that another story would be more advantageous for his client. That is why no experienced defense attorney will ever permit his client to speak to the police or the DA, contrary to what we see on some TV lawyer shows where the defendant and his lawyer are often seen meeting with the police, the DA or both. Such meetings are extremely rare and would usually occur, in my experience, only when the defense attorney is inexperienced, or is not a Club member, or when a defendant agrees to plead guilty and testify against a co-defendant. In this latter situation, the investigating officer and the prosecutor will meet with the attorney and his client to discuss the client's proffered testimony.

During the O.J. Simpson case, O.J. disregarded his attorney's advice and made a statement to the police. Soon thereafter, the *Los Angeles Times* interviewed several of the best criminal defense attorneys in Los Angeles to obtain their views about the advisability of defendants talking to the police.[9] Loyola Law School professor Laurie Levensen told the *Times*, "Simpson locked himself into a statement before his lawyer could explore the case with him." "If your client wants to talk to the police, you chain him to your desk at your office," said top criminal defense attorney Harland Braun. One of the best criminal defense attorneys in the business, Bradley Brunon, told the *Times*, "Whatever Simpson said will have a serious effect on his attorney's range of options. Without that interview [attorney Robert] Shapiro would be playing on a much more open field and could be more creative in his strategy without having to worry about a possible credibility deficit."

It is risky for a suspect charged with a crime to hire an attorney who is not a member of the Criminal Justice Club. I recall a case in which we were considering filing a home burglary charge against a young man. The suspect's father was a successful businessman. He called his company lawyer, a civil lawyer—clearly not a Club member. The father persuaded him to represent his son. The son told his father and the lawyer he was innocent. The lawyer believed him and made an appointment with me to "straighten out this unfortunate mistake." I made sure my investigating officer (I/O) was in attendance.

The lawyer showed up with the burglary suspect and permitted the suspect to speak with my I/O. The suspect vehemently denied committing the burglary. The I/O told the suspect where the house was located and showed the suspect photos of the outside of the house. The young suspect said he had never seen that house or been on that street or even in that area of town. But the I/O kept asking the suspect if he was certain about that. The suspect repeated his denials. The I/O then told the suspect and his attorney that the suspect's fingerprints were lifted from the window at the point where the burglar had entered the house. The suspect could offer no explanation inasmuch as he had denied ever being in that area of town. The suspect was left with no options but to plead guilty to residential burglary.

The suspect's father's big mistake was in believing that his company lawyer would be able to handle a criminal case. The father or the company lawyer should have referred the case to a Club member. No criminal lawyer I know would have brought his client to the DA's office and permitted him to speak to my I/O. An experienced criminal lawyer would have waited to see the police reports. He then would have seen that the police had lifted the suspect's prints from the window. The defendant would then have been free to be "creative."

For example, the defense might have been that the defendant had gotten a flat tire in the area. He wanted to use a phone. He knocked on the door of the burglarized house and thought he heard noises, but no one answered the door. He went around to the side of the house and looked in the window to see if someone was home. In doing this, he must have touched the window. Or, perhaps better yet: After the flat tire he had the urge to urinate. He went to the side of a house to relieve himself. The defendant would tell the jury, "I guess I must have touched the window." But, because of the civil attorney's lack of criminal law experience, he allowed his business client's son to paint himself into a corner from which there was no escape.

The media can mislead us in more subtle ways. Recently, my wife and I were in a clothing store in a mountain-resort town east of Los Angeles. We entered into an extended conversation with the lady who owned the store. After about 15 minutes, she asked what I did for a living. I told her I was a retired deputy DA. "Oh no," she said. "You're too nice to be a prosecutor." I asked her where she got the idea that prosecutors are not supposed to be nice people. She replied that she had always thought prosecutors were cold and tough. Where did that stereotype come from?

Like the word "only" that almost always precedes the phrase, "circumstantial evidence," it dawned on me that the media often precedes the word "prosecutor" with the word "tough." "Tough prosecutor." Haven't we heard and read this coupling innumerable times? Why the stereotype? Most prosecutors I know could never be described as "tough" if "tough" means hard, callous or unfair. Most deputy DAs I know could never compete with criminal defense attorneys in the area of "toughness." To be an effective defense attorney, he must be able to rip into a rape or child-molest victim or other crime victims on cross-examination and try to make them look like liars or sluts in front of the jury—even when the defense attorney knows or believes the victim is telling the truth. I know many DAs who could not do this. So who is "tougher," the deputy DA, trying to convict a violent rapist or murderer by seeking to present what she believes is the truth, or the defense attorney, who is doing his best to get the jury to acquit his client—even if he believes or knows his client is guilty? No, in the area of "toughness" we DAs are often no match for the most competent defense attorneys. This "tough prosecutor" stereotype is, for the most part, just another media-created fiction.

Why do the media perpetuate this "tough prosecutor" stereotype? The traditional, mainstream media is comprised mainly of liberal Democrats who generally have an anti-prosecutor/pro-defense bias. Sometimes, but rarely, the bias is admitted. For example, on June 6, 2005, television personality Larry King was interviewing one of his regular guests, criminal defense attorney Mark Geragos. Near the end of the show Geragos said, "I could never be a prosecutor, could you?" King responded, "It would be hard." In my liberal youth, neither I nor any of my liberal friends liked prosecutors because we were all raised to believe the myth that many of the people they prosecuted were innocent, and that prosecutors were not very nice or fair people. This image was validated each week by such TV shows as *Perry Mason* and *The Defenders* which portrayed the prosecutor as a person who often obstructed justice and the search for truth.

When a criminal justice story appears in the *Los Angeles Times*, there will often be a reference in the story to the views of some well-known criminal defense attorney or liberal law school professor. It is far less common to see a reference in such a story to the views of the District Attorney. The *Times* often presents only the side of criminal justice issues they favor. My plea to the *Times* is for more balance.

I do not recall ever reading in the *Los Angeles Times* that the Los Angeles County District Attorney's Office rejects a high percentage of cases presented by the police for the filing of criminal charges. It is important for the public to understand that the DA's office files charges in only the strongest cases and that thousands of suspects arrested for serious crimes are released annually without charges being filed because of the high filing standards of the Los Angeles County DA's office. This is the price we pay for a justice system we can believe in and which is dedicated to achieving justice.

We frequently read criminal justice stories in the *Los Angeles Times* that are factually incorrect and would cause a fair-minded person to think the criminal justice system was cruel or the laws overly harsh. For example, the *Times*, in 2000,[10] and again in 2001,[11] said that a 17-year-old charged with murder in California could receive the death penalty. Each article involved the same defendant, but each article was written by a different writer. After the second story, I wrote a letter to the editor and enclosed a copy of the California law that precludes the death penalty for anyone under 18. To the *Times'* credit, they did print a correction the following week.

In spite of that correction, the *Los Angeles Times* continues to mislead their readers about the death penalty. For example, on January 17, 2005, the *Times*, in an editorial titled "California's Death Penalty Lie," asked Governor Schwarzenegger to commute the sentence of Donald Beardslee, who was sentenced to death for the 1981 murders of two women. The editorial suggested that it was unfair to execute Beardslee because, in unrelated cases, two other men who had also been convicted of killing two people had been sentenced to life in prison. The *Times'* argument for commutation was thus based on the fact that it would be unfair to execute Beardslee when he too had only killed two people. The *Times'* editorial stated, "Three men, each convicted of two murders, yet only one is sentenced to death." The editorial went on to complain that "Judges in California cannot throw out a capital sentence on the ground that defendants, who committed similar crimes, were not sentenced to die."

The *Times* neglected to mention in this editorial that Beardslee had been convicted of another murder he committed in 1969. He killed a 52-year-old woman in St. Louis, Missouri. He slit her throat and left her nude body in a bathtub where it was discovered by her son-in-law. The ugly part of this story is that the *Times'* editorial writer had to be aware of Beardslee's first murder conviction, because two days prior to this editorial Beardslee's prior murder conviction was described in a *Los Angeles Times* story titled "Killer Makes Bid to Avoid Execution."

The editorial's main argument for asking Governor Schwarzenegger to commute Beardslee's death sentence to life in prison was that it would be unfair to execute Beardslee when others, who had also killed two people, had received life sentences. Any reasonably objective person must conclude that the editorial's failure to mention that Beardslee had been convicted of three murders—not two, was misleading and disingenuous. The editorial ends with this charge: "By erecting a death penalty scheme that sentences so many to death and executed so few, the state lies to itself and the people about what it's doing." Look who's calling the state a liar!

One can only conclude that the *Times* must believe that all the legitimate arguments against the death penalty are not sufficient to sway public opinion. Otherwise, why would they resort to misleading their readers by failing to mention in their editorial requesting commutation of Beardslee's death sentence the very significant fact that he had killed three times. The *Times* must believe they are justified in continuing to mislead their readers on criminal justice issues because they feel so certain they are right. Put more simply, they believe the end justifies the means. What other explanation could they have for their long history of not being honest with their readers?

One thing is certain. The jury that imposed the death penalty on Donald Beardslee was aware that in 1969, twelve years before he murdered two women in 1981, he had murdered another woman.

In a January 19, 2005, story of Beardslee's execution, the *Los Angeles Times* stated that Beardslee had served only seven years for his first murder conviction. This *Times* story also said, "Because of the complicated appeals process, condemned California prisoners wait an average of more than 20 years between the date of sentencing and execution. In fact, most inmates on the state's death row die of natural causes." This statement is not completely accurate. The reason California's death-row inmates wait more than 20 years before execution, and that most die of natural causes, is not because of the "complicated appeals process." Other states that have the death penalty have a far shorter interval between sentencing and execution even though all states must follow the same federal procedures, called habeas corpus, in death penalty cases.

There are two main reasons for the longer delays in California. The first is attributable to the Ninth Circuit Federal Court of Appeals which is regarded as the most liberal federal appeals court in the nation and is the court whose decisions are reversed by the U.S. Supreme Court more often than any other federal appeals court. Texas, with 402 executions since 1982 (at this writing), must follow the same federal appeals procedure as California.

The second reason for the longer delay in California is that death-row inmates often must wait years before an attorney is appointed to represent them in their appeals. Why? Because of the failure of the Democrat-controlled legislature to allocate sufficient funds to pay attorneys representing death-row inmates. Ronald George, Chief Justice of California's Supreme Court told the Associated Press that "The legislature's inability to adequately fund capital punishment has led to a de facto moratorium on executions in California."[12] The public doesn't know why murderers on California's death row wait decades before their sentences are carried out. It is clear, however, that the "complicated appeals process" is not the main reason California has only executed 13 murderers (at this writing) since 1978.

When reading stories in the *L.A. Times* dealing with the death penalty, the reader is urged to read with caution. The *Times'* opposition to the death penalty is so strong, it seems they have lost their ability to report death penalty stories objectively. For example, on February 18, 2006, the *Times* reported that Governor Schwarzenegger denied clemency for Michael Morales, who has been on death row for about 25 years for the rape and murder of a 17-year-old high school girl in 1981. The last paragraph of this story says, "The growing list of people urging clemency include Kenneth W. Starr, dean of the Pepperdine School of Law and former Whitewater independent counsel. Starr has said it [the execution] would amount to a 'grievous injustice of profound proportions.'"

Would it not have been more forthright if this *Times'* story had also mentioned that Kenneth Starr is one of Morales' attorneys? Would it not have been ludicrous if the *Times* had run a story during the O.J. Simpson trial that said, "The growing list of people urging that O.J. be acquitted includes Johnnie Cochran"?

Relative to the number of murders in this country, the death penalty is rarely used. Since the U.S. Supreme Court permitted capital punishment to resume in 1976, there have been approximately 576,000 murders in this country. Since that time, as of December 2005, only one thousand murderers have been executed. In 2003, there were 16,503 murders in this country. Yet, in 2003, only 65 murderers were executed nationwide. At this writing, California's death row houses 667 murderers.

To the *Los Angeles Times* (in the event any *Times'* executives are reading this): My purpose here is not to make a pitch for the death penalty. We could live without it, although some murders are so cruel, so heinous, or the perpetrator has hurt or killed so many people in his criminal career, that nothing short of the death penalty seems appropriate. My purpose is only to implore you to stop misleading us. I know it's hard to do when you believe so strongly in the righteousness of your cause. But you must realize it is not in anyone's interest if we reach the point that we cannot trust anything we read in the newspapers or see on the network news. There are legitimate arguments against the death penalty. You need not sacrifice your integrity by resorting to misleading your readers to enhance these arguments. You must know that sooner or later your false and misleading statements will be discovered by your readers and what little is left of your credibility will come crashing down.

When super-pop star Michael Jackson was on trial in 2005 for child molesting, newspapers and television news commentators falsely told the public repeatedly that if Michael Jackson was convicted he would face 20 years in prison. That was not true. Even if the maximum sentence for his alleged crimes was 20 years, if he had been convicted and was given the maximum sentence of twenty years, which would have been highly unlikely, he would serve at most only 10 years. The reason is that most felons sentenced to state prison in California serve only one half, or less, of the sentence pronounced in court by the judge. This 50%-off rule is for good behavior and work credits but does not apply to murderers and three-strikers, who earn no credits. Inmates convicted of "violent felonies," as defined in Penal Code section 667.5(c), earn 15% credits, and two strikers earn 20% credits.

What if, instead of most inmates receiving 50% credits, the legislature again increased the credits for prison inmates, this time to 75%, resulting in the inmate serving only five years on a 20-year sentence? Would it still be OK for the media to tell the public that Michael Jackson was facing 20 years in prison?

If Jackson had been convicted, it would have been his first conviction. It is unlikely he would have been sentenced to the maximum. He could have been sentenced to probation. But if the judge had denied probation and sentenced Jackson to prison, the most that a first-offender child molester would likely serve in prison for molesting one victim, without the use of force, would be about two or three years of actual time served.

Several times during Michael Jackson's trial, TV anchors kept telling us that if Jackson was convicted he would be housed at Corcoran Prison with Charles Manson. Where did this come from? California has 33 prisons. Nobody is able to tell the press, or even the DA, where a nonconvicted defendant would be housed if he is convicted. That is determined by prison authorities *after* a defendant is convicted. It is doubtful this information given to the media came from a legitimate, official source.

Common sense dictates that many jurors would feel increased pressure to cast a "not guilty" vote if they heard and believed false reports from the media that their vote for a guilty verdict would result in 20 years of imprisonment and that Jackson would be housed with Charles Manson, a national symbol of evil. All I'm asking is that the media use reliable, legitimate sources and start telling the public the truth.

On March 5, 2005, an article titled "3 Face Murder Charges in Disappearance of Boat Owners" appeared in the *L.A. Times*. One of the suspects arrested was said to have a criminal record. The *Times* said that this suspect "was jailed in December and charged with grand theft for allegedly failing to pay $7,000 for boat repairs." This statement is misleading. Nobody can be charged in this country with a theft for failing to pay for repairs—or for failing to pay for anything. We no longer have a debtor's prison in this country.

The media often fail to tell the entire story when they report a defendant's sentence. The *News-Press* is a small-town newspaper which circulates in the L.A. suburbs of Glendale, Montrose, La Crescenta and La Canada Flintridge. The *News-Press* is owned by the Tribune Company, the same company that owns the *Los Angeles*

Times. In September 2004, the *News-Press* reported on its first page that a defendant, who had been in jail for four years during very lengthy criminal proceedings, was sentenced to the maximum 18 years in prison for involuntary manslaughter.[13] The writer of the story said, "[Judge] Johnson's sentence means [the defendant] will spend another fourteen years in prison. He has served four years of the 18-year sentence." Of course, this is not true. At the most, considering his 50% good-time/work-time credits, the defendant would serve five more years. But even that is misleading because the crime of involuntary manslaughter calls for a sentence range of two, three or four years[14]—actual time to be served being 12 months, 18 months or 24 months. Thus, if the defendant received a sentence of 18 years, it had to be for something more than just involuntary manslaughter. Prison inmates in California have been receiving 50% off their sentences for about a quarter century. Is it possible the media are not aware of this? Highly unlikely.

On July 29, 2005, the *Los Angeles Times* headline on page one of the "California" section said, "Boy, 13, Gets 12 Years for Murder." The sub-headline said that the boy received the "maximum CYA [California Youth Authority] sentence...." The first paragraph of this story said that the boy was sentenced to "confinement at the California Youth Authority until the age of 25." All three of these statements are, at the very least, misleading. The boy was not sentenced to CYA for 12 years or until he is 25, although it is legally possible for the CYA to keep the boy until he reaches age 25. Most juveniles sentenced to CYA for murder are released long before they serve 12 years. Also, when a judge sentences a juvenile to the CYA, there is no mention of any specific time period. Why? Because the sentence is indeterminate—meaning the CYA may parole the boy anytime they determine parole would be appropriate. The judge's alternative was to sentence this boy, convicted of second-degree murder for killing a 15-year-old boy with a baseball bat, to a juvenile camp—not an appropriate sentence for juveniles convicted of murder. It was only near the end of this story on page seven that the *Times* quoted the prosecutor as saying, "Though the California Youth Authority legally can parole the 13-year-old at any time, it is likely that he will remain detained for at least three or four years because of the severity of his crime."

When the editor who wrote the headline and sub-headline to this story read the prosecutor's estimate that the boy was likely to serve only three or four years for this murder, why would he tell *Times'* readers that the boy was sentenced to 12 years for murder— when the judge never mentioned 12 years? Why would the editor and the writer tell *Times'* readers that the boy was sentenced to "confinement at the California Youth Authority until the age of 25"—when the judge never said that? If the *Times'* writer or editor doubted the prosecutor's three- or four-year estimate, they could have called the CYA for confirmation. Why didn't they make that call? One thing is clear: unless this boy kills or seriously injures someone while in the CYA, he will not remain there until he is 25.

These are just a few examples of the liberal media misleading their readers into believing the criminal justice and penal systems are unjustly harsh, and it seems there are few people out there who have the inclination or courage to challenge them. We deserve the truth from our media and we are not getting it. The *Los Angeles Times* has no significant competition in the Los Angeles area. Perhaps this is just another example of the truism that "Power corrupts and absolute power corrupts absolutely."

One of the clearest and most pervasive examples of liberal media bias is on the subject of gun control. John R. Lott Jr. is a resident scholar at the American Enterprise Institute. He received his Ph.D. in economics from UCLA. He has been a senior research scholar at the Yale University School of Law, a fellow at the University of Chicago, School of Law, a professor at UCLA and the Wharton School at the University of Pennsylvania. Professor Lott is the author of two books on the hot topic of guns: *More Guns, Less Crime* and *The Bias Against Guns*.

Professor Lott claims the media misleads us by failing to accurately report stories when guns are used in self-defense. He cites, as an example, studies that show in 2002 about 2.3 million defensive uses of guns occurred over the previous one year. The professor says that although simply brandishing a gun stops crime 95% of the time, we rarely see a story in the media where the brandishing of a gun prevented a crime. Why? Because much of the media has a bias against guns.

Professor Lott, in a May 25, 2004, speech, cited what he called, "A Case Study in Bias."[15] In January 2002, a shooting at Appalachian Law School in Virginia left three people dead. The event made international headlines and resulted in more calls for gun control. Yet one critical fact was missing from nearly all the news stories: the attack was stopped by two armed students.

When the killer, Peter Odighizuwa, started shooting, Michael Gross and Tracy Bridges, both law school students, heard the shots and ran to their respective cars. They retrieved their guns and confronted the shooter who was still shooting. Tracy and Michael pointed their guns at Odighizuwa and yelled at him to drop his gun. Odighizuwa immediately dropped his gun. The fast responses of these two students undoubtedly saved many lives.

A study by Professor Lott showed that out of 218 news stories about this shooting, only four mentioned that the students who stopped the shooter had guns. The liberal *Washington Post* wrote, "Three students pounced on the gunman and held him until help arrived." New York's *Newsday* noted only that the attacker was "restrained by students."

About ten days after the shooting, Professor Lott appeared with Tracy Bridges on a Los Angeles radio show. Tracy related that he had been interviewed by over fifty reporters about the shooting and had told all of them the shooter only dropped his gun after he and Michael Gross pointed their guns at him and yelled at him to drop his gun. Yet nearly all the media had reported the incident had ended by the students "tackling" or "pouncing" on the killer.

Professor Lott called the *Washington Post* and spoke with reporter, Maria Glod. Ms. Glod told Professor Lott she had interviewed both Tracy and Michael. She explained that her failure to mention in her story that the two students had brandished their guns to end the shooting was not intentional but was the result of "space constraints." As Tommy Smothers once said, "If you believe that, you would believe that chickens have lips."

The anti-gun bias is pervasive in the media. Professor Lott's research shows, for example, that in 2001, out of 104 gun-crime news articles in the *New York Times*, they published only one story about a person using a gun in self defense. In the same year, the *Chicago Tribune* and the *Los Angeles Times*, both owned by the same company, each reported three such stories.

Bias is revealed not only by what a newspaper prints and the manner in which a story is told, but also by the stories it chooses not to print. Professor Lott, in the same speech, noted that an analysis of *New York Times* news articles from 2000 to 2002 shows that *Times* reporters cited nine pro-gun-control academics a total of twenty times. The *New York Times* did not mention a single academic in this two-year period who was skeptical that gun control reduces crime.

There are plenty of academics who are not in favor of gun control. For example, Professor Lott reports that in 1999, 294 academics from institutions as diverse as Harvard, Stanford, Northwestern, the University of Pennsylvania and UCLA released an open letter to Congress stating that the new gun laws being proposed at that time were "ill advised." Not one of these 294 academics was quoted in the *New York Times* over this two-year period—the same newspaper that claims they print "All the news that's fit to print." Apparently the *New York Times* did not believe the views of these 294 academics, with whom they disagreed, was news that was fit to print.

We desperately need an honest, courageous press we can all trust; a press that will keep its opinions on its editorial page, a press that is not afraid to fairly present both sides of an issue—even when the newspaper publisher or TV network heads believe strongly that one side is clearly right. Am I being naïve and unrealistic to even hope for fairness and objectivity from this nation's leading media, whose reporters and editorial writers are overwhelmingly liberal Democrats?

The American Society of Newspaper Editors published a 1999 study that showed 78% of Americans believe there is bias in the media. According to a 2004 poll from the Pew Research Center, conducted by the Princeton Review Research Associates, only 7% of journalists described themselves as conservatives.

11

EARLY RELEASES FROM THE LOS ANGELES COUNTY JAIL

Most defendants convicted of felonies in Los Angeles County receive a county jail sentence. The actual amount of time the defendant spends in jail depends on the extent of jail overcrowding. In 1988, a federal judge, in a lawsuit by the ACLU, gave the Los Angeles County Sheriff authority to release as many inmates as necessary to control overcrowding. This authority is still in effect.

A story titled "Jail Inmates Freed Early to Save Money" was published on page one in the *L.A. Times* on March 25, 2004. In this piece, the *Times* made more erroneous statements about sentencing. For example, the article stated that "Nearly all felons are sentenced to state prison." This is not true. The majority of defendants convicted of felonies in Los Angeles County are placed on probation— 63% in 2003 (65% in 2005) according to DA's office statistics. Probation is usually for three years and, as earlier mentioned, is customarily conditioned on the defendant serving a few days, weeks, weekends or months in the county jail. The maximum county jail sentence for a felony offense is one year. In 2005, only 34% of convicted felons sentenced in Los Angeles County courts were sentenced to prison. Why does the *Los Angeles Times* continue to mislead us when it is so easy for their reporters to check their story for accuracy? If it were just a matter of not knowing the law or the facts, all they need to do is ask the DA's office. Why don't they make that call?

The same story states that in the prior year, 47,500 Los Angeles County Jail inmates had been released early, serving only about 10% of their sentences ordered by the judge. Sheriff Lee Baca said the early releases were necessary because there was not enough money in his budget to pay for the number of deputy sheriff's needed to guard the inmates.

The same piece said that from 1998 to April 2003, jail inmates served their full sentences. This is not true. Most Los Angeles County Jail inmates have not served their "full sentences" for many years. A "full sentence" in county jail is regarded as two-thirds of the sentence pronounced by the judge. County jail inmates are entitled to a one-third sentence reduction for good behavior.[16] For many years, most L.A. County Jail inmates have been serving only a small fraction of their sentences—far less than two-thirds. As a Deputy DA, I became aware of many instances of early releases in the late 1980s and 1990s. If the *L.A.Times* had a desire to be accurate, it would be easy for the them to simply examine a sampling of inmates' files, which are open to the public, to learn what the sentence was, when the inmate entered the jail and when he was released. If the *Times* did this and reported the results accurately, it could not claim that from 1998 to April 2003 jail inmates served their full sentences.

There is so much misinformation published in the press about the criminal justice system, there is no way a citizen can know what is true and what is false. In a March 27, 2006, *Los Angeles Times* story titled "Inmate Plan May Be Scuttled," both Sheriff Baca and David Janssen, the county's chief administrative officer, implied that only low-risk inmates convicted of misdemeanors are being released from jail early. But the above-mentioned March 25, 2004, *L.A. Times* story said that in one year (March 2003 to April 2004) 972 inmates convicted of assault with a deadly weapon (ADW to Club members) and 682 inmates convicted of robbery were released early from the L.A. County jail. Convicted robbers and those guilty of assaulting another with a deadly weapon are not low-risk inmates who were convicted of misdemeanors. In California, a robbery conviction can never be reduced to a misdemeanor.

Sheriff Baca announced in November 2004 that his previous announcement eight months earlier of 47,500 early releases was wrong. He said that since June 2002, 119,577 inmates had been released early. More than half, 62,090, left jail within a day or two despite having been sentenced to jail for up to three months.[17] Yet, Sheriff Baca has contracted with the state of California to house up to 1,300 of the state's prisoners in exchange for $27 million.

On January 17, 2005, it was reported in the *Los Angeles Times* that a defendant had been convicted of misdemeanor ADW in April 2004 and was sentenced to probation. In December 2004, he violated his probation and the judge sentenced him to 60 days in the county jail. He served only three days of this sentence—or 5% of his time. After he was released, he allegedly killed both of his parents and kidnapped his girlfriend who was killed when he tried to shoot it out with police. The girlfriend left four small children. The sheriff placed some of the blame for the defendant's early release on the voters who failed to pass a one-half cent sales tax in November 2004, which would have paid for more deputy sheriffs he could have assigned to the county jails.[18]

On May 14, 2006, the *Los Angeles Times* published a page one story titled "Releasing Inmates Early Has a Costly Human Toll." Kudos to the *Times* for publishing the consequences of the sheriff's early release program. The story said that from July 2002 to December 2005, 148,229 Los Angeles county jail inmates were released early. After their release, *and during the time they should have still been serving their sentences*, 15,775 were rearrested. Of these 15,775, 1443 were charged with assault, 653 were charged with DUI, 641 were charged with a weapons offense, 518 were charged with robbery, 215 were charged with a sex offense, 20 were charged with kidnapping, and 16 were charged with murder. Of the 16 men charged with murder, nine were found guilty and seven were awaiting trial, the story said.

The *Times* story said that of these 15,775 inmates released early and rearrested during the time they should have been serving their sentences, 2,000 of them were again released early after being convicted of their subsequent offense.

The story said that although 32 of California's 58 counties release jail inmates before they complete their sentences, Los Angeles County Jail sentences are among the weakest in the nation. The story said that "…nearly everyone now sentenced to 90 days or less is let go immediately." The *Times* story said the typical county jail inmate who is sentenced to one year in the Los Angeles County Jail actually serves just 24 days.

The *Times* story said that "In recent years, sheriff's clerks have routinely disregarded sentences handed down by judges. In some cases, inmates are freed despite instructions from a judge that they must serve their full sentences." This extraordinary power of sheriff's clerks to disregard judges' sentences flows from the 1988 ACLU federal lawsuit in which the judge empowered the sheriff to release inmates early to control overcrowding.

The *Times* story correctly points out that "Many of these inmates probably would have committed new offenses even if they had served their full sentences. But the early releases have given career criminals more time on the streets to commit additional crimes, endangering the public," the story said.

I do not recall ever reading another *Times* article that spoke so disparagingly of career criminals, although the *Times* often laments the daily violence on the streets of Los Angeles. Also, I do not recall the *Los Angeles Times* ever conceding that there might be a correlation between the number of career criminals on the street and their responsibility for an increasing crime rate. Why is there no public outrage over so many convicted felons in Los Angeles County going unpunished? Perhaps it is because much of the public does not know. Also, many of us have higher priorities. One thing is certain: the defendants who plead guilty to felonies in Los Angeles County and are placed on probation on condition they serve a county jail sentence (65% of all convicted felons in 2005) all know they will serve very little or no jail time for that crime—regardless of the sentence pronounced by the judge.

12

THREE STRIKES, SENTENCING AND MEDIA MISINFORMATION

The Los Angeles Times, like most liberal papers, does not like the Three-Strikes law. They editorialized against it before and after its passage. California's Three-Strikes law was enacted in 1994 by a vote of the people. The law provides that if a defendant is currently charged with *any* felony and has been previously convicted of two "serious"[19] or "violent"[20] felonies, as defined in the *California Penal Code*, upon conviction of the currently charged felony, he could be sentenced to 25 years-to-life. The currently charged felony (the third strike), need not be on the list of "serious" or "violent" felonies.

In addition, if the defendant is currently charged with any felony and has one prior "serious" or "violent" felony conviction (this is called a two-strike case), the sentence for the current felony is doubled and the defendant must serve 80% of his sentence instead of the usual 50%.

For example, assume an inmate was recently paroled from prison after serving a sentence for robbery, a "serious" felony, which therefore constitutes a strike. While on parole he commits the crime of grand theft (not a "serious" felony) which has a sentencing range of either 16 months, 2 years or 3 years. The DA most likely would not dismiss the strike (the robbery prior), at least not in Los Angeles County. The defendant would not be placed on probation because of the strike allegation. If he pled guilty, he would probably be sentenced to the low term of 16 months for the grand theft. But because of the strike, the 16-month sentence is doubled to 32 months and the defendant would have to serve 80% of 32 months or about 26 months.

Prior to the Three-Strikes law, the same defendant could have been placed on probation for the grand theft conviction. But if the judge had denied probation and sentenced him to prison, it would most likely have been for 16 months. He would have received one additional year for the prior robbery prison term for a total of 28 months. He would earn good-time/work-time credits of 50% and, therefore, would serve 14 months in state prison. Fourteen months before the Three-Strikes law—26 months after the Three-Strikes

law—a big difference to the inmate serving the time. Because there
are so many more two-strike defendants than three-strike defendants, I believe the convictions of two-strike defendants have had a
greater impact in reducing crime in California than three-strike
defendants.

In September 2004, two college professors wrote an op-ed
piece for the *Los Angeles Times* in support of the Three-Strikes law.[21]
The professors pointed out that in the ten years since the Three-
Strikes law was passed by the voters, the crime rate in California
had fallen 45%. This was the steepest decline in crime rates in the
nation in that ten-year period.

No drug offenses, with the exception of selling certain drugs
to a minor, constitute a "serious" felony and hence cannot count as
strikes. Therefore, even if a defendant is currently charged with
robbery, rape or even murder and has several prior felony convictions for selling large quantities of drugs to adults, he is not
regarded as either a two- or three-striker as a result of his drug convictions. The same rule applies to prior theft convictions. That is,
even if the defendant has several prior grand theft convictions and
has served prison time for stealing millions of dollars from many
victims, these prior theft convictions are not "strikes" and therefore,
no matter how many prior grand theft convictions a defendant has,
he will not be a two- or three- strike candidate. This fact is rarely, if
ever, reported in the media.

The media rarely, if ever, tell us how often deputy DAs and
judges dismiss prior strike allegations. If a defendant is charged in
a three-strikes case and the sentence of 25 years-to-life appears to be
too severe, after considering the nature of the current offense and
the two prior felony convictions, and the time spread between
them, the Los Angeles County deputy DA will dismiss one of the
strikes, i.e., one of the alleged prior convictions. This converts the
case into a two-strike case. If, after considering all of the circumstances of the current case, and the nature and age of the two prior

convictions, the DA decides not to dismiss a prior strike, the judge still has the power to dismiss a prior conviction over the DA's objection. If both the DA and the judge refuse to dismiss a prior conviction, there is good reason to believe this defendant constitutes a continuing public threat and deserves to be treated as a three-striker and to be sentenced accordingly.

But it doesn't end there. The defendant has a right to appeal. Defendants who cannot afford to hire a lawyer, and few say they can, get a free attorney on appeal. The defendant's lawyer can argue to an appellate court that the judge abused his discretion by refusing to dismiss a prior conviction. If an appellate court upholds the trial judge's refusal to dismiss one of the strikes, the public can feel confident this defendant deserved to be treated as a three striker and was sentenced appropriately.

The media rarely mention that in many three-strikes cases, the DA's office does not pursue the case as a three-strikes case even when the defendant is legally eligible for a three-strikes sentence. My experience as a prosecutor is that in close calls regarding what charges to file, whether to pursue three strikes, whether to seek the death penalty, what kind of plea agreement to offer the defendant, we give the benefit of the doubt to the defendant, a fact I cannot recall seeing reported in the media.

When the media are critical of a 25-year-to-life sentence in a three-strikes case, they often fail to mention the nature of the defendant's prior serious or violent felony convictions, how recent they were or whether the defendant was on probation or parole at the time he committed the current offense. For example, in the infamous case of the three-strike pizza thief who stole pizza from children, how many people knew this was the defendant's *fifth* felony conviction? Did the *L.A. Times* ever tell us that this defendant, after an appeal, ended up being sentenced to six years in prison—for his fifth felony? The *Los Angeles Times* rarely gives its readers an objective view of both sides of a criminal justice issue when they favor one side.

The *Times* continues to rail against the Three-Strikes law. In an article published on page one of the California section on March 5, 2004, the headline was titled "Three-Strikes Law Has Little Effect, Study Says." The article states that "Three strikes inmates in California now number 42,000—one fourth of the state's prison population...." A reasonably objective person reading this sentence would believe there are 42,000 inmates in California prisons serving a three-strikes sentence. But this is not true. Of this 42,000, 35,000 inmates are two strikers. The remaining 7,000 are three strikers. By claiming that "Three strikes inmates in California now number 42,000," it seems clear that the *Times* wanted its readers to believe that nearly one fourth of the state's 170,000 prison population is serving a three-strikes sentence of 25 years-to-life. Aside from the issue of the *Times* again misleading its readers, 42,000 two- and three-strikers is a large number of violent and career criminals incarcerated —prisoners who might well be on the streets committing thousands of crimes if it were not for the Three-Strikes law.

When I hear a statistic like this, 42,000 career criminals in prison under the Three-Strikes law, I think of the thousands of people who would have been victims of these 42,000 career criminals, but now will not be victims because of the Three-Strikes law. That thought would never have entered my mind in my earlier life when I was a stereotypical liberal. Like most liberals, I never gave much thought to crime victims. I was insensitive to their suffering because crime victims receive so little attention from the press. I was also unaware of the high recidivism rates of career criminals. But even had I been aware of the statistics, I would have sided with the criminal—as most liberals do. I had a great deal of emotion invested in my liberalism. I was so sure I was right.

In March 2004, the *Los Angeles Times* published an article about a woman sentenced in a three-strikes case.[22] The *Times* stated that her first two strikes were robbery convictions. As mentioned, the crime of robbery is a "serious" felony and thus, a strike. In describing the facts of each of her prior robbery convictions, the *Times* again misled its readers. With respect to the defendant's first robbery conviction, the *Times* stated that the defendant said, "She lent her car to friends, who held up a liquor store." Doesn't it sound unfair to convict this woman of robbery simply because the people to whom she loaned her car decided to commit a robbery? Of course, it would be terribly unjust if this had actually occurred. But be assured that in California, and everywhere else in this country, one cannot be guilty of the crime of robbery by simply lending one's car to friends who then decide to commit a robbery. Is it possible that perhaps the *Los Angeles Times*, with their large legal staff and numerous defense attorney consultants, did not know this? Was this just another mistake—like the story in which the *Times* falsely told its readers, on two occasions, that a 17-year-old could receive the death penalty in California?

In describing the woman's other robbery conviction, the *Times* stated, "She was convicted of second-degree robbery for shoplifting at Sears and leading a security guard on a chase." Again, this is misleading because this description of the facts underlying the woman's second robbery conviction cannot possibly be accurate. Why? Because the crime of robbery requires that the personal property, whether it is money or merchandise, be taken by the use of force or fear. This woman who shoplifted at Sears, and ran away and was pursued and arrested by a security guard, cannot be guilty of robbery unless she, at some point, used force or fear against a store clerk or the security guard. For example, she would have had to strike the clerk or security guard or use or threaten to use a weapon against the clerk or the security guard in an effort to escape with the property taken.

If the *Times* were to claim they only printed what the woman told their staff writer about her two robbery convictions, and her explanations did not appear to the staff writer to make any sense, does not a reputable newspaper have an ethical obligation to call the DA's Office and ask for their version? Or, they could have looked at the court file, which is open to the public, before printing these false stories in their newspaper and leaving the impression on their readers that the defendant's version is accurate—and the justice system unfair.

Remember, about 90% of all defendants charged with felonies in Los Angeles plead guilty. Wouldn't it be helpful for the reader to know whether the defendant in these examples had pled guilty? This defendant was almost certainly represented by an attorney, most likely a deputy public defender. No criminal defense attorney would have permitted his client to plead guilty to the crime of robbery if the defendant had only loaned her car to friends who then decided to rob a liquor store clerk. Or for merely shoplifting at Sears and then running from the security guard. No prosecutor would ever charge anyone with robbery if the *Times'* version of the facts was accurate. These kinds of false stories about the criminal justice system are not unusual. I was raised on them and believed them until my experience as a deputy DA taught me I could not trust the media.

The big question is why the *Los Angeles Times* continues to mislead its readers. One might reasonably conclude that these false stories are evidence of the *Times'* continuing campaign against the Three-Strikes law and are designed to prejudice the public against the criminal justice system by making the system appear to be unfair.

In the same article involving the two alleged robberies, the *Times* stated that inmates get 20% credit on their state prison sentences. The *Times* neglects to point out that this 20% reduction only applies to two-strike cases. In all other "determinate" state prison sentences in California, defendants are released from prison after serving only 50% of their sentences, except those convicted of "violent felonies" (as defined) who receive only 15% credit. Nearly all crimes in California call for a determinate sentence other than crimes which call for a maximum sentence of life in prison.

For example, the determinate sentence range (see Chapter 24) for residential burglary is either two years, four years or six years. Assume the defendant is sentenced to the middle term of four years; because he gets one-half off his sentence, he actually spends two years in prison, or even less if he is released to a half-way house or receives extra credit for participating in educational programs. It is misleading for the media to fail to tell the public that a defendant sentenced by the judge to four years really serves only two years—or less.

It is clear the *Los Angeles Times* is on a continuing campaign to weaken or repeal California's Three-Strikes law. For example, on June 26, 2005, the cover story of the *Los Angeles Times Magazine* was titled "Price of Punishment." The cover-story description says, "California prisons are teeming with older inmates who run up staggering medical costs before their release. Their numbers are only growing in the wake of the Three-Strikes Law. Is the punishment worth the price?" This story, like so many other *L.A. Times* stories dealing with criminal justice issues, contains several false statements.

For example, the story says, "The state's 1994 Three-Strikes law mandates life sentences without parole for certain repeat felons, and these recidivists—42,240 second and third strikers as of June 2002—will inevitably grow old and die in prison." This one sentence contains two untruths. First, nobody is sentenced to "life without parole" under the Three-Strikes law. A three-striker sentenced to 25 years-to-life will come up for a parole hearing. (The *Times* repeated this false statement on March 9, 2007.) Second, it is not true that 42,240 second and third strikers will die in prison. All inmates sentenced as second-strikers have a right to be paroled. I have no doubt that the great majority of third-strikers will also be paroled.

The same story says that a 69-year-old woman was convicted of conspiracy to commit murder because she delivered cash to a hit man who turned out to be an undercover police officer. The story says the inmate thought she was just doing her son a favor when she delivered the cash to the cop who was posing as a hit man. There is no mention of the DA's evidence submitted to the jury to prove she knew she was paying a hit man. The evidence in such cases nearly always involves the defendant's tape-recorded conversation with the undercover police officer she thought was a hit man. She was convicted because the DA had proved beyond a reasonable doubt to all 12 jurors that she knew she was hiring a hit man.

The same story says that "In California, a life sentence almost always means just that, even if the Board of Prison Terms recommends parole. Former Governor Gray Davis, a Democrat, stated that murderers would leave prison during his term only in a pine box. Republican Governor Schwarzenegger is on exactly the same page."

This statement is false. As of March 2005, Governor Schwarzenegger had approved the paroles of 82 convicted murderers—all serving maximum terms of life in prison. By March 2006, this number had grown to over one hundred murderers. Why does the *Los Angeles Times* continually publish editorials and articles that mislead their readers on three-strikes facts and other criminal justice issues?

I have read countless examples of these types of misleading criminal justice stories in the *Los Angeles Times*. If this constitutes a continuing pattern of deception, and I certainly believe it does, the question is, why do they continue to do it? Many of these "errors" have one thing in common: They make the criminal justice system appear excessively harsh, unreasonable and unjust. Could the *Times* possibly believe, as they view the world through their biased, liberal lenses, that their continuing pattern of deception is somehow in the public interest?

I want to make clear that I am not criticizing the media solely for their editorial positions. Both print and television media have a right to express their opinions on the issues of the day if they make clear it is only their opinion. My gripe concerns their consistent attempts to mold public opinion by misleading their readers, slanting news stories to reflect their own point of view, omitting facts and views which are inconsistent with their position, or failing to mention legitimate authorities with whom they disagree.

13

CRIME, MAYBE A LITTLE PUNISHMENT

I discovered early in my career that the public, including police officers, attorneys who are not in the Criminal Justice Club, and even some DAs, have little knowledge of the actual sentences served for various crimes. We are frequently told by the media that sentences are too long. But the media rarely tells us how much time a defendant actually serves in prison for a given crime. I know of one notable exception: an op-ed piece published in the *Los Angeles Times* on November 24, 1992, titled "Crime, Maybe a Little Punishment," authored by Joseph Bessette. Kudos to the *Times* for publishing these startling statistics.

Joseph Bessette is currently a professor of government and ethics at Claremont McKenna College and the former Acting Director of the U.S. Bureau of Justice Statistics. His article was so enlightening that I have included some relevant excerpts. At my request, Professor Bessette updated the statistics cited in his 1992 article. I have included the updated statistics in brackets immediately following the statistics cited in his 1992 piece.

Professor Bessette asserts that there is a myth in this country, fostered by advocacy groups, columnists, and academics that we send people to prison for too long. The professor says the purpose is clear: to mold public sentiment against punishment and incarceration. The professor says that a growing body of data, most of it published by the Bureau of Justice Statistics of the U.S. Department of Justice, tells quite a different story. These data demonstrate the striking contrast between this myth of American punitiveness and the reality of crime in the United States.

Professor Bessette points out that very few people arrested for felonies in the United States end up sentenced to state prisons. Felonies are the most serious criminal offenses and include such crimes as murder, manslaughter, rape, child molestation, robbery, aggravated assault, residential burglary, arson, drug trafficking, and weapons offenses.

When Professor Bessette's op-ed piece appeared, the most recent published data showed that the odds that a person arrested for a felony would eventually be sentenced to state prison for a year or more were about one in ten, and for violent felonies, about one in eight. Data for 2002, the professor says, show that less than one in seven of those arrested for the violent felonies of murder, rape, robbery, and aggravated assault are convicted and sentenced to prison.

The professor says many convicted felons are not incarcerated at all. He presented data from a 1988 national survey showing that state courts throughout the nation convicted 667,000 people of felonies that year [1,051,000 in 2002]. Federal courts convicted another 31,000 of felonies [63,217 in 2002]. State courts sentenced 44% of the convicted felons to state prison [41% in 2002] and 25% to local jails [28% in 2002]. That means more than 200,000 convicted felons [more than 325,000 or 31% of felons convicted in state court in 2002] received no prison *or* jail time.

Professor Bessette says the Department of Justice statistics for 1991 show that about 60% of state prison inmates had at least one violent crime conviction [62% in 1997]; that 79% of state prison inmates were serving at least their second sentence to prison or probation [75% in 1997]; 60% at least their third [59% in 1997]; 45% at least their fourth [43% in 1997]; and 18% at least their seventh [The 18% figure remained the same in 1997]. Ninety-three percent of state prison inmates were either convicted violent offenders or recidivists [91% in 1997].

Professor Bessette asserts that "Over and over we are told that we keep criminals in prison "too long" but never how long. And the reason is clear, he claims. "Those who promulgate the punitiveness myth do not want us to know just how little time criminals actually spend behind bars in the United States." Professor Bessette offers some examples: Half of the several hundred thousand inmates released in 1988 served a year and a month or less in prison. [In 2001, one-half of the state prison inmates released had served $1\frac{1}{2}$ years or less in prison.] The median time served for drug traffickers was one year, [$1\frac{1}{2}$ years in 2001]; for burglars, 13 months [20 months in 2001]; for arsonists, 17 months [23 months in 2001]; for rapists, three years [5 years, 8 months in 2001]; and for those convicted of murder, $5\frac{1}{2}$ years [8 years, 8 months in 2001].[1]

Data from the end of 1990 show that of the 4.4 million offenders then serving criminal sentences in the United States [6.9 million in 2003], 74% of them—more than 3 million—[70% of them, more than 4.8 million in 2003], were serving their time in the community on probation or parole while the balance were in prisons or jails. Professor Bessette asks rhetorically, "Is this kind of ratio—three convicted criminals on probation or parole for every one in prison or jail—the mark of a society obsessed with locking up criminals and throwing away the key?"

Professor Bessette concludes by saying that "Those who argue that we punish criminals too severely have been less than forthcoming about the consequences of their schemes to lessen punishment for criminal offenses. They should say straight out that they want to see even more than 200,000 [325,000 in 2002] convicted felons released by courts to our communities each year without time behind bars...and that they want murderers to serve less than 5 $^1/_2$ years in prison [8 years, 8 months in 2001], rapists less than three years [5 years, 8 months in 2001], burglars less than 13 months [20 months in 2001], and drug traffickers less than a year [18 months in 2001].

In Los Angeles, local news programs often show a car being chased by the police that sometimes consumes nearly the entire news program. One of our most experienced Los Angeles television-news anchors, the late Hal Fishman, often editorialized during these car chases, expressing his view that if the people who drive recklessly while attempting to run from the police were given a five-year prison sentence, there would be fewer car chases. On March 5, 2005, Fox TV's Bill O'Reilly called for a sentence of ten years for such chases. What these TV personalities seem not to realize is that the median time served for murder in this country is less than nine years—an increase from 5 $^1/_2$ years in 1988. Long ago I stopped being surprised how uninformed most people are about how much prison time criminals actually serve in this country— even professional news people who we assume should know.

I have a suggestion. Some news anchor should do a follow-up story on a few car-chase defendants. Watch them get convicted and sentenced. Then wait for them to be released. It won't be a long wait—unless a particular defendant is a two or three striker. Then do a story about what *really* happens to the people who are chased by the police at high speeds through city streets and on freeways. I can safely guarantee that the public, as well as the news anchor, will be surprised at how quickly most of these car-chase defendants are released. It will usually be a matter of days, weeks or a few months—not years. One caveat: The news organization cannot reveal to the court or prison authorities that they are monitoring a particular case. I have been in the Club long enough to know that official conduct is sometimes influenced by the presence of a reporter or TV camera.

14

CALIFORNIA'S PROBATION SUBSIDY ACT

In the Los Angeles County District Attorney newsletter, *Amicus*, published in March 1976, it was revealed that in 1974, in our own L.A. County DA's office, 72% of all robbers, 93% of all burglars, 70% of all rapists, 80% of the drug dealers, and 36% of defendants convicted of murder and voluntary manslaughter were placed on probation or given non-prison sentences. In September 1976, the magazine, *Prosecutor's Brief*, published by the California District Attorney's Association (CDAA), revealed that, statewide, 41% of defendants convicted of their fourth felony were sentenced to probation. Who knew? Who cared? The press was silent. A sentence to state prison was the very last resort. One reason for this reluctance to sentence felons to prison had little to do with justice. It had to do with money. It was called The Probation Subsidy Act.

To discourage judges from sentencing felons to prison and to encourage them to place felons on probation, thus avoiding the necessity of having to spend hundreds of millions of dollars to build more prisons, the California legislature, in 1965, enacted The Probation Subsidy Act.[2] This law authorized the state to pay the counties up to $4,000 for every convicted felon who was placed on probation instead of being sentenced to prison. The counties made a profit on every convicted felon who was *not* sentenced to state prison, because the amount the state would pay the county was more than the county probation services cost.

One of the functions of county probation officers is to prepare probation reports for judges for every convicted felon. The report sets forth a summary of the facts of the defendant's current crime, his family history, his work history, his criminal history, and the probation officer's sentencing recommendation for the current felony offense. Judges follow the probation officer's sentencing recommendations about 80% of the time.

In the mid-1970s, I spoke to a Los Angeles County probation officer about the Probation Subsidy Act. He told me that because the county lost money for each convicted felon who was sentenced to state prison, probation officers were under great pressure from their supervisors to recommend in their probation reports to the judges that convicted felons be placed on probation. He told me the pressure became so great that before a probation officer could recommend a state prison sentence, even for a violent or career criminal, he had to make an appointment with his supervisor to try to persuade him that the defendant presented too great a threat to the public to be placed on probation. He told me that very often the area outside his supervisor's office was crowded with deputy probation officers waiting to make their arguments for state prison. He told me this procedure became so time consuming that most of the probation officers in his office finally got the message, gave up, and recommended probation for the great majority of felony defendants—including violent and career criminals.

The pressure placed on county probation officers to recommend probation sentences instead of state prison sentences, even for violent and career criminals, helps explain why, in the mid-1970s, 72% of all robbers, 93% of all burglars, 70% of all rapists, 80% of the drug dealers, 36% of those convicted of murder and voluntary manslaughter, and 41% of fourth-time convicted felons were placed on probation or given non-prison sentences. In 1976, 11,806 defendants were convicted of felonies in Los Angeles County. Only 14.3% were sentenced to prison.[3]

The Probation Subsidy Act also helps explain the reason California's prison population remained at about 20,000 inmates for much of the 1970s, during a period of increasing crime, thus allowing the state to delay for many years having to make the large investment for new prisons. It cost far less for the state to pay the counties $4,000 for each felon not sentenced to prison. Public safety was clearly sacrificed. This could not have occurred if we had had lawmakers who had concern for crime victims or a press that was vigilant and concerned with public safety.

In 1976, an attempt by then Republican State Senator George Deukmejian to terminate the Probation Subsidy Act was defeated in the Assembly Criminal Justice Committee. The Committee's only two Republicans voted to repeal the law. Four votes were required for passage. All the Democrats voted "no" *or failed to vote.*[4]

Failing to vote (called "abstaining") is a way that legislators can kill bills without having to explain a "No" vote to their constituents. On August 28, 2005, the *L.A. Times* published a story about legislators' practice of abstaining. The story was appropriately titled "Not Yes, Not No, Not Even Maybe." The story referred to a study showing that on bills that failed, Democrats abstained from voting more than twice as often—an average of 32% of the time, as Republicans—13.5% of the time.

The Probation Subsidy Act was finally terminated in 1978, but not before it diverted 45,000 felons from receiving state prison sentences, according to the California Research Bureau.[5]

I finally began to realize that if this was an example of liberal compassion— releasing all these violent and career criminals to victimize thousands more people, with no criticism from the liberal press—I had been on the wrong side of the criminal justice issue for many years throughout college and law school, and even as a young attorney. The only people who seemed terribly upset seeing violent and career criminals sentenced repeatedly to probation, aside from some DAs, were their victims—who have rarely been the focus of the press. The police were often not aware of what was going on. It is rare that the I/O is in court when the defendant is sentenced and oftentimes is not aware of the sentence.

15

TRUTH IN SENTENCING–NOT

Since I began my career, the criminal justice system has changed substantially for the better. In California, until 1978, the sentence for second-degree murder (for those not placed on probation) was five years-to-life in prison. However, in reality, a defendant convicted of second-degree murder and sentenced to prison was eligible for parole after serving twenty months in prison. The median time actually served for second-degree murder in 1976 was fifty-eight months—four years and ten months. One-half of second-degree murderers served less time. Convicted murderers, age sixteen and seventeen, served about two years. Very few people knew about this, because the press rarely told us. I would think most people reasonably assumed that defendants who were convicted of murder and sentenced to life in prison, or a maximum of life in prison, served an actual sentence of something closer to life in prison.

There were some influential people in California who knew how little prison time was served by convicted murderers. They were frustrated with their inability to lengthen murder sentences through the liberal, Democrat-dominated legislature. In 1978, they bypassed the legislature and went directly to the people through the initiative process and enacted a law which increased the sentences for first- and second-degree murder. More about this initiative later.

In 1988, as mentioned, the median state prison time actually being served by all convicted murderers *nationwide* was 5 $^1/_2$ years. Of course, 5 $^1/_2$ years was not the sentence the judge announced in court when he sentenced the defendant for murder. The sentence which the judge announced in court in almost every state, and reported by the press, was either life in prison or a maximum life sentence. The public was rarely told that the sentences actually served by convicted murderers were far less than that pronounced by the judge and published in the media.

For every felony defendant, a rap sheet is ordered. The rap sheet contains the entire adult criminal record of the defendant. In the 1970s it was not uncommon, when I was handling a robbery, burglary or drug case, to see a prior murder conviction on the defendant's rap sheet. This was one of my biggest shocks upon becoming a deputy DA. I remember asking another, more senior DA, "How can this convicted murderer be out committing burglaries and robberies a few years after his murder conviction?" To paraphrase Walter Cronkite, "That was the way it was."

Even today, the law in California states that a person sentenced to "life" in prison is eligible for parole in seven years. However, only a few California crimes, including willful, deliberate, and premeditated attempted murder, call for a "life" sentence. Even a sentence of "life in prison without parole" (L-WOP to Club members) does not guarantee that the defendant so sentenced will actually have to spend the rest of his life in prison.

In 1984, in a case called *People vs Zimmerman*,[6] authored by Justice Stanley Mosk, the California Supreme Court stated:

"As we concluded in *Williams* [another Supreme Court case] (at p.489 fn.10, of 30 Cal. 3rd), this does not mean that for practical purposes there is 'no such penalty' as life without possibility of parole; it means only that persons so sentenced do not necessarily 'remain in prison for the rest of their lives.' [case citation] Thus, although defendant's sentence herein purports to deny him all possibility of parole, there is in fact 'no insurmountable barrier against mitigation of the sentence if the time should come when the sentence appears to have served its purpose.' " [case citation]

I am not aware of any defendant who was serving a sentence of life without parole who has been paroled. However, Justice Mosk's language in *People vs Zimmerman* does not inspire confidence that a sentence of life without parole means that a defendant so sentenced will spend the rest of his life in prison.

There is very little truth disseminated to the public about the actual sentences served by convicted felons. This is the fault of the media who certainly have the resources to determine and periodically publish the *actual* prison time convicted felons serve for various crimes and how such actual sentences compare with the sentence the judge pronounced in court. One might reasonably conclude that the press will not give us this information periodically, because they do not want to alarm their readers by informing them of the short sentences (other than two and three strike and murder cases in California) actually served by most convicted felons.

The press nearly always tells us the maximum sentence a defendant is facing. If, for example, the maximum sentence for a particular crime is five years, and the defendant received the maximum, which is rare, he would still only serve half, or 2 ½ years, after he receives his good-time/work-time credits. But remember, about 90% of all defendants plead guilty, and defendants almost never agree to plead guilty for the maximum sentence.

16

A PERRY MASON MOMENT

In one of my more memorable cases, the defendant was charged with a double murder. He killed a man while trying to steal his methadone. The victim's nine-year-old niece was awakened by the commotion. She came out of her bedroom and witnessed the defendant stabbing her uncle to death. The little girl had a sweater loosely hanging over her shoulders with the arms tied in front. To eliminate the only witness to the murder of the little girl's uncle, the defendant strangled the little girl to death with the arms of the sweater. The defense attorney, the late Carl Jones, was one of the best in Los Angeles County. Carl established a great rapport with jurors. You just had to like him.

During a trial attorney's career, there are very few, if any, what I call Perry Mason moments; that is, where something truly unexpected and dramatic occurs in front of the jury. I've had a few of these Perry Mason moments, and one of them occurred in this case. During the defendant's scuffle with the man he murdered, the defendant's eyeglasses fell off. When the police detective later collected evidence at the murder scene, a pair of prescription eyeglasses were recovered, placed into an evidence envelope, and booked into the evidence room at the police station. After that, the eyeglasses were largely forgotten.

My strongest evidence came from a tow-truck driver. After the defendant killed the man and the little girl and left the victims' apartment, he discovered his car would not start. The defendant had to call a tow truck to have his car towed to his house. During the ride to the defendant's house, the defendant sat in the tow truck with the driver. In court, the tow-truck driver positively identified the defendant as being near the murder scene. I was able to tenuously tie the defendant to the killing by establishing the approximate time of death, the fact that the defendant and the victim both received their methadone from the same clinic, and that they were acquainted with each other. In addition, while the defendant was in jail, he tried to hire his cell mate, who was soon to be released, to kill the tow-truck driver—the only eyewitness against him. But, I had no evidence that placed the defendant inside the apartment where the two victims had been murdered.

During the trial, the defendant's wife was seated in the back row of the spectator section of the courtroom. After I rested the People's case, the defendant took the witness stand in his own defense. During my cross-examination of him, I showed him a document and asked him to identify his signature. The document simply showed that he was enrolled in the same methadone program as the victim. The defendant looked at the document and said he was not able to read it without his glasses. I asked him where his glasses were. He said he didn't know. I walked back to the counsel table and retrieved the glasses found on the floor at the murder scene. I showed the glasses to the defendant and asked him to try them on. When he tried on the glasses, his wife, from the back row of the courtroom, started waving her hands wildly and screaming, "No, no." But it was too late. The defendant testified that these were his glasses and asked me where I found them.

This testimony placed the defendant at the murder scene and corroborated the eyewitness testimony of the tow-truck driver. A rare Perry Mason moment indeed! The jury found the defendant guilty of two counts of first-degree murder. Although this kind of courtroom drama occurred every week on the fictional television-lawyer show, *Perry Mason*, a real trial attorney is lucky if this kind of courtroom surprise happens once or twice in his career.

Another interesting thing happened in this trial. The defendant's cell-mate, who the defendant tried to hire to kill the tow-truck driver, had been charged with auto theft. He had such a long record, the DA's office decided to spend the money to extradite him from Pennsylvania to stand trial in L.A. County where he stole the car. But his attorney was able to show that he was not brought to trial within the strict time limitations set by the extradition statute and his case was dismissed. Of course, the defense attorney in my murder case claimed that we had dismissed his case in exchange for his testimony that the defendant tried to hire him to kill the tow-truck driver. To rebut this tactic, I called, as witnesses, both the judge who dismissed the car thief's case as well as the deputy DA who argued against the dismissal. Both testified they were not even aware the alleged car thief was a witness in my double murder case.

In addition, the car thief testified that he was not even asked to kill the tow-truck driver until *after* his case was dismissed. It was only then, when he told my murder defendant he was going to be released from jail, that the defendant tried to hire him to kill the only eyewitness. The car thief testified proudly that he had stolen cars for many years, and that he was a very good car thief, but that he was not a killer, and that is why he told the police the defendant tried to hire him to kill the tow-truck driver.

17

MY GLADYS ROOT RAPE CASE

In the mid-1970s, I tried a rape case with the legendary defense attorney, Gladys Towles Root. Whenever Gladys Root entered the courtroom everything stopped. Her presence commanded attention. She was a large woman who dressed like no woman I had ever seen. Her dresses were not really dresses but simply fabric wrapped tightly around her body and pinned. She wore very large broad-brimmed hats. Her perfume was so strong, you could sometimes smell her before you saw her. Rape cases were her specialty. She was famous for her jury tactics in rape cases. One of her more successful ploys in arguing to juries was to hold up a needle and thread. Then, while moving the needle around with one hand, she would try, unsuccessfully of course, to put the thread through the needle—at the same time proclaiming loudly to the jury that it is impossible to thread a moving needle. This was her way of demonstrating that if the victim really had not wanted to engage in sexual intercourse, she could have resisted her client's advances. The fact that the intercourse occurred proved, she claimed, that the victim had consented to the intercourse. She told juries that most often when women said "no," it did not really mean no and that "no" often really meant yes. Gladys had a reputation for being very successful in getting rapists acquitted.

Rape cases are difficult cases to prosecute, because it often comes down to the victim's word against the defendant's, inasmuch as few rapes are committed in front of witnesses. According to the U.S. Department of Justice, in 2002 about half of all rapes in the nation went unreported. Nationwide, of those cases that prosecutors chose to prosecute, only 58% resulted in convictions, according to the National Center for Policy Analysis. In contrast, the Los Angeles County DA's Office, in 2002, convicted 83% of the rapists it chose to prosecute.[7] But in Los Angeles County, there is a high rejection rate in rape cases. If we are able to prove that intercourse occurred because of DNA evidence, we know the defendant's defense will be that the woman consented. If the case comes down *solely* to his word against hers, the case will not be filed—because we know from long experience that we cannot convince twelve jurors beyond a reasonable doubt that she is telling the truth and he is lying.

It was reported that in 2001 California had DNA evidence from 20,000 unsolved rape cases that had not been compared to the statewide DNA database. Los Angeles County alone had a backlog of 2,600 rape kits in which the DNA had not been analyzed.[8]

The best evidence a prosecutor can have in a rape prosecution is another rape victim who had been raped by the same defendant who used the same unique modus operandi (method of operation or M.O.) with her as with the rape victim in the case on trial.

I would often stay in the DA's office until late at night when preparing cases for trial and also during trials. In the 1970s, before we had computers, I would sit in our records section on the 17th floor of the Criminal Court's Building where we stored thousands of old filed and rejected cases. I would look for cases we had rejected on the same defendant. It sometimes paid off.

In the case I tried with Gladys Root, the defendant's M.O. was quite distinctive. The defendant was good looking with a deep, resonant voice. He was a professional actor and very charming. He met his victims in an acting class at Los Angeles City College. He complimented them on their acting ability and offered to take them to a producer friend of his to have them audition. In the current case, the defendant did actually take the victim, a very sweet girl, to a Hollywood producer who gave the defendant a script and told him to take the acting student somewhere and have her cold-read the script. The producer told the defendant that if he thought she performed well, to make an appointment and he, the producer, would audition the young lady. The young, aspiring actress was very excited.

After leaving the producer's office, the defendant suggested to the victim that they go to his apartment he shared with his fiancée. He warned the victim they would have to hurry because his fiancée would be home soon from work and they would then have to stop. Of course, this story about the fiancée coming home soon gave the victim a feeling of security. Once at the apartment, instead of giving the victim the script the producer had given him, the defendant set up his own scene for the two of them to play. The defendant told the victim that he would assume the character of her fiancé, a soldier coming home from Vietnam. He would knock on the front door. The victim, who had not seen her fiancé in over a year, would answer the door and be very surprised to see him standing there handsomely in his army uniform. The victim was supposed to throw her arms around him and greet him joyously— which she did. The defendant, upon entering the apartment, responded with joy and affection, kissing the victim while moving in the direction of the bedroom.

The victim explained to me that although she felt uncomfortable doing this scene, she saw women's clothes in the apartment and did not want to appear young, inexperienced, and unprofessional. Once in the bedroom, the defendant forced himself upon the victim and accomplished an act of sexual intercourse against her will. After the victim got dressed, she asked the defendant to take her back to the school where she had left her car. The defendant insisted they first have a cup of coffee, and then he would drive her to her car. The victim sat and had coffee with the defendant after which he drove her to her car.

I cannot imagine any deputy DA filing rape charges in this case. The defense attorney would tell the jury that the adult woman went willingly to the defendant's apartment. She agreed to play a love scene with him. Then she had sex with him. Then she sat and had coffee with him. Hardly the actions of a woman who has just been raped, the defense attorney would argue. The victim had not been hit. There was not a mark on her. There is no way we could convince all twelve jurors of the defendant's guilt of forcible rape beyond a reasonable doubt.

So why did I file a forcible rape charge against this defendant? Because while sitting in the DA records section late one night,

I found a rape case we had rejected a few years earlier that involved this same defendant. That rape victim was also an acting student at L.A. City College. She was also taken by the defendant to the same Hollywood producer, then to the defendant's apartment, followed by the same Vietnam-soldier scene. But that case was rejected for filing because it was the victim's word against the suspect's, and because she had not been hit and had no marks on her, there was insufficient evidence to prove to all twelve jurors beyond a reasonable doubt that she was telling the truth and he was lying.

I asked a DA investigator to try to locate this former victim whose case we had rejected. We found her living in Northern California. She agreed to come down to Los Angeles and testify. Unfortunately, I could not file rape charges with respect to her, because the statute of limitations had expired. But my hope was that I could use her to help establish the defendant's M.O. and thereby prove the defendant's guilt in his current rape case.

I knew if I could persuade the judge to admit into evidence the testimony of the prior victim relating her almost identical experience with the defendant, we would have a good chance of convicting the defendant. If I lost this pretrial motion to allow the jury to hear the testimony of the former victim, there was no way I could convince 12 jurors that the defendant raped the current victim. I wrote a 32-page motion pointing out every element of similarity between the defendant's actions with each victim. I won the motion. I flew the former rape victim down from Northern California.

But Gladys Root was brilliant. Gladys had a beautiful girl sitting in the front row of the spectator section. Each time the judge called a court recess, Gladys made sure the jury saw the defendant's alleged girlfriend stand up and throw kisses to the defendant. Of course, Gladys' strategy was to make the jury wonder why the defendant would rape this young acting student when he had this gorgeous woman waiting for him. I wondered if the defendant even knew this alleged girlfriend in the front row. Gladys was very wily and I thought it was a brilliant tactical move. I even complimented Gladys for staging it so well—putting the girl in the front row so the jury could not miss the kiss blowing. Gladys just laughed.

But Gladys' scheme did not work. The former rape victim's testimony was too convincing. These two women had never met. The chance of two women who had never met fabricating such similar stories was highly unlikely. The defendant was convicted of forcible rape and sentenced to prison. But, as I later discovered, when another deputy DA requested a copy of my 32-page motion, the defendant had been paroled in less than two years and had raped another woman employing the same M.O. Since that time, thanks largely to the women's movement, sentences for sex crimes have been substantially increased. Also, we now have the Three Strikes law, no thanks to the media, that would put this type of defendant in prison for a very long time on his third felony conviction.

18

"YOUR HONOR, I DON'T NEED ANOTHER FATHER"

Judge Richard Francis Cavanaugh Hayden was a very bright and compassionate judge. He sympathized with defendants who found themselves in the unfortunate situation of being charged with a felony and facing the possibility of a state prison sentence. Judge Hayden put more convicted felons on probation than any judge I can remember. He would sentence them to consecutive years in the Los Angeles County Jail—one year for each count—as a condition of granting them probation. He ordered most of the defendants to go to baking school while in jail so when they were released they would have a skill. This was in addition to ordering them to earn their high school diploma while in jail. His sentences would often contain an order to the sheriff that the defendant was to be released from jail when the defendant had achieved a "C" average in the courses he was ordered to take while in custody. Judge Hayden was very sincere in wanting to rehabilitate all the defendants who appeared before him. Even some defense attorneys would kid him about his lenient sentences. Judge Hayden's reputation for lenient and creative sentences was widely known.

Although Judge Hayden was likable, he was also thin-skinned and had a quick temper. He always kept a pitcher of water on the bench and in his chambers. When his temper would start to flare, he would reach for the pitcher and pour himself a glass of water.

I was assigned to Judge Hayden's courtroom for about a year as his "calendar deputy." The calendar deputy in the L.A. County DA's office is the senior DA assigned to a superior court. Although there might be one or two subordinate DAs also assigned to the court, the calendar deputy is the chief representative of the People in that courtroom. It is the calendar deputy's duty to determine what plea bargains to offer defense attorneys for the cases set in that courtroom. The calendar deputy may also try jury trials occasionally, but still must prepare for a heavy caseload each day and decide what plea bargains to offer the defense attorneys in each case. Some cases involve multiple defendants, each with his own attorney.

I remember a case in which a defendant was charged with several armed robberies of convenience store clerks. This defendant had a serious and lengthy criminal history. He liked to pistol whip his victims *after* they gave him the money. Some of his victims had suffered serious head injuries. The defense attorney asked me if we could go into the judge's chambers to discuss a plea bargain. This attorney had a very dry sense of humor. Judge Hayden always began each plea-bargaining discussion by asking the defense attorney, "What are your goals?" The defense attorney began his pitch with an absolutely straight face. He told the judge that he realized his client was charged with very serious crimes and had a long criminal record. Nevertheless, the attorney explained, still holding his poker face, his client desired to go to medical school while in the county jail, and he wondered if he could be released if he achieved a "C" average.

The judge became tight-lipped and reached for his water pitcher. He hated being made fun of for his compassionate sentencing practices. The judge, without saying a word, rose from his seat. That was a clear signal that this plea-bargaining session was over. However, the attorney knew Judge Hayden to be an honorable man, and he knew that trying to have some fun with him would not hurt his client. And he was right. Judge Hayden would never make a defendant pay by imposing a longer sentence because of his anger toward his attorney.

In the afternoons, Judge Hayden conducted probation violation hearings for convicted felons who were on probation to him. In the typical case, the probation officer was requesting Judge Hayden to revoke probation and sentence the defendant to prison. But Judge Hayden strongly resisted sending any defendant to prison no matter how many times the defendant had violated his conditions of probation. He would often find fault with the probation officer's supervision of the defendant rather than blame the defendant.

One of Judge Hayden's probation cases became famous nationwide. It even made the CBS news with Walter Cronkite. The defendant was a habitual pickpocket. He had been convicted numerous times for pickpocketing. It was how he made his living. Pickpocketing is a felony and the crime is called grand theft from the person. For his most recent pickpocketing conviction, Judge Hayden had sentenced him to probation on condition he serve some time in the county jail. He remained on probation to Judge Hayden for many years, which the law permitted in the 1970s, but he continued to get arrested for pickpocketing. Nevertheless, Judge Hayden wanted desperately to save him from the prison experience and refused to terminate probation and commit him to prison, as was recommended repeatedly by the probation officer.

Finally, after one of the defendant's many pickpocketing arrests, he was brought again before Judge Hayden for a probation revocation hearing. But Judge Hayden again refused to follow the probation officer's recommendation to terminate probation and sentence the defendant to prison. Instead, he amended the conditions of probation by ordering that whenever the defendant left his house, he had to wear heavy wool mittens—which made it very difficult to pick pockets. The defendant was again released from jail.

The defendant plied his pickpocketing trade in downtown Los Angeles. The police officers assigned to the downtown area knew the defendant and were made aware of the defendant's new condition of probation requiring him to wear his wool mittens whenever he was out in public. Well, you guessed it. On a hot summer day, a police officer saw the defendant not wearing his mittens. He arrested the defendant for violating his probation, and the defendant was again brought before Judge Hayden. I was in the courtroom to hear the probation violation hearing; and so was the press.

The police officer took the witness stand and testified to seeing the defendant on a downtown street not wearing his mittens. The defendant did not testify. Judge Hayden found the defendant in violation of probation. Judge Hayden was about to place the defendant back on probation because, after all, it would have been cruel, the judge thought, to enforce the wool-mitten rule on such a hot summer day. But a surprise occurred. The defendant refused probation and asked to be sentenced to prison. The law in California says a judge cannot place a defendant on probation if the defendant refuses probation. I had never heard of a defendant refusing probation, which is understandable, because the alternative is prison. However, here was this defendant telling Judge Hayden he was refusing probation and asking to be sent to prison. The judge told the defendant he was making a big mistake and that he was going to continue the case until the next day so the defendant could spend the night in jail and think over his decision.

The next day the defendant appeared before Judge Hayden. The judge asked him if he had thought about his decision. The defendant replied that he had, and his decision remained the same. Judge Hayden tried his best to change the defendant's mind by telling him how bad prison was. But it was no use. The defendant's mind was made up. The judge asked the defendant why he preferred prison over freedom, and the defendant replied that he had been on probation to Judge Hayden for many years. He told Judge Hayden that if he had been sentenced to prison several years before when he was first sentenced, he would have been out long ago. He told Judge Hayden that he knew he meant well, and he appreciated the judge's concern. He told the judge that he knew he had let him down, but he finally decided he couldn't take it any longer and, besides, he didn't need another father.

With that, it was checkmate. Judge Hayden could not continue the defendant on probation, and he believed dismissing the case would be inappropriate. He therefore had no alternative but to send this career-criminal pickpocket to prison. I actually felt sorry for Judge Hayden. I knew how difficult it was for him to send this man to prison—even though the actual prison time to be served would only be a few months inasmuch as all defendants who are sentenced to prison in California receive credit for the time they had spent in the county jail.

19

THE LOS ANGELES TIMES AND THE INITIATIVE

For many years, some legislators tried repeatedly to get tougher criminal laws through the California state legislature. But Assembly Speaker Willie Brown appointed the committee members. He made sure the chairman and other members of the Assembly Criminal Justice Committee (now called The Assembly Public Safety Committee) were liberals who would kill all meaningful criminal justice legislation.

Finally, those advocating tougher criminal laws gave up on the legislature. They turned to the initiative process. California has a provision written into the state Constitution permitting direct action by the people to recall politicians, to enact laws through the initiative process, and to repeal laws through the referendum. Few initiative proposals make it to the ballot and become law. According to the California Secretary of State, between 1912 and 2002, advocates tried to gather sufficient signatures to place 1,187 measures on the ballot in California. In those 90 years, only 290 got on the ballot and only 99, or 8.3% of those originally proposed, were approved by the voters and became law.[9]

The *Los Angeles Times* and the liberal establishment dislike the initiative. They state many reasons for not liking the people's exercise of direct democracy but, in truth, I believe they have a deep distrust of the voters. In addition, the *Times* finds it difficult to lobby millions of voters to vote in favor of their ultraliberal, soft-on-crime agenda. The *Times* believes they can be more effective by persuading individual state senators and assemblymen to their point of view. In addition, criminal laws passed by the legislature almost always contain loopholes and exceptions. By contrast, criminal laws set forth in initiatives tend to be more straightforward and contain fewer loopholes and exceptions that weaken the law.

The *Times* has been editorializing against the initiative process for many years. Since 1978, California's voters have passed, and thereby enacted into law, many initiatives reforming the criminal justice system. In every one of the many substantive criminal justice initiatives submitted to the voters since 1978, the *Los Angeles Times'* editorial positions, either supporting or opposing the initiatives, have been rejected by the voters. It is no wonder the *Times* dislikes the initiative.

Proposition 7

All initiatives in California are called "propositions" and all propositions are assigned numbers. In 1978, Proposition 7 was on the ballot. Prop 7 was an initiative that provided for a sentence of twenty-five years-to-life for first-degree murderers and fifteen years-to-life for second-degree murderers. In the campaign for Prop 7, the public was finally made aware of how little prison time convicted murderers served. Prop 7 also said that if the murder was of the first degree, and was committed during the commission of one or more "special circumstances" (as defined in the initiative), the murderer could be sentenced to death *or* to life without parole (L-WOP). The *Los Angeles Times* opposed Proposition 7,[10] but it passed with 71% of the vote.

Even in those first-degree murder cases in which the defendant is legally eligible for the death penalty, the L.A. County DA's office seeks the death penalty in relatively few of these cases. The death penalty is reserved for the most egregious of the special-circumstance murder cases.

For many years, Curt Livesay was the Chief Deputy District Attorney, the second in command of the office. Livesay made the final decision on whether we sought the death penalty. Livesay was regarded by defense attorneys as eminently fair. It was his policy to invite the defendant's attorney to his office in close cases to make his best arguments against the death penalty and in favor of L-WOP. Livesay would notify the attorney of his decision with what came to be known as the "Livesay Letter." Today, in the Los Angeles County DA's Office, a committee of supervising deputy DAs decides if the trial deputy DA should seek the death penalty.

Rose Bird and the *Los Angeles Times*

The extremely liberal Chief Justice of the California Supreme Court, Rose Bird, was also on the ballot along with Prop 7. Rose Bird had been appointed to the court in 1977 by Governor Jerry Brown.

During her tenure on the court, Rose Bird voted to reverse the death sentence of every defendant whose death penalty sentence was reviewed by the Supreme Court—62 in all. She never saw one case where the jury imposed the death penalty that she did not find reversible error. Rose Bird squeaked by in the 1978 election. She was supported enthusiastically by the *Los Angeles Times*. In their October 29, 1978 editorial endorsing her, the *Times* stated that "Judges must stand above partisanship. Their role is to interpret the law, not to twist it this way or that...." One can only imagine how much twisting of the law was necessary to find reversible error in every death penalty case that ever came before her: sixty-two murderers sentenced to death and 62 votes by Rose Bird to reverse the death penalty. She was later removed from office in 1986 by a vote of the people—over the strong editorial endorsement of her by the *Los Angeles Times*.

Proposition 8

In 1982, the proponents of criminal justice reform, still striking out with the liberal California legislature, collected sufficient

announced U.S. invasion. The *Times'* editorial said, "Deceiving the enemy is one thing, but lying to the public is out of bounds." The *Times* went on to say, "Credibility once lost will not be regained." If only the *Los Angeles Times* would practice what they preach.

Proposition 67

In 1988, sufficient signatures were collected to put Proposition 67 on the ballot. Prop 67 provided that defendants convicted of second-degree murder of a police officer, while the officer was in the performance of his duties, shall be sentenced to 25 years-to-life in prison. Also, the defendant would have to serve 25 years before he is eligible for parole. John Van de Kamp, my former boss, who was then California's Attorney General, signed the ballot argument in favor of Prop 67.

In an editorial dated June 2, 1988, the *Los Angeles Times* opposed Prop 67. Nevertheless, 82% of the voters voted for Prop 67 and it is now the law in California. Only a newspaper on the far Left fringe would feel comfortable opposing a minimum sentence of 25 years in prison for one who murders a police officer. The fact that over 80% of the voters rejected the *Times'* soft-on-crime position indicates how far the *Times* is from mainstream voters.

Proposition 89

In November 1988, Proposition 89 was on the ballot. Prop 89 provided that the Governor could modify or reverse any decision of the California parole board, known as the Board of Prison Terms. The impetus for Prop 89 was the parole board's granting of parole to murderers who, when released, murdered again. The "Argument in Favor of Proposition 89," which appeared in the ballot pamphlet, revealed many instances in which murderers paroled from California prisons murdered again after their release. Prop 89 was opposed by the *Los Angeles Times* in an editorial dated November 2, 1988, but 55% of the voters voted for it and it is now the law.

Ever since the late 1970s, the *Los Angeles Times* has been editorializing against the death penalty. One of their reasons for their opposition to the death penalty is their contention that the public would be just as safe if convicted murderers received life in prison. In a November 20, 2005 editorial titled "A Rush to Executions," the *Times* said, "Americans would be just as safe...with an ultimate sentence of life in prison." But again, the *Times* was being disingenuous. During Gray Davis' five years as California's governor (1999-2003), the *Times* frequently criticized him for his reluctance to approve the parole of murderers. The Governor only had this approval power because it had been given to him by Prop 89. The truth is, the *Los Angeles Times* is not just against the death penalty. The *Times* also opposes a true sentence of life in prison for convicted first-degree murderers. And that is the reason they opposed Prop 89. The *Times* saw Prop 89 as another hurdle (the Governor's approval) which might prevent convicted murderers from gaining their freedom.

Proposition 115

Proposition 115 was on the ballot in June 1990. Prop 115 was the most important criminal justice reform since I had become a deputy DA in 1968. Prop 115 was a very important initiative for crime victims, DAs and their clients, the People of the State of California. It brought about many important changes in the system.

Prop 115, for the first time, gave the People (and their attorney, the DA) the right to a speedy trial. Prior to June 5, 1990, defense attorneys could get judges to continue cases sometimes for years and there was nothing the DA could do about it. Our witnesses would disappear and cases were dismissed; witnesses would forget details of the crime that occurred years before and would consequently make a poor impression on cross-examination by the defense attorney. Sometimes witnesses would die, evidence was lost; it was a terrible situation. And that was the way it was for my entire career until June 1990—when everything changed.

The U.S. Constitution and state law guarantee the *defendant* a speedy trial, but the People had no corresponding right—until Prop 115. For the first time, the People were permitted to appeal if the trial judge continued (delayed) the case without good cause over the People's objection. Every criminal defense attorney knows that delaying a criminal trial almost always helps the defendant. As mentioned earlier, "justice delayed is often justice denied." Nobody knows this better than defense attorneys.

Prop 115 added a special circumstance for defendants who were convicted of first-degree murder for killing a witness to prevent his testimony. For the first time, such a murderer was eligible to be sentenced to life without parole or death.

Prop 115 prohibits trial judges from dismissing, without legal cause, a special circumstance allegation that had been found true by a jury. Prior to Prop 115, it was not uncommon for judges to dismiss special circumstance allegations that the jury had found to be true, thereby precluding the DA from seeking a sentence of death or life in prison without parole. Prior to Prop 115, there was nothing the DA could do when a judge dismissed the special circumstance allegation. Since Prop 115 was enacted, the DA has had a right to appeal if a judge, without legal cause, dismisses a special circumstance allegation which had been found true by a jury.

For the first time, Prop 115 provided for reciprocal discovery in criminal cases. The law says that a prosecutor must give the defense attorney a list of all the witnesses the DA intends to call and all the exhibits he intends to introduce into evidence, as well as all police reports and lab reports. Until Prop 115 passed, the defense attorney had no obligation to tell the DA anything. For example, he could call surprise witnesses who had long felony records. But the DA had no prior notice and therefore no time to find out who the defense witnesses really were. Only defense attorneys, never the DA, could call surprise witnesses. Prop 115 requires the defense attorney to inform the DA of the names of the witnesses he intends to call.

I remember a pre-Prop 115 robbery case one of our DAs was prosecuting. The defense attorney called a surprise alibi witness who testified that the defendant was with him in a location many miles away from the location of the robbery at the time the robbery occurred. The defendant was found not guilty and was released from jail. After the trial, we learned that at the time of the robbery in Los Angeles, the alibi witness had signed in as a visitor at a northern California prison visiting an inmate.

Of course, the trial was over and because of the double jeopardy rule, there was nothing we could do about it. The double jeopardy clause in the U.S. Constitution prohibits trying a person again for the same crime once the person has been acquitted. There is an exception in the relatively rare case when the defendant's crime violates both state law and federal law. An acquittal in state court, in such cases, does not bar another trial in federal court. The reader might recall the Rodney King case in which the officers who beat King were acquitted in state court, but later some of the same officers were convicted in federal court of violating King's civil rights.

The reader might think that surely we could file a perjury charge against the witness who falsely testified he was with the defendant at the time of the robbery. Not so. As a practical matter, we would not file a perjury charge in a case like this. The reason is, the DA cannot win it. We have to prove perjury, like any other crime, beyond a reasonable doubt to all twelve jurors. If we had filed a perjury charge against this witness, he most certainly would have testified that he had gotten his days mixed up, and that his false testimony was not willful but simply a mistake. To convict someone of perjury, the DA must prove that his false testimony was intentional and not the result of a mistake. The DA can rarely prove this, and for this reason, very few perjury charges of this type are charged. In fact, I have only seen a handful of perjury charges filed resulting from giving false testimony in a trial. In addition, even if the DA can prove intentional lying under oath, it is not necessarily perjury in California. The lie must relate to a "material" issue in the case to constitute perjury.

Prop 115's requirement that the defense attorney provide the DA with a list of the witnesses he intends to call was a significant change in the law because it gives the DA time to check out a defense witness's background, including whether he has prior felony convictions which the DA can use to impeach his testimony, i.e., to cast doubt on his truthfulness.

Prop 115 also allows the investigating officer to testify to hearsay at preliminary hearings. For example, before Prop 115, in a burglary case we always had to subpoena the victim home-owner to come to court to testify that she did not give the defendant permission to enter her home. Sometimes the victim was elderly or sick, and it was difficult or sometimes impossible to get her into court. If we could not get her to the preliminary hearing, the case was dismissed and the burglar went free.

But after Prop 115, the investigating officer was permitted to testify at the preliminary hearing that the burglary victim told him that she did not give anyone permission to enter her home. This Prop 115 rule allowing limited hearsay testimony at the preliminary hearing does not apply to the trial. If the case went to trial, we would have to get the victim in court to testify. But remember, about 90% of all defendants plead guilty and there is no trial. This very practical Prop 115 rule saves a great deal of time and avoids incon-venience for crime victims and witnesses, but in no way affects the defendant's right to have a jury trial and to confront and cross examine all the witnesses against him—*at the trial.*

Prior to Prop 115, one of the strategies used by defense attorneys was to force a severance in multiple-defendant cases. For example, if three defendants are charged with the robbery and murder of a convenience-store clerk, defense attorneys would almost always prefer to go to trial with one defendant at a time, that is, without their co-defendants.

Before Prop 115, in such a three-defendant robbery-murder case, one of the three defense attorneys would demand a speedy trial for his client. The other two defense attorneys would tell the judge they were not ready for trial. Before Prop 115, the judge had no choice but to sever the case and the DA had to go to trial with just the one defendant who demanded his speedy trial. Then, later, the second and third defendants would each use the same tactic, causing the DA to have three separate trials. This was very expensive and time consuming. All defense attorneys know that separate trials favor the defense. It is easier for a jury to sympathize with one defendant than with three. Also, the single defendant on trial can try to shift the blame to the other defendants, who are not in court, by claiming that the other guys were the real bad guys, and that his role was relatively minor, or that he was forced or coerced to participate in the robbery by his two crime partners. Prop 115 put an end to this defense strategy of forcing the DA to have three separate trials, one for each defendant, instead of one trial for all three defendants.

In an editorial dated May 29, 1990, the *Los Angeles Times* opposed Prop 115. One of the *Times'* reasons for opposing Prop 115 was that "Attorneys appointed to represent the poor would be compelled to prepare their cases more rapidly than lawyers retained by wealthy clients." There is nothing in Prop 115 that discriminates between poor defendants and wealthy defendants. And there is nothing in Prop 115 with respect to how rapidly attorneys representing wealthy defendants must prepare their cases as contrasted with attorneys representing poor defendants.

In this same editorial, the *Times*, in their desperation to defeat Prop 115, told its readers that if Prop 115 passed, it could put at risk, "the right of women to obtain, safe, legal abortions." There was no mention of abortion in Prop 115. In California, as well as all other states, the right of women to obtain safe, legal abortions is guaranteed by the Supreme Court of the United States. And even if *Roe v Wade* were overturned by the U.S. Supreme Court, California law protects a woman's right to an abortion. The California law permitting abortion was signed by Governor Ronald Reagan in 1967, six years before *Roe v Wade* was decided. Once again, the voters rejected the soft-on-crime philosophy of the *Los Angeles Times* and passed Prop 115 with 57% of the vote.

Proposition 184: Three Strikes and You're Out

Then came the really big initiative in 1994: Proposition 184, Three Strikes and You're Out. The proponents of the Three-Strikes initiative had collected sufficient signatures to put Three-Strikes on the November 1994 ballot, but only after liberal Democrats had killed a similar Three-Strikes bill in the legislature. The impetus behind Three-Strikes was Mike Reynolds, a Fresno resident whose 18-year-old daughter, Kimber, had been murdered in 1992 by a career criminal who tried to snatch her purse. When she resisted, he shot her in the head. Mr. Reynolds, a wedding photographer, was determined to do something about the revolving-door prison system in California. He called his Republican Assemblyman, Bill Jones, who wrote and introduced a bill in the legislature called "Three Strikes and You're Out." Like all criminal justice legislation, the bill was sent to the Assembly Public Safety Committee, known as the "graveyard" for criminal justice bills.

The Speaker of the Assembly, Willie Brown, had stacked this committee with soft-on-crime liberal Democrats. It was an eight-member committee, but Willie Brown only appointed seven legislators to the committee, five Democrats and two Republicans. Because it was designated an eight-member committee, five votes were needed to pass any legislation to the floor of the Assembly even though the committee had only seven members. Three of the seven members of the committee were liberal, soft-on-crime Democrats: John Burton, Barbara Lee, and Tom Bates. John Burton and Barbara Lee refused to even meet with Bill Jones or Mike Reynolds to discuss the bill. Mike Reynolds, in his excellent book, *Three Strikes and You're Out*, said he was surprised how rude the liberals were on the Public Safety Committee. The committee vote was four to zero in favor of passing the bill, but Bates, Burton, and Lee abstained. Inasmuch as any bill needed five votes for committee approval (a simple majority of what was supposedly an eight-member committee), the Three-Strikes bill died.

It was only after the Three-Strikes bill was killed by the California legislature that Mike Reynolds decided to go the initiative route. Signature gathering began slowly, but when a little girl named Polly Klass was kidnapped and murdered, the initiative took off. When the legislators in Sacramento saw the groundswell of support for the Three-Strikes initiative set for the November 1994 ballot, they revived and passed the Three-Strikes bill despite almost universal opposition from the press. Even many legislators who voted for the Three-Strikes bill criticized the bill, but voted for it anyway because it was very popular and because every member of the Assembly faced re-election in November 1994.

Governor Wilson signed the Three-Strikes bill into law on March 7, 1994, and it took effect that day. But Mike Reynolds did not trust the legislature. He believed, with good reason, that had he not continued to collect signatures for his Three-Strikes initiative, the legislature would have gutted the Three-Strikes law in subsequent revisions to the law. But they were not able to gut the Three-Strikes law with the threat of the popular initiative hanging over their heads, and the initiative required a two-thirds vote in each house to weaken it.

The Three-Strikes initiative really seemed to drive the *Los Angeles Times* crazy. They editorialized against it vehemently. On March 1, 1994, the *Times* printed a story on page one citing a study that predicted by the year 2000, if the Three-Strikes initiative passed, California would need to build 20 new prisons, in addition to the 12 that were already planned. The story also predicted that by 2001, 109,000 more inmates would be in our prisons because of Three Strikes for a total of 229,000. The reality is that instead of having to build 32 new prisons by the year 2000, California has only built five new prisons since 1994, from 28 then to the current 33. Instead of adding 109,000 new prisoners by 2001, we added 37,000 by 2001 for a total of 157,000.

The *Times* even printed a piece on their op-ed page by law professor Gerald Uelman, one of O.J. Simpson's lawyers, who said that if the Three-Strikes initiative passed, it would eliminate the death penalty for career criminals. Of course, that did not happen either. The voters passed the Three-Strikes initiative by 71% of the vote. If the *Times* had believed that the Three-Strikes initiative would have eliminated the death penalty for career criminals, they surely would have been in favor of it, given their strong opposition to the death penalty.

It is not uncommon for the liberal media to attack a criminal justice initiative on the grounds that it would cost too much. It seems that liberal legislators, who are supported by the liberal media, have historically spent freely for social programs and have shown no reluctance to run massive budget deficits. Yet, they suddenly become fiscal conservatives when it comes to funding public safety. The *Los Angeles Times* points out repeatedly how much it costs to keep an inmate in prison. Yet, what I have not read in the *Times* is how much crime costs its victims and society.

In a 1996 study published by the National Institute of Justice titled *"Victim Costs and Consequences: A New Look,"* researchers found that personal crime in the U.S. is estimated to cost $105 billion annually in medical costs, lost earnings, and public program costs related to victim assistance. If pain and suffering and reduced quality of life were also considered, the annual cost would rise to $450 billion. Violent crime, (including drunk driving and arson) accounts for $426 billion of this total. Property crime accounts for the remaining $24 billion. These estimates exclude several crimes that were not included in the study but that also have large impacts, notably many forms of white-collar crime (including personal fraud) and drug crimes. From a monetary perspective, incarcerating violent and career criminals is a bargain for society.

Proposition 195

Proposition 195 was on the California ballot in March 1996. Prop 195 added two new special circumstances to the Penal Code: the murder of the victim during a carjacking and the murder of a juror in retaliation for the juror's verdict.

In California, the only way a convicted murderer can receive either a sentence of life without parole or the death penalty is if the DA alleges, and the jury agrees, that one or more special circumstances apply, as defined by the Penal Code.[11] Examples of special circumstances are multiple murders, murder with a prior murder conviction, murder for hire, murder by poison, and murders committed during the commission of robbery, rape or kidnapping. In California, a convicted first-degree murderer cannot be sentenced to death or to life without parole simply because the murder he committed was willful, deliberate and premeditated. The murder must also have been accompanied by a "special circumstance."

Proponents of Prop 83 resorted to the ballot only after Democrats killed similar measures in the legislature. The *Times* came out against this initiative even before it qualified to be on the ballot. In their editorial, the *Times* said that extending the ban around schools and parks from 1300 feet to 2000 feet "is another dubious idea." The *Times* will always come up with some reason to oppose measures that protect victims by keeping the predators in prison longer—no matter how unlikely the prospect of rehabilitating the predators. Prop 83 passed 70% to 30%.

On July 6, 2004, the *Los Angeles Times* published an editorial titled "Mexico's Anti-Crime Wave." The *Times* criticized the Mexican government for not doing enough to control crime—especially kidnappings for ransom. The *Times* applauded Mexican citizens for demanding action and said that the *Mexican* government's most basic obligation is to provide public safety. The editorial stated that "The [Mexican] politicians must prove they heard the message and are ready to do whatever is necessary to solve the problem." Can this be the *Los Angeles Times*? Are they really getting serious about controlling crime—*in Mexico*? The same newspaper that has opposed every major effort since 1978 to control crime in California? Is this not the height of hypocrisy?

The chances of justice prevailing in our criminal courts in California are far greater today than at any time since I became a deputy DA, primarily because of California's initiative process, which permits the people to take direct action when the legislature fails to act.

None of these initiatives would have been necessary if the legislature had been doing its job. None of the laws contained in these initiatives is unfair to defendants. How does a liberal legislator defend the median sentence of four years, ten months for murder? How can the liberal community defend their opposition to a minimum sentence of 25 years for the murder of a police officer? But, as a former liberal I really do understand it. In my college- and law-school days, and even as a new lawyer, I would also have opposed these reforms. I would have argued that it really isn't the criminal's fault. He is a product of his environment: poverty, racism, broken home, etc. I argued that we all share collective guilt for the criminal's crimes. It is society's fault. It is unfair to punish the criminal by locking him up in a cage like an animal. After all, I argued, as does Willie Brown, that he too is a victim.

I remember all of my passion-filled arguments. But, I realized years later that as the compassionate person I thought I was, I gave almost no thought to the criminals' past or future victims. Like so many liberals, my compassion was misplaced. One of the reasons for this is that before I became a prosecutor, I had never seen or spoken to victims of violent crimes. I never empathized with them. I was only concerned with the criminal's unfortunate situation. It was his situation that received the publicity. We tend to look where the spotlight shines. Victims and their families are often forgotten by the media, except in the relatively rare celebrity case.

20

PROPOSITION 66

In November 2004, two important criminal justice initiatives were on the ballot. One was Proposition 66, an initiative that would have substantially weakened the Three-Strikes law. In addition to providing that the third strike must be either a serious or violent felony, as is required for the first two strikes, Prop 66 would also have removed many crimes from the list of serious felonies, such as residential burglary, arson, felony-gang crimes, and drunk driving in which people are seriously injured or killed. These crimes would no longer have been strikes under Prop 66.

Under Prop 66, juvenile sex offenders would no longer have received a strike for seriously injuring an elderly or disabled person during an assault with intent to commit rape. In addition, Prop 66 had a limitation of one strike per prosecution. Therefore, a defendant convicted of multiple forcible kidnappings, robberies, and rapes in one trial would only have received one strike.

Governor Schwarzenegger signed the ballot argument opposing Prop 66, along with then Democrat California Attorney General, Bill Lockyer. Even the former Democrat Governors, Jerry Brown and Gray Davis joined former Republican Governors Pete Wilson and George Deukmejian in opposing Prop 66. Every District Attorney in California from all 58 counties opposed Prop 66. Even liberal Democrat Senator Barbara Boxer opposed Prop 66. The California District Attorney's Association estimated that the passage of Prop 66 would result in the release of 26,000 career criminals from California's prisons.

On October 5, 2004, the *Los Angeles Times* endorsed Prop 66 and proclaimed in their editorial that Governor Schwarzenegger, former Governor (and current Attorney General) Jerry Brown, Los Angeles County District Attorney Steve Cooley, and Attorney General Bill Lockyer were all wrong when they warned that Prop 66 would flood the streets with predators. On criminal justice issues, the record shows that the *Los Angeles Times* positions itself to the Left of even the most liberal politicians.

But again, it is not just the *Times'* consistently soft-on-crime positions that are objectionable. It is the misleading manner in which they present the debate. On October 31, 2004, two days before the election, the *Los Angeles Times* published an article titled "Gov. Pounds Away at Prop. 66." In this article, the *Times* quoted a woman who favored Prop 66: "I have a son who is serving a 25-year-to-life mandatory minimum sentence for watching someone sell drugs. The guy who sold the drugs got a four-year sentence." Of course, this cannot be true. It is not against the law for someone to watch another person commit a crime, any crime, unless the person watching was proven to be a co-conspirator or an aider and abettor, that is, one who instigates or encourages the commission of a crime. Is it possible that the *Los Angeles Times* does not know this? No deputy DA would charge someone with a crime for merely watching another person commit a crime. Why would the *Times* accept at face value such a preposterous story and print it—unless they were trying to mislead their readers—in this case to persuade them to vote for Prop 66?

Michael Kinsley is the former Editorial and Opinion Editor of the *Los Angeles Times*. I saw Mr. Kinsley interviewed on KCET, the Los Angeles public television channel. Mr. Kinsley told his interviewer that the *Times* keeps its opinions on its editorial page. Even a cursory read of the *Los Angeles Times* will leave no doubt that this is not the case. The opinions of the *Los Angeles Times*, or of the staff writer, are frequently included in their news stories. For example, in a page-one story titled "Battle Over 3-Strikes Measure Heats Up," October 29, 2004, the *Times* stated, "The two sides [of Proposition 66] have tangled repeatedly over how many prisoners might be freed if Proposition 66 passes. In his ads, the governor [Schwarzenegger] says '26,000 dangerous criminals will be released from prison'—*a statement that exaggerates the proposition's effect.*" [Emphasis added] Nobody is quoted as having made this statement. The emphasized portion is clearly the *Times*' opinion—which was, as is often the case, embedded in its news story.

The *Times* repeated this same opinion in another Prop 66 news story, "Prop. 66 In Tough Fight," published November 1, 2004, the day before the election. In this story, the *Times* pointed out that Governor Schwarzenegger and the California District Attorney's Association (CDAA) claim that 26,000 inmates would be eligible to be resentenced if Prop 66 passes. The story then said that support-ers of Prop 66 claim only 4,200 inmates would be eligible to be resentenced if Prop 66 passes. The *Times* then chose sides in this news story and said the Governor's 26,000 figure "exaggerates the potential impact [of Prop 66]." The point is that the *Times* often expresses its opinions in its news pages—a practice the *Times* denies.

On October 20, 2004, the front-page headline of the *Los Angeles Times* reads, "Voters Favor Scaling Back 3-Strikes Law." A *Times* poll showed that 62% of the voters favored Prop 66 with only 21% opposed. At the time these poll results were published, there had been no television spots on either side of the issue. Prop 66 was bankrolled by the wealthy father of a state prison inmate whose son was in prison serving eight years for two counts of vehicular manslaughter. Because of the way Prop 66 was written, if Prop 66 had passed, his son would have been entitled to be resentenced, resulting in an early release.

As mentioned, between 1994 when the Three Strikes law was enacted, and 2004, California had a 45% drop in crime, the largest of any state. Although other states also had decreases in crime, the drop in California's crime rate after the the Three Strikes law passed was twice the national average, according to FBI statistics.[12] The *Times* never told its readers that if Prop 66 passed, inmates serving Three-Strike sentences would have an absolute right to be resentenced by the court within 180 days of Prop 66 taking effect. This right to be resentenced applied to all three-strikers whose prior strikes included serious felonies which would have been dropped from the Prop 66 list of crimes that constituted strikes—such as residential burglary and arson. There is no question that if Prop 66 had passed, many thousands of career criminals would have been released, resulting in a sharp spike in California's crime rate. The *Times*, ostrichlike, will not concede there is any connection between the longer sentences given to two- and three-strike career criminals and the sharp reduction in California's crime rate.

One week before the election, Governor Schwarzenegger's anti-Prop 66 TV spots hit our TV screens and continued up until the election. These numerous TV spots were the result of $3.5 million that billionaire Henry T. Nicholas III gave to the anti-Prop 66 campaign 12 days before the election. Nicholas also had a personal interest. His sister was murdered by her boyfriend who is serving a sentence of 17 years-to-life.

On November 2, 2004, California voters defeated Prop 66 by a margin of 53% to 47%. The *Los Angeles Times* thus maintains its perfect record. Its positions on all the major criminal justice initiatives since 1978 have been rejected by California's voters.

It is noteworthy that a wealthy man whose son was in prison, and who would have benefited from the passage of Prop 66, bankrolled the Prop 66 campaign, while a billionaire, whose sister was a murder victim, pumped millions into the anti-Prop 66 campaign at the last minute, turned the electorate around, and caused Prop 66 to fail at the ballot box.

But the liberal Democrats in the California legislature are not giving up. After Prop 66 was defeated, State Senator Gloria Romero introduced SB (Senate bill) 1642, a bill that would have substantially weakened the Three Strikes law. If SB 1642 had become law, several thousand violent and career criminals would have been resentenced and released from prison. Opposing this bill were the California District Attorneys Association, the California Police Chiefs Association, and Crime Victims United of California. On April 4, 2006, the Senate Public Safety Committee gave its approval to SB 1642. All four Democrats on the committee voted in favor of the bill. The committee's two Republicans voted "no." This committee's action to substantially weaken the Three Strikes law was not reported in the *Los Angeles Times*. SB 1642 died on November 30, 2006. But Senator Romero is determined to weaken the Three Strikes law. If she ultimately succeeds, our crime rate will surely increase after thousands of career criminals are released from prison. Of course, this will create thousands more crime victims.

21

PROPOSITION 69

The other significant criminal justice proposition on the November 2, 2004, ballot was Proposition 69. Prop 69 would expand California's DNA database. Upon passage, all persons *convicted* of any felony and all suspects *arrested* for murder, voluntary manslaughter, and felony sexual offenses must submit a DNA sample by permitting the swabbing of the inside of their cheek with a Q-tip-like cotton swab. In 2009, DNA samples would be taken in the same manner from all suspects *arrested* for committing *any* felony crime.

Prop 69 has built-in privacy protections. Prop 69 makes it a felony for anyone to sell or disclose a DNA sample to any unauthorized person. Prop 69 also provides that a defendant who has been acquitted of the crime may have his DNA removed from the database.

On October 11, 2004, the *Los Angeles Times*, in an editorial titled "A Risk-Filled Use of DNA," opposed Prop 69. The *Times* based its opposition to expanding the DNA database on their claim that even if the defendant is acquitted, "the [DNA] samples would stay on file forever." What the *Times* did not tell its readers is that Prop 69 clearly states that a person who is acquitted can have his DNA sample removed from the database. Again, the *Times* misled its readers on a matter of great public importance—the solving of murders and sexual assaults through DNA analysis as well as the exoneration of those who were wrongly convicted. The ACLU joined the *Los Angeles Times* in opposing Prop 69.

The *Times'* argument against Prop 69, that "the DNA of a suspect who has been acquitted would stay on file forever," was very weak. Aside from the fact that Prop 69 provides that an acquitted defendant can have his DNA sample removed from the database, the fact is that everyone who is arrested for any crime must be fingerprinted. The suspect's fingerprints remain in the fingerprint database forever. There is no law that would permit an acquitted defendant to have his fingerprints removed from the database. Could there be any doubt that if the police were not already permitted to collect a suspect's fingerprints when he is arrested, that such a proposal would encounter similar objections from liberal Democrats, the *Los Angeles Times* and the ACLU?

The voters approved Prop 69 by a margin of 62% to 38%. Why would the *Los Angeles Times* not want to give our police and crime labs this valuable tool to solve the numerous murder and sexual assault cases that an expanded DNA database would solve?

Even in my most liberal days, I do not believe I would have opposed obtaining a suspected felon's fingerprints or DNA or taking his photograph—which also remains in police files. Anyone who has worked in the criminal justice system knows that solving old murder and rape cases, and incarcerating those held responsible, will surely prevent future murders and rapes.

Prop 69 was placed on the ballot for one reason: because one wealthy man, Bruce Harrington, invested nearly $2 million in the Prop 69 campaign. Why would one man make such a sacrifice? Because Bruce Harrington's brother, Keith, a medical student, and Keith's wife, were murdered during a robbery in 1980 in a case that remains unsolved. Harrington hopes that an expanded DNA database will catch the killer.

A bill requiring all felons to submit DNA samples was killed in the Democrat-controlled California legislature in 2003. Because the legislature again failed to act, Harrington was left with no alternative but to finance the collection of the hundreds of thousands of signatures required by the initiative process to put the issue before the voters.

There are those who believe that a mere citizen should not be able to circumvent the legislature and invest his own money to finance and promote an initiative. I see it differently. How many countries in the world would permit a citizen to spend his own money to put great questions of public policy before the voters? I cherish this freedom. I am familiar with the arguments against the initiative: no legislative committee hearings, ballot propositions resulting from the efforts of millionaires and big corporations to benefit themselves or their favorite causes, the possibility of badly drafted legislation and the like. But in the end, the question is whether the public would be better off if they relinquished this power and put their faith in the politicians to always do the right thing. The answer to this question is not difficult for me.

California's pre-Prop 69 DNA database contained about 200,000 DNA samples, but California's database, in contrast to 40 other states, did not require all felons to submit DNA samples, that is, until November 2, 2004, when Prop 69 passed. When the California database includes DNA samples from all felons, the database will include more than one million samples. There is no dispute that an all-felon DNA database will result in solving many more rapes, murders, and other crimes. In a *Los Angeles Times* story titled, "Expanded Cold-Case Operation is Sought," (April 6, 2006), Los Angeles Police Chief William Bratton said that he will need 18 additional detectives in LAPD's cold-case unit (triple the current number) to keep up with the growing number of potential DNA matches in old cases.

And there is a somewhat surprising DNA development. According to a Florida State study,[13] 52% of DNA database hits in murder and sexual assault cases matched individuals who had prior convictions of burglary. The police are beginning to solve an increasing number of violent crimes by matching DNA from a sexual assault victim or homicide scenes to DNA samples taken from those arrested for burglary, drug, and other less serious felonies.[14]

Credit must be given to L.A. County Deputy DA Lisa Kahn, who not only is largely responsible for writing Prop 69, but also has the responsibility of helping numerous police departments implement it. It is a huge task. Many of us say we would like to think we made a difference. Lisa Kahn has definitely made a difference. I cannot think of any deputy DA who has made a greater contribution to the criminal justice system in California than Ms. Kahn, whose efforts have helped make Prop 69 a reality.

On September 14, 2006, the *Los Angeles Times* disclosed that because of inadequate funding, 287,000 DNA samples from convicted felons had not been processed. Barry Fisher, director of the Los Angeles County Sheriff's Crime Lab, said, "It was shocking that the program [Prop 69] had not been adequately funded, given its potential to solve cases and to prevent crimes by identifying perpetrators before they strike again." The following day, a *Times* editorial said that collecting DNA samples from suspects arrested for felonies is an invasion of their privacy.

22

THE POLICY OF PATRONIZATION

My former fairy-tale view of the world ignored reality. It ignored the high recidivism rate among convicted felons. It ignored the pain and the injuries that would be inflicted upon future victims of paroled career criminals. As a deputy DA, I saw the pain, the injuries and the wrecked lives of crime victims and their grieving families. I have seen the media disparage grieving crime victims and their families by suggesting that they are seeking "vengeance"—not justice. I have been very moved, and changed, by what I have seen. I finally awoke to acknowledge that the liberal policies I so passionately espoused have resulted in anguish and injustice for countless thousands of crime victims.

I have also seen the anger and frustration experienced by the families of the victims of crime. Many do not know how government works, and they don't know where to turn to vent their frustrations or to make changes. For example, many don't understand that in California the powerful Speaker of the Assembly selects the legislative committee members. If a liberal Speaker selects members of the Assembly Public Safety Committee who are soft on criminals, as Speaker Willie Brown did for so many years, criminal justice reform will not pass out of that committee and the public will have no choice but to seek reform of the criminal laws through the initiative process.

Another reason for my conversion from liberalism is that I had children. I now had two kids who depended on me to care for them and protect them. We have all heard the old saying attributed to Churchill, "If you are young and conservative you have no heart; and if you are old and liberal, you have no brains." I think one of the main reasons young liberals turn into old conservatives is that when one is young and has no dependents, talk is cheap. For example, in my college and law school days, I was an advocate of busing as a way to circumvent de facto school segregation. I reasoned that inasmuch as we were all to blame for segregation, we must collectively pay the price to try to end it. But then I had no kids. After my two children were of school age, I would have worked two jobs to send them to a private school, if the only alternative had been to bus them to a school in a high-crime area. Also, it dawned on me much later that many of my fellow liberals, who so fervently promoted busing, either did not have children or they had their own kids in private schools, and it was other people's kids they wanted bussed.

A 1990 survey revealed a dismal statistic: one-third of all black men in their twenties, 667,556 men who reside in California, were behind bars, on parole or on probation for a criminal offense.[15] By 1995, this figure had grown to 40%.[16] By contrast, 5.4% [5% in 1995] of white male Californians in their twenties and 9.4% [11% in 1995] of Latino males in their twenties were in the same situation.

A study by the Justice Department's Bureau of Justice Statistics, published in August 2003, revealed that at the end of 2001, 5.6 million people in this country had served a state or federal prison sentence. Almost 17% of all black men, about one out of six, have served a state or federal prison sentence. This compares with 7.7% of Hispanic men and 2.6% of white men. These statistics do not include those convicted of felonies who have served only a county jail sentence—who represent the largest number of convicted felons.

On July 14, 2005, the *Los Angeles Times* published a report by the Los Angeles Urban League and the United Way of Greater Los Angeles titled "The State of Black Los Angeles." One of the co-sponsors of the report was the *Los Angeles Times*. The report predicted that "An estimated 32% of black men born in Los Angeles in 2001 are likely to go to prison in their lifetimes…."

More depressing statistics were published in a March 30, 2006 *Los Angeles Times* op-ed piece by columnist Jonah Goldberg. Regarding black unemployment, Goldberg said, "If you include blacks in prison or not seeking work—which conventional unemployment surveys don't—the true jobless rate for black men in their 20s without a high school diploma is 72%." Goldberg said, "A UC Berkeley researcher found that black [high school] dropouts in their late 20s are more likely to be in prison than working." Goldberg said that when World War II ended in 1945, 80% of black children were born to married parents. Today, nearly 70% of black children in this country are born out of wedlock, according to the 2005 World Almanac. Goldberg says, "By every measure, racism, particularly official racism, has declined even as these problems have worsened."

These statistics and projections should be viewed as a national tragedy. Instead, all one hears from the black leadership and the liberal community, with few exceptions, is either silence or words similar to the position of Willie Brown: "They are victims." The words spoken by the liberal media and much of the black leadership may be a bit different, but there is one theme: it is somebody else's fault: society in general, the criminal justice system, poverty, racism, unjust laws, police harassment, slavery 144 years ago, etc, etc.

As a deputy DA for about the last third of the 20th century, I have read thousands of probation reports. It was the rare case that the convicted male, black felon grew up with a father in the home. How could government possibly solve this problem if the father will not remain in the home to help raise his kids and be a good role model for his children? The government cannot force fathers to care for their children.

I have seen thousands of young black men sentenced to jail and prison for committing felonies. It is relatively rare to see either parent of the young, convicted black felon in court at the time he is sentenced. Where are they? What could be more important? I see only one solution: there must be a radical change in values, child-rearing and a commitment to a moral, as well as an academic education. The pressure for this change must come from within the black community. It cannot be imposed by government. It would help greatly, however, if there were some stigma attached to abandoning one's children. But, again, from the liberal community, including the politicians and the media, one hears only silence on this crucial issue.

It was reported in the *Los Angeles Times* on September 29, 2005, that minority employees were suing FedEx Corp for discrimination. The minority employees alleged they were paid less and not promoted as often as white employees. The lawyer for the minority employees said, "Twice as many minorities as whites failed promotional tests." He said, "FedEx knows that blacks and Hispanics fail at a much higher rate, but yet has not changed the test." What could be a more racist statement? It is extraordinarily demeaning for this attorney to say that blacks and Hispanics need to have the promotional tests simplified for them to pass. This lawyer's statement is a good example of the "soft bigotry of low expectations." I have no doubt that many blacks and Hispanics would be outraged and humiliated by such patronization.

Shelby Steele is a research fellow at the Hoover Institution at Stanford University. Dr. Steele is one of a new breed of black intellectuals who believes that preferences for blacks hurt blacks. Dr. Steele received his Ph.D. in English from the University of Utah and his M.A. in sociology from Southern Illinois University. Dr. Steele is the author of, *The Content of Our Character: A New Vision of Race in America*. The book received the National Book Critic's Circle Award. *Harper's* Magazine published an essay by Dr. Steele on November, 30, 1999, titled "The Age of White Guilt: and the Disappearance of the Black Individual."

In this essay, Dr. Steele says, "Ethnic groups that have asked a lot from their individuals have done exceptionally well in America even while enduring discrimination." Dr. Steele asks the reader to imagine a young, black Harvard student and to consider what is expected of him today. To be acceptable to his group, he must, for example, defend affirmative action in college admissions. Dr. Steele writes, "All that is creative and imaginative in him must be rallied to argue the essential weakness of his own people. Only their weakness justifies the racial preferences they receive decades after any trace of

mainly by the liberals and the Democratic Party. The Democrats desperately want to hold onto the 90% black vote that went to Al Gore in 2000 and nearly the same amount that went to John Kerry in 2004. Without it, the Democrats are in deep trouble—and they know it.

Thomas Sowell is a black, Harvard-educated economist, syndicated columnist and author of a dozen books. He received his Ph.D. in economics from the University of Chicago. In a column published May 24, 2005, titled "Liberals, Race, and History," Sowell writes, "If the share of the black vote that goes to the Democrats ever falls to 70%, it may be virtually impossible for the Democrats to win the White House or Congress because they have long ago lost the white, male vote and their support among other groups is eroding." Sowell says, "Liberal Democrats, especially, must keep blacks fearful of racism everywhere..." He says, "Blacks must be kept believing that their only hope lies with liberals." He says, "Achievement is not what liberalism is about. Victimhood and dependency are." Sowell says, "Black self-reliance would be almost as bad as blacks becoming Republicans, as far as liberal Democrats are concerned."

But Republicans are just as eager to win over black voters. The result is that both political parties, as well as society in general, tread very delicately in the area of race. That is the reason we don't hear Democrats or Republicans say anything either critical or constructive that could possibly offend black voters.

The consequence of this policy of patronization, rooted in fear of the racist label and fear of losing traditional black voters—or not winning over new black voters—is to have a double standard for criticizing blacks and whites. They say that criticizing or trying to change Social Security is the third rail of politics. Do it and die politically. The same can be said of any politician who would say, "It is not the fault of racism or the criminal justice system that 33% [40% in 1995] of all black males in their twenties in California were under the jurisdiction of the criminal justice system. It is largely a consequence of so many of these kids having no father in the home—no male role model whose example is worth following." Can you imagine any politician saying this? One thing seems certain: enlightened, courageous blacks must say it first. And they are beginning to say it. This is the basis for my long-range optimism.

23

WOMEN'S INFLUENCE ON THE CRIMINAL JUSTICE SYSTEM

Women's groups brought about big changes in California's criminal justice system. Although the initiative deserves great credit for bringing justice to California crime victims, we should not forget the contribution of women's groups. When I was in law school, and I heard such words as "justice" or "fairness," I always assumed it meant justice and fairness for the people *accused* of crime. It really never occurred to me, in any meaningful way, that the criminal justice system must be fair to crime victims as well.

MADD

In 1980, drunk drivers killed 28,100 people in this country. Hardly anyone seemed to pay much attention to this awful statistic. It was common for comedians like Red Skelton and Dean Martin to get a lot of laughs by pretending to be drunks. As a Los Angeles deputy city attorney from 1965 to 1968, I handled hundreds of drunk driving cases. In those days it was office policy to reduce a drunk driving (more accurately, "driving under the influence" or DUI) charge to a lesser offense, usually a "reckless driving," for any defendant with a blood alcohol content of 0.14% or less—almost twice California's current legal limit.

In 1980, 13-year-old Cari Lightner was killed by a drunk driver. Two days before Cari was killed, the drunk driver who killed her had been released on bail for a hit-and-run, drunk driving crash. At the time he killed Cari, he had a valid California driver's license in spite of the fact that he had two prior convictions for drunk driving and one prior conviction for reckless driving. Cari's mother, Candace, is not the type of person who just gets upset. She is the type who makes things happen. Candace Lightner met in a Sacramento restaurant with friends who decided it was time for a change. Candy Lightner started MADD, Mothers Against Drunk Drivers. By the end of 1981, MADD had 11 chapters in four states. By 1982, 70 MADD chapters were operating. In 1990, MADD had grown to 407 Chapters. In 2000, MADD had more than 600 chapters in all 50 states—all because one woman was mad as hell and decided she would change public attitudes toward drunk drivers. After the MADD women successfully urged the media to publicize how many thousands of people were being killed and injured each year by drunk drivers, drunkenness ceased being as funny as it had been. Today, I rarely see a comedian get laughs by pretending to be drunk and out of control.

Today, in California, a driver is presumed to be under the influence of alcohol if he is driving with a blood alcohol content of 0.08% or more. Although the laws are much tougher on drunk drivers today, in California there is still no requirement for a convicted drunk driver to serve any jail time on a first offense. The women of MADD deserve much of the credit for changing the public attitude towards drunk drivers. With respect to urging tougher laws against drunk driving, I have to give credit to the *Los Angeles Times*. The DUI law seems to be the one law that the *Times* has urged the legislature to toughen—in terms of reducing the blood-alcohol level for DUI from 0.10% to 0.08%. Is it a personal experience with a drunk driver or is DUI seen as a liberal or women's cause and therefore passes the political correctness test? Whatever their reason, the *Times* deserves credit.

In the late 1970s, other women's groups learned that most forcible rapists convicted in the California courts were sentenced to probation with a few months in the county jail. They went to Sacramento and raised hell with the legislators who responded by passing a law that prohibited judges from granting probation to forcible rapists.[17] The irony is that many of these women were well-educated, wealthy liberals who discovered how lenient our laws and sentencing practices were in the area of sexual assault and child molestation. These women were tough and became quite politically sophisticated. If a legislator was reluctant to vote for tougher laws for rapists and child molesters, these women were not above threatening to back a candidate to run against him. They used their formidable clout to toughen the laws in both of these areas, and they deserve kudos for their successes.

The Mentally Disordered Sex Offender Law

In the 1970s, California had a law called the Mentally Disordered Sex Offender Act, or MDSO, as it was called. The idea, and the hope, was to rehabilitate sexual offenders and child molesters by sending them to a prison/hospital setting in Atascadero, California where they would undergo psychiatric treatment in the form of group therapy, individual therapy, aversion therapy, and any other kind of therapy the psychiatrists could think of to learn more about sexual offenders and how to "cure" them. The doctors tried many different approaches. When a convicted rapist or child molester was fortunate enough to be referred to the MDSO program, the time he would spend in the hospital undergoing treatment was far less than if he were sentenced directly to prison for the same offense. Of course, many defense attorneys tried to get their convicted sex-offender clients into the MDSO program.

As the story was told to me, a serial rapist, convicted of

several forcible rapes in the San Fernando Valley (which is in the city of Los Angeles), was referred to the MDSO program. He underwent treatment and was released in about a year. One of the women's groups, who had earlier helped toughen the sentences for rape, heard about the serial rapist's short sentence in a hospital setting. The women's groups had not been aware of the MDSO law. They were under the impression that they had successfully persuaded the California legislature to end probation and short sentences for rape. They felt betrayed by the legislature. Their new objective was to end, once and for all, the possibility of short sentences for forcible rapists and child molesters. They saw the MDSO program as a loophole that allowed dangerous sex offenders, even serial rapists, to escape justice.

So back to the legislature these angry women went. A small group of them met with the Chairman of the Assembly Criminal Justice Committee—now called the Public Safety Committee. Under pressure from these women, who were now playing the kind of hardball legislators understand, the chairman made an appointment with the chief psychiatrist of the MDSO program at Atascadero State Hospital.

The chief psychiatrist had his entire psychiatric staff of doctors present at this meeting. The chief psychiatrist told the committee chairman that in preparation for the meeting with him, he and his staff had done a study comparing the recidivism rates of the sexual offenders who had undergone treatment in the MDSO program with the sexual offenders who had been sentenced directly to prison. The study revealed that the MDSO graduates and the sexual offenders paroled from the standard prison setting had almost identical recidivism rates.

The chief psychiatrist told the committee chairman that he had discussed the results of this study with his staff. They all realized, he said, that if the study results were made public, it would probably result in the termination of the MDSO program and the elimination of their jobs, or at the very least, transfers to other psychiatric positions within state government. Nevertheless, the chief psychiatrist of the MDSO program and his staff of psychiatrists decided to give the committee chairman the results of the study which showed clearly that the MDSO program was a failure. The chief psychiatrist told the chairman there was even a split among his staff psychiatrists on the basic question whether sexual offenders even suffered from any recognizable mental disorder. The chief psychiatrist reported to the committee chairman that assuming the rapist or child molester suffers from some mental disorder, they had not discovered an effective treatment.

With this stunning confession of failure by the professionals who would be expected to be the most aggressive defenders of the MDSO program, the chairman returned to Sacramento, reported to his colleagues in the legislature what he had learned, and the state legislature repealed the MDSO program, effective January 1, 1982. The MDSO law had been ineffective, had cost the state millions of dollars, and had released hundreds of sex offenders back on the streets of California after relatively short hospital stays.

The California legislature declared that "In repealing the mentally disordered sex offender commitment, the legislature recognizes and declares that the commission of sex offenses is not in itself the product of mental diseases."[18]

Domestic Violence

Women are also largely responsible for substantially changing the attitudes of the public, the legislature, law enforcement, and the courts in the area of domestic violence. When I was a new deputy city attorney in 1965, my first assignment was to "The Pit" where all new deputy city attorneys were assigned. The Pit was where we would interview domestic violence victims and schedule informal office hearings between husband and wife, boyfriend and girlfriend. We would counsel and warn, usually the husband or boyfriend, that if he kept beating his wife or significant other, he would go to jail. But in truth, we rarely filed criminal charges in domestic violence cases. Monday mornings were especially difficult. The women were lined up waiting to see a deputy city attorney. Some had eyes swollen shut. Some had teeth that had been knocked out.

I will never forget my first day in The Pit. It just happened to be my first day on the job, a Monday. Remember, I was the committed liberal who had become a prosecutor only to find out how the racist criminal justice system operated. With respect to the issue of domestic violence, my first day on the job validated my preconceived ideas. Nearly all the female victims of domestic violence who were interviewed in The Pit were black. And, in 1965, I came to learn very quickly that neither the police nor the prosecutors—not even the judges—took domestic violence cases seriously. It was assumed by all of us that it was a private affair between the man and the woman—a family affair.

That first day on the job as a prosecutor, I interviewed a woman whose face was swollen and discolored and who had one eye swollen shut. I was really green—and not just as a deputy city attorney. I had never seen domestic violence up close. I don't even recall getting a spanking as a child. So, there she sat, this poor black woman looking at me through her one good eye. I had great sympathy for her. But I really didn't know what I could do for her. "Who did this to you?" "My common-law," she replied. "Has he ever hit you like this before?" "Yeah, every time he gets drunk." "How often does he get drunk?" "Just about every weekend," she replied. "He hits you like this almost every weekend?" I asked incredulously. She nodded her head, "yes." "Have you ever thought of leaving him?" Indignantly, she shouted at me: "Leave him! I love him! I just want y'all to make him stop beatin on me."

It was a strange new environment for me, but I soon adapted.

Today, thanks to various women's organizations, domestic violence is treated as a serious public, not private, offense. However, these cases are very difficult to prosecute. The reason is that the great majority of women who call 911 and have their boyfriends or husbands arrested for domestic violence later refuse to prosecute. Some of these women are contacted by the defense attorney who gives her what I call, *The Speech*.

I have found that very few women victims of domestic violence can resist *The Speech*. Here is how it goes: The defense attorney for the husband or boyfriend tells the victim that her husband/boyfriend feels terrible about what he did. "He told me to tell you that he loves you and the kids more than anything in the world. He is sitting in jail and he cannot seem to stop crying. He is so ashamed of himself. I guarantee you he has learned his lesson and he will never hit you again. But don't take my word for it. He wants to go to therapy. I am enrolling him in a special counseling program for domestic violence. If you testify in this case, he will go to prison. He will be in prison with *real* criminals like dope dealers, robbers, burglars and rapists. He will lose his job, and you will have no money coming in. Please don't do this to him and to you and the kids. I promise you that if you drop the charges in this case, I will enroll him in the counseling program immediately. If he ever lays a hand on you again, you should take the case all the way. But please, give him this one last chance. He loves you so much."

Bingo! We have just lost our victim. In the L.A. County DA's office, there is a policy not to drop the charges, even if the victim begs us—which they often do. Legally, the victim has no power to drop the charges, but the legalities do not really matter if the victim is uncooperative. Very often, we cannot find her to serve her a subpoena to appear in court and the case is dismissed. I tried to warn domestic violence victims when I was filing cases to expect to hear *The Speech* from the defense attorney, and I told her what he would say. I found the women I dealt with were much better able to resist *The Speech* if they knew it was coming.

If the DA can persuade the domestic violence victim to testify, she will usually prevail in trial. Judges and jurors are not nearly as indifferent to the issue of domestic violence as they were in 1965 when I started my career as a prosecutor in The Pit—thanks to the women's groups who spotlighted the problem.

When I said the victim cannot legally "drop the charges," this calls for an explanation. The district attorney is not the victim's lawyer—in any criminal case. The DA represents all the People of the State. All crimes are considered, by law, an offense against the People of the state. A victim of a crime is simply a witness, perhaps the most important witness, but a witness nevertheless. That is why no crime victim is empowered to drop the charges or to order the district attorney not to prosecute a case.

Consider the ludicrous possibilities if a crime victim had the power to drop the charges: Mary Jones is a bank teller in a small town. Mary Jones' estranged boyfriend enters the bank, displays a gun to Mary and demands she give him the bank's money as well as her own. Mary complies with the robber's demands out of fear. Mary is the person robbed. Mary is therefore the victim of the robbery—not the bank—even though we all call this crime bank robbery. Remember, only a "person" can be the victim of the crime of robbery—not a building or a business. Mary and the robber reconcile, and Mary tells the DA she wants to drop the charges. Of course, the DA need not comply with Mary's request. The same rule would apply even if Mary was at home when she was robbed of her own money. Neither she, nor any crime victim, is authorized by law to order the DA to drop the charges. In addition, it is a felony in California for anyone to attempt to dissuade a witness or crime victim from either reporting a crime to the police or from testifying in court.[19]

24

THE SEA CHANGE IN SENTENCING

In the late 1970s, the California criminal justice system's sentencing laws went through a major change. Prior to this change, California had an indeterminate sentencing scheme for virtually all crimes. For example, the sentence for first-degree murder was "life," and the convicted first-degree murderer had to serve seven years before he was eligible for parole. The media would report the "life" sentence but would rarely report the seven-year parole eligibility. As mentioned earlier, the sentence for second-degree murderers was five years-to-life with parole eligibility in twenty months. Interestingly enough, the sentence for armed robbery was also five years-to-life, and armed robbers also had to serve twenty months in prison before they became eligible for parole. Burglary of a residence also carried the same sentence as second-degree murder and had the same twenty-month parole eligibility. So, there was no difference in the sentence and the parole eligibility date for second-degree murderers, armed robbers, and residential burglars. In practice, however, the murderers stayed in prison about twenty-one months longer than the robbers and two years longer than the burglars.

When I first discovered this in the early 1970s, I did not understand how it was possible that a murderer would serve only two years more than a burglar and less than two years more than a robber. Such a lack of proportionality made no sense to me. I finally came to the conclusion that the only possible reason for this absurd sentencing scheme was that very few people knew about it, because the media rarely told us and the lawmakers didn't care. After all, there was not one dollar in it for the politicians. I have never heard of anyone making a campaign contribution to a politician for voting for a sensible sentencing scheme. Besides, longer sentences mean more prisons, and more prisons mean spending more tax dollars.

Prior to July 1, 1977, the crime of assault with a deadly weapon (ADW) carried an indeterminate prison sentence of six months-to-life and the inmate was eligible for parole in six months. In court, the judge announced a sentence of six months-to-life in prison. The media reported that the defendant could spend the rest of his life in prison. They rarely reported that he could be paroled in six months.

The indeterminate sentencing scheme in California gave the parole board wide discretion in setting parole dates. Partly as a result of this wide discretion, the California prison population stayed right around 20,000 inmates for many years in the 1970s, even as crime increased.

But in 1977, this all changed when the California legislature adopted the new "determinate" sentencing law (DSL). This did not affect first- and second-degree murderers who continued to be sentenced under the indeterminate sentencing law. Also, the following year, California voters passed Prop 7 which fixed the sentences for first- and second-degree murder at 25 years-to-life and 15 years-to-life, respectively. Almost every other California felony came within the new DSL and had a low, middle, and high-term sentencing range with specific guidelines for the judge to consider when choosing either the low, middle, or high term. After California adopted determinate sentencing, the parole board no longer had any authority as to when, for example, a robber, whose sentencing range was two, three, or five years, would be released.

For many years, prison inmates had received one-third off their sentences for good-time/work-time credits. But a new study, conducted after the new determinate sentencing law was enacted, projected that California would need to start building many new prisons. The basis for this projection was that, under the new determinate sentencing law, the parole board could no longer control prison population by granting more paroles as the prison population increased, as it had done for many years under the indeterminate sentencing law. But neither the Democrats nor the Republicans wanted to spend hundreds of millions of tax dollars for new prisons. What to do?

After the determinate sentencing law was enacted, a representative of the California Department of Corrections was interviewed on a Los Angeles television show. He explained how the new determinate sentencing law would work. He said if an inmate was sentenced to three years and he received credit for one-third of his sentence for good behavior and work credits, he would have to serve two years, and there was no way for the parole board to legally release him earlier. He referred to the recent study that projected a large increase in the prison population as the result of the new sentencing law. He asked his television interviewer if the press didn't ever wonder, with crime increasing every year and more people being sent to prison, how the prison population could remain about the same, year after year. He seemed to be chastising the press for not asking the obvious questions. Well, he was there to tell them. He said that under the indeterminate sentencing law, if one hundred new inmates enter the prison system in a given week, the parole board would sign one hundred "Certificates of Rehabilitation" and release one hundred inmates in order to keep the prison population stable. That is how, for many years, the state had avoided spending hundreds of millions of dollars to build new prisons, he said. It was really a fraud on the public insofar as the Certificate of Rehabilitation indicated that the prisoner had been rehabilitated.

I do not want to leave the impression that the Democrats are always the villains in the area of criminal justice and the Republicans always the good guys. This is not the case. Doug McKee was a Los Angeles County deputy DA. I knew Doug fairly well. The District Attorney picked McKee to be our representative (lobbyist is really more descriptive) to the California legislature. Doug was very personable and fit in well with the Sacramento lawmaker crowd. I recall a conversation that Doug and I had after the determinate sentencing law was enacted. The legislators had been given the Department of Corrections study which projected the need for many more prisons if the parole board lost its power to determine when prisoners, sentenced under the DSL, were to be released.

According to Doug, the liberal Democrats were most upset about the possibility of inmates doing more prison time under determinate sentencing, and the Republicans were most upset at the prospect of spending hundreds of millions of tax dollars for building new prisons. The new determinate sentencing law was supposedly designed so that inmates would do about the same amount of time for a given crime as they had before the DSL, but many doubted that would be the result. The conversion from indeterminate to determinate sentencing (for most crimes) in 1977, followed by the repeal of the Probation Subsidy Act in 1978, proved the doubters were correct.

In this same conversation, McKee told me a story I would not forget. He said he was in a Republican caucus meeting when the Republican lawmakers were complaining about having to spend so many tax dollars building new prisons as a result of the new determinate sentencing law. One Republican suggested, tongue in cheek, that if they reduced the sentences for all felony crimes, they would not have to build as many new prisons. That was shouted down derisively as political suicide. McKee said one Republican, who had not been participating in the conversation, said that he had the answer to the problem. He said his idea would have the effect of reducing the sentences for most prison inmates, but it would have the advantage of being so clouded in bureaucracy that it would be practically invisible, and the media would not even notice it. Thus, he explained, it could be accomplished with minimal political risk.

McKee said everybody was all ears. This unnamed Republican explained to his colleagues that all they had to do was increase the good-time/work-time credits from one-third off the inmate's sentence to one-half off. This, he explained, would effectively reduce the sentences for everyone in state prison serving a determinate sentence. McKee told me that the Republican who offered this clever suggestion was hailed as a hero by the other Republicans. The idea was accepted enthusiastically by liberal Democrats—but for a different reason. The liberals were able to reduce the sentences for thousands of prison inmates, and they had excellent political cover. The majority of the legislators, including Governor Jerry Brown, were happy. Others, including Doug McKee and I, were not happy. That is the story, according to Doug McKee, that explains why most state prison inmates now only serve one-half, instead of two-thirds, of their sentences.

Despite the increase in prison credits from one-third to one-half off the sentences, the prison population exploded, causing a prison-building boom, due in large part to the DSL which prohibits the parole board from granting paroles to inmates sentenced to a determinate sentence. But also, the repeal of the Probation Subsidy Act freed probation officers to use their best judgment in recommending the appropriate sentence for convicted felons. This resulted in thousands more state prison sentences for felons who would have been sentenced to probation when the Probation Subsidy Law was in effect. During George Deukmejian's eight years as governor (1983-1991), he oversaw a doubling of the number of prisons and an increase in the number of prison inmates from 40,000 to more than 100,000. Of course, the *Los Angeles Times* does not like the determinate sentencing law.

On December 10, 2003, the *Los Angeles Times*, in what ranks among their most disingenuous editorials, came out for the repeal of the determinate sentencing law. To support their position, they quoted former liberal Governor Jerry Brown as saying that the law, which he signed, had been, "an abysmal failure...a scandalous merry-go-round of crime [that] saddled California with parolees who are ill-prepared for release." The *Times'* editorial said the law "all but eliminated the [parole] board's discretion to keep dangerous felons behind bars longer and release reformable ones earlier." The *Times* cited the case of Richard Allen Davis who is on California's death row for the murder of Polly Klass. The *Times* complained that the, "parole board was forced to set [Davis] free in 1993 because the act [determinate sentencing law] deemed that he had served his 'uniform' amount of time."

What hypocrisy! As if the *Times* objects to the law because dangerous criminals are being released too early. As we have seen, the *Times* has opposed *every* initiative proposition that sought to keep dangerous and career criminals in prison longer. If the *Los Angeles Times* were really concerned about releasing dangerous criminals too early, why did they not complain about the four-year-ten-month average prison term served by second-degree murderers in the 1970s? Why did they not complain when 70% of all rapists, 72% of the robbers, 93% of burglars, 80% of drug dealers, 36% of those convicted of murder and voluntary manslaughter, and 41% of defendants convicted of their fourth felony, were given probation or other non-prison sentences in the mid-1970s? Why did they not complain when only 14.3% of the felons convicted in Los Angeles County in 1976 were sentenced to prison? Why did they oppose Proposition 67 in 1988 which called for a minimum sentence of 25 years for the second-degree murder of a police officer and every other initiative that increased sentences for violent and career criminals? When has the *Times*, in the last 25 years, *ever* urged longer sentences for *any* crime? No, the true intent of the *Times*, when considering their editorial positions on criminal justice issues over the last quarter century, is transparent.

The new Governor, Arnold Schwarzenegger, barely in office for about one month at the time of the *Times* editorial, was facing a staggering budget deficit. The goal of the *Los Angeles Times*, in urging the repeal of the determinate sentencing law, was to again permit the parole board to control the growth of the prison population by reverting to the past practice of releasing the same or greater number of inmates each month as are committed to California prisons. This would stop prison inmate population growth and save millions of tax dollars. The *Times* understands that this was powerful bait for a Governor looking for a way out of California's financial morass. Hopefully, the Governor, who has been advised by former Governors Pete Wilson and George Deukmejian, understands that compromising public safety is not the best road to a balanced budget—nor to maintaining popularity with the voters.

For several years, the *Los Angeles Times* has had an editorial series titled "State Prison's Revolving Door." This title is misleading to the extent it implies that the *Times* believes sentences are too short. To my knowledge, the *Los Angeles Times,* since the mid-1970s, has never editorialized in favor of longer sentences for *any* crime. If the *Times* had its way, the prisons' revolving doors would look more like windmills on a windy day. Thousands more criminals would be released and many prisons would be closed.

To the extent the *Times'* "State Prisons' Revolving Door" series means inmates should receive more job training, education, and counseling in prison to better prepare them for release, this is good public policy. I would be willing to pay my fair share of taxes for the effort, but I doubt that many career criminals would be amenable to such efforts. In my long career as a prosecutor, I have seen judges, on numerous occasions, place violent and career criminals on probation and refer them to countless different kinds of programs in an attempt to rehabilitate them. Relatively few successfully completed these programs, got jobs and stopped committing crimes.

But there is a way to stop those felons who have proven themselves to be career criminals and who continue to victimize others: keep them in prison until they are too old to continue their lifestyles of crime. Statistics show that most career criminals, other than child molesters and white-collar criminals, start to slow down when they reach their late 40s or early 50s. The average age of the California state prison inmate is 35. Eighty-one per cent of inmates are between 20 and 44. Inmates 45 and over make up only 17% of the California prison population. The Three-Strikes law accomplishes this goal. This is a major reason California has had a 45% reduction in crime, the greatest drop in crime in the nation between 1994, when the Three-Strikes law was enacted, and 2004. This dramatic decrease in crime must not be seen as just numbers. It must be understood that many thousands of people have been spared being crime victims since 1994 because of the Three-Strikes law.

2 5

MY FIRST OFFICE MATE – THE EAST COAST DA

My first assignment, as a new deputy DA, was to the Van Nuys office in the San Fernando Valley. I had to share an office with a deputy DA from an eastern city who was visiting the L.A. County DA's office for a few weeks as part of an exchange program. He was tall, balding and wore a pin-stripe suit. I learned from this man how different our DA's office is from his DA's office on the East Coast.

The first day we met, this fellow asked me how I got into the DA's office. I told him I filled out an application and was interviewed by three lawyers, a deputy DA, a deputy public defender, and a deputy county counsel, who represents the county in civil matters. I told him I received a passing score on the interview and was asked to report to the DA's office for a follow-up interview. I was hired after the second interview. The eastern DA then asked how I *really* got in the office. I said I just told him. He said where he comes from you need some "juice" to get into the DA's office. Prior to this conversation, I had never heard the word "juice" unless it was preceded by some kind of fruit. I asked him what he was talking about. He explained that there is no way a new lawyer can get a job as a deputy DA in an eastern city unless he knows someone who has influence with the DA—like a big campaign contributor or some other politician in the DA's political party. I told him it doesn't work that way in Los Angeles. He looked at me in a way that told me he had a tough time believing me.

He asked me how we decide whom to support for DA in the election. I told him I had only been a deputy DA for a short time, and it had never crossed my mind. He said that in eastern cities, if a deputy DA supported the losing candidate for District Attorney, he would not be a deputy DA after the election. I told him that in Los Angeles, deputy DAs are civil service employees and that joining the Los Angeles County District Attorney's Office is a career choice. I told him we had job protection and could not be fired without legal cause. He told me that when a new DA is elected in eastern cities, all the prosecutors submit letters of resignation and that those deputy DAs who supported the victorious DA are asked to remain. He told me that in his DA's office, most prosecutors only remain prosecutors for a few years in order to get trial experience.

He asked me what would happen if my supervisor ordered me to reduce the charges or dismiss the case of the son of a big campaign contributor to the DA. I told him that under our system how little prison time most inmates actually serve. Within 24 months after their release, about 70% of paroled felons are returned to prison for parole violations or for committing new crimes. In 2005, over 61,000 parole violators were returned to prison. In California, inmates who are returned to prison for parole violations serve an average of five months. In 2005, 40% of California's parolees, nearly 47,000, absconded from parole and their whereabouts were unknown. Only 21% of all paroled felons in California are able to successfully complete their paroles.[1]

Many in the liberal community blame the prison and parole officials for these dismal statistics—not the criminals. As mentioned, there currently is much pressure being exerted, mainly by the liberal community, including the *Los Angeles Times*, to abandon the determinate sentencing law and return to indeterminate sentencing. Indeterminate sentencing has *longer-sounding* sentences. In reality, the return to indeterminate sentencing would result in shorter sentences, because the parole board would again be given the power to control the prison population by granting early paroles.

Can it be questioned that if 70% of the 122,000 felons released from prison in 2005 will return to prison within 24 months for parole violations, or for committing new crimes, that the crime rate will increase if even more felons are released each year because of shorter sentences? And, shorter sentences would surely occur if we return to indeterminate sentencing, as is being urged by the *Los Angeles Times*.

In November 2003, California's Little Hoover Commission recommended that, instead of sending so many parole violators back to prison, they should be given short jail sentences, home detention, drug treatment and electronic monitoring. The California Department of Corrections (recently re-named the California Department of Corrections and Rehabilitation— CDC&R) decided to implement these recommendations starting in

2004. The CDC&R projected that this new policy will mean 15,000 fewer prison inmates and as many as five fewer prisons in California.[2] If this projection proves accurate, I predict a sharp spike in the crime rate resulting directly from the fact that prisons will be closed, and thousands more felons will be kept in the community instead of returning to prison after they violate their parole or commit new felonies while on parole.

In a May 10, 2006, *Los Angeles Times* story titled "Woman Stomped to Death on Skid Row," it was reported that a state prison parolee stomped to death a 49-year-old woman on skid row. This parolee had been arrested in March 2006 for a parole violation, failing to report to his parole officer. Instead of being returned to state prison, he was released after serving ten days in the county jail. The *Times* story said that the killer had a criminal record "dating back 30 years, with at least 42 arrests as an adult for violence, narcotics and burglary." LAPD police chief Bratton called the killer a "career criminal preying on society. He should not have been out on the street." Why was this career-criminal parole violator given only ten days in the county jail instead of being returned to the state prison? Was it because of the ill-advised Little Hoover Commission recommendation of keeping some parole violators in the community instead of returning them to prison? The *Times* story said that, according to authorities, "this was the fourth death on skid row that police linked to state parolees."

Another plan that other so-called "reformers" have urged on the legislature and the governor is to shorten the period of parole supervision for certain "low-risk" parolees to six months from the current three years. How do these reformers define "low risk"? Does "low risk" mean "nonviolent" drug dealers, burglars or con men who repeatedly steal from innocent victims? The result of this proposal for shortening parole supervision to only six months will be fewer parole violators. This will *look* better and reduce the prison population, but not the crime rate.

liberals did not complain and the few complaints from disgruntled Republicans were muted. In 1973, the draft ended under Nixon.

As governor of California, Ronald Reagan signed the bill that permitted the state to withhold income taxes from our paychecks. He had earlier vehemently opposed the bill, proclaiming, "Taxes should hurt," meaning that if the taxpayer is forced to pay state income taxes in one lump sum, it would hurt more and thus the taxpayer would presumably be more attentive in monitoring government spending and choosing more frugal candidates. Reagan told reporters at the time, "My feet are in cement" on this issue, meaning he had no intention of signing the bill. He later signed the bill, survived politically, and became president.

Governor Reagan, a strong pro-life politician, signed California's first, and very liberal, abortion bill in 1967; and this was six years before the Supreme Court decided *Roe v Wade.* In 1986, President Reagan signed the Immigration Reform and Control Act which gave permanent amnesty to 2.7 million illegal aliens.

California's most liberal Governor in my memory, Jerry Brown, signed the "use a gun—go to prison" bill, imposing a mandatory prison term for using a gun in the commission of a crime. This was a significant and positive change for criminal justice. Prior to this law, it was common for convicted armed robbers to be placed on probation.

President Clinton signed a tough welfare reform bill that caused a furor within his cabinet, angered the liberal community and attracted vociferous opposition from the liberal press, including the *Los Angeles Times.*

I recall one time where the rule of opposites failed—or perhaps it didn't apply—when our 41st President, George H.W. Bush, said, "Read my lips, no new taxes" and then signed a bill increasing taxes. My gut feeling is that if this president had been viewed as more conservative "in his heart," as Reagan was perceived, he might have been forgiven by his political base and won a second term.

The Rule of Opposites is not limited to the United States but is a universal phenomenon. Who would have thought that Ariel Sharon, the hard-nosed Israeli general who had championed the establishment of settlements in the occupied Gaza and West Bank, would be the leader to coerce settlers in the Gaza Strip to abandon their settlements and promote the establishment of a Palestinian state?

29

CAN WE REHABILITATE CAREER-CRIMINAL SOCIOPATHS?

Our current California legislature is controlled by Democrats. Democrat State Senator Gloria Romero is currently a key player in setting criminal justice and prison policy. Senator Romero, described by even the *Los Angeles Times* as "liberal," is co-chairwoman of a Senate select committee to investigate problems within the state prison system. Governor Schwarzenegger appointed former Republican Governor Deukmejian to lead a panel to investigate and recommend changes to the prison system. In March 2004, Senator Romero told the *Times*, "For a moment my heart sank" when she learned that Deukmejian had been named chairman of the commission. Romero told the *Times*, "[Deukmejian] as a governor was tough on crime and fiscally responsible. He should respond to the argument that rehabilitating criminals is cheaper than incarceration in the long run."[5]

The *Los Angeles Times*, in an editorial dated April 15, 2004, said, "Until the Legislature and the Governor support a return to effective rehabilitation, California prisons will keep turning out better criminals." When the *Times* uses the phrase, "return to effective rehabilitation," do they mean return to the 1970s when the parole board would sign the same number of "Certificates of Rehabilitation" and release as many allegedly "rehabilitated" inmates as would enter the prison system in any given period? If the *Times* is claiming that there was a time in California when we were able to successfully rehabilitate violent and career criminals, the *Times* should bear the burden of identifying that period and offer proof in the form of reduced rates of recidivism.

Liberals who claim that sentences are too long and that rehabilitation is preferable should be more specific and more direct. As Professor Bessette says, they should tell us which sentences for which crimes are too long. Of course, rehabilitating violent and career criminals would be great. Most people would be all for it—myself included. When liberal newspapers like the *Los Angeles Times*, and liberal politicians like Senator Romero, urge that we stress rehabilitation over incarceration, there is an implication that they know of some program that has been successful in reforming child molesters, rapists, violent and career criminals. They should tell us which programs have *proved* successful—and not by using tricks, such as keeping parole violators in the community instead of returning them to prison, or shortening parole supervision to six months, thus giving the *appearance* of declining recidivism rates.

We tried for years to rehabilitate sexual predators through the MDSO program. It did not work. The program's own psychiatrists confessed failure. It is incumbent upon those who are willing to risk more victims of violent or career offenders to identify which rehabilitative programs have worked, and for which type of crime, as measured by reduced recidivism, if they are so opposed to long incarceration for rapists, child molesters, violent, and career criminals. When liberals urge shorter sentences and more rehabilitation for violent or career criminals, they do not think of it in terms of risking more victims. They think of it as giving the career criminal one more chance, and one more, and one more, and then one more. The fact that innocent victims are paying in horrific ways for their misplaced "compassion" is not in their thoughts.

In the summer of 2004, it was reported that a Ventura County Superior Court judge was being asked to end a gang injunction in a 6.6 square-mile area in Oxnard, California, an area victimized by gang killings. The writers of an op-ed piece, who I'm certain think of themselves as compassionate and "progressive," wanted instead to "attack the root causes of crime," a phrase I've heard all my adult life, and which I mouthed as part of my liberal script for many years. They wanted, "an expansion of social programs, job opportunities, and recreational activities...." The liberals seem to believe that we cannot use both approaches simultaneously. They seem to not want to do anything punitive to protect us from the career criminals. I have no objection to more job opportunities for gang-bangers. This assumes, however, that gang-bangers are fervently looking for jobs. My experience has shown me that, for the most part, this is not the case. When we have a crisis in gang killings, we have to take immediate action to save people's lives. It is naïve to believe that the killings will be reduced if there are more jobs, parks, or playgrounds available for armed robbers and drive-by killers.

Six months after this gang injunction took effect, it was announced that violent crime in this 6.6 square-mile area had dropped more than 80%. Officers reported that the streets in this area had never been so quiet. But to the so-called "civil libertarians" who continued to challenge the gang injunction in court, it didn't matter that crime had dropped 80%. It didn't matter that this dramatic crime drop translated into saving numerous people from becoming victims of the gang-bangers. Victims are simply not in their thoughts. And yet, these self-described "progressive" people see themselves as compassionate. I know this is true because for

many years I was one of them, along with all my equally sophisticated, "progressive," compassionate, liberal friends.

It is the parents' responsibility to make sure their child does
not join a gang. I know, this is easier said than done. Nevertheless,
I have no doubt that caring, determined parents can accomplish
more than any government program. But this requires parents who
will not abandon their parental responsibilities. We must break the
ugly legacy of generations of kids being raised in fatherless homes.
I see no alternative to this basic, first requirement. It is tough
enough to raise a child even if both parents are in the home,
especially in these times when the child is confronted with so many
negative influences. But it makes it far more difficult for the
developing child who is growing up on a diet of violent videos, rap
music, and pressure to join a gang when there is no principled,
responsible, employed, male role model for the child to emulate.

I have yet to see the program that can convert a lifelong liar,
career-criminal sociopath into a law-abiding citizen. Remember,
over 90% of the inmates in state prisons have either been convicted
of violent crimes or are recidivists. I have seen judges refer
defendants to all kinds of programs during my career. If there was
a program that could really turn around career-criminal sociopaths,
we in the Criminal Justice Club would surely have heard about it.
Perhaps, someday, science will provide the answers. We do not
have them yet. But science is beginning to produce some interesting
findings.

A *Los Angeles Times* story titled "Some Minds Appear Wired to
Lie," October 1, 2005, reported on the findings of a USC study
published in the October 2005 issue of the *British Journal of
Psychiatry*. The findings of the study "suggest that the talent for
compulsive deception is embedded in the structure of the brain."

The study involved 108 volunteers who were sorted into
groups based upon how often they lied, used aliases, cheated,

conned people, malingered or gave false reports to the police. Their brains were then scanned to obtain detailed anatomical images of their brain tissue.

"The group of compulsive liars had 25.7% more white matter in their prefrontal cortex and 14.2% less grey matter than the normal control group." The prefrontal cortex is the area of the brain, just behind the forehead, that enables people to feel remorse, learn moral behavior, and plan complex strategies. University of Southern California psychologist Adrian Raine, the senior scientist on the project, said, "Some people have a biological advantage in lying."

Again, I want to emphasize, I have no objection to having educational, vocational and counseling programs available in prison if the career criminal desires to take advantage of them. Professor of Criminology, Joan Petersilia, in an October 16, 2005 op-ed piece in the *Los Angeles Times*, said, "Prisoners who take vocational education...are 15% less likely to return to crime when released." One must closely examine such claims. How does one conclude the parolee has not returned to crime? How long was he tracked after his release from prison? One year? Eighteen months? Is it possible that he was committing crimes but was not caught? Criminals are arrested for a very small percentage of the crimes they commit. (See Chapter 41)

I am not optimistic that many inmates will take advantage of these programs—unless, of course, they can reduce their sentences by enrolling in the programs. I have a suggestion: make the inmate *really* earn his 50% credits by earning a high school diploma and/or college degree, as well as learning a trade. Insist he achieve a C-plus grade average. The courses must be taught by a legitimate educational institution.

The inmates, other than those who are severely mentally impaired, must be given the same standardized exams that are now

Prop 36 allocates $600,000,000 from the general fund over a five-year period to pay for treatment programs, but specifically prohibits the use of any of that money for drug testing. Of course, this makes it nearly impossible for the treatment program officials to know if the drug user is still using drugs.

The proponents of Prop 36 spent over $3,700,000 to promote this measure. Over $3,000,000 of this amount came from just three people, including the liberal billionaire, George Soros, who gave over $1,000,000. The opponents of Prop 36 included former Governors Gray Davis and Pete Wilson, U.S. Senator Diane Feinstein and numerous other office holders from both parties. Also opposed were many district attorneys and police chiefs. To their credit, even the *L.A. Times* editorialized against Prop 36, saying that it went too far. But the opponents only raised $442,000—which helps explain the reason Prop 36 passed with 61% of the vote.

Another reason for the lopsided vote in favor of Prop 36 was its title describing the measure as a "Crime Prevention Act." I would like to see an objective study on the number of crimes Prop 36 has prevented. Under the guise of promising "drug treatment" and "crime prevention," two very attractive-sounding phrases, Prop 36 took California down the road towards de-penalizing the possession of every kind of restricted and addictive drug.

Before the election, The Rand Corporation, a California-based think tank, published a study of Prop 36. Among other findings, the study found that the failure of Prop 36 to provide funds for drug testing was a serious flaw.

It was announced in September 2004 that, in the first year after Prop 36 became effective, 76% of the defendants diverted under Prop 36, and ordered by the judge to participate in a drug treatment program, failed to complete the program.[7] Included in this 76% are thousands of defendants who did not even bother to show up for the treatment program. Of those who did start a treatment program, about one third completed it. The convicted drug user has little incentive to complete the program, because he knows he will face no possibility of jail time for failure to complete the program.

Another reason for this dismal completion rate is that the convicted drug user did not really agree to enroll in a drug program voluntarily. He enrolled in a Prop 36 treatment program only because it was the most attractive alternative. His other choices were either immediate incarceration or probation coupled with a non-Prop 36 drug program in which the penalty for failure to succeed in the program was jail or prison. Under Prop 36, the consequences of failure to successfully complete the drug program are two more chances.

Officials at UCLA were designated to issue annual evaluation reports on Prop 36. In their September 2004 report, they opined that many drug offenders do not complete their treatment programs because they lack jobs, transportation or housing, and some are mentally ill or seriously addicted or ambivalent about treatment.

Why was there no mention of the big reason drug users do not complete the treatment program? They like taking drugs! It makes them feel good. They enjoy the lifestyle. Many of their pals and/or crime partners take drugs, and they enjoy the camaraderie. By failing to even mention these reasons, it leaves the false implication that most of these thousands of defendants convicted of drug possession really want to get off drugs, but are simply too weak to do so. This is not true. The question is, why do the media, and in this case the academics, continually feed the public the myth that most drug offenders would like to stop using drugs but are just too weak to stop, or because they "lack jobs, transportation or housing."?

I doubt that many of the people who voted for Prop 36 realized that even prior to Prop 36, judges diverted defendants charged with drug possession out of the criminal justice system and into treatment programs. Under the pre-Prop 36 drug-diversion programs, if the defendant successfully completed the drug program, the criminal charges against him were dismissed. The difference was that prior to Prop 36, if the defendant failed to complete the program, the judge was not compelled by law to give the defendant multiple chances to fail before probation could be revoked.

It can reasonably be assumed that a large percentage of the 76% of addicts who did not complete the Prop 36 treatment program were on the street committing crimes to get the money to support their habits. Every Club member knows that many criminals commit crimes to finance an expensive drug habit and their chosen lifestyle. Is it really wise policy for the law to tell these drug users they will not face penal consequences until they have been convicted of possessing restricted drugs three times—and then for only a few days? Prop 36 went into effect on July 1, 2001. As of September 2004, over 70,000 convicted drug users, who had little fear of incarceration, were diverted out of the criminal justice system and into Prop 36 drug rehab programs. And only a relatively small percentage of these defendants have completed the treatment program. This is the situation in California as a result of Prop 36.

But the Prop 36 story gets worse. On November 26, 2004, the *L.A. Times* reported the results of a study which revealed that 31% of offenders in Prop 36 drug programs were rearrested for a new drug offense within a year of starting treatment, compared to only 18% of those defendants in other court-ordered drug treatment programs. A later UCLA study, released April 5, 2006, found that 58% of all offenders referred to Prop 36 programs were rearrested within one year—which was 48% higher than the rearrest rate for non-Prop 36 drug programs.

It was reported that the lead researcher of the study, a research psychologist at UCLA, said he was surprised by the high recidivism rates for Prop 36 defendants. "I would have assumed that they [the arrest rates for Prop 36 defendants] would be comparable to other criminal justice clients...." "I wouldn't have assumed that the arrest rates [for Prop 36 defendants] would be significantly higher," he said.

The fact that the lead researcher was surprised that Prop 36 defendants were more likely to be rearrested than drug defendants referred to non-Prop 36 drug treatment programs illustrates the extent to which some academics are disconnected from reality and common sense. A defendant who is convicted of a drug offense, and is referred to a traditional, non-Prop 36 drug treatment program, and fails to complete the program, will be found in violation of probation and faces a possible state prison or jail sentence.

A Prop 36 defendant knows that Prop 36 promises him that he will serve no jail time if he violates his probation by failing to complete his drug program, or even if he is convicted again for using or possessing restricted drugs, unless the DA can prove to the judge that the defendant "poses a danger to the safety of others," something the DA can rarely prove. The Prop 36 defendant knows if he gets convicted for possessing restricted drugs a third time, he faces only three days in jail in Los Angeles County. How does he know this? Because his attorney and his friends have told him. Given these facts, why would anyone be surprised that so many more Prop 36 drug defendants are rearrested for a new drug offense than defendants who are placed on probation and ordered to participate in a non-Prop 36 drug program?

If you tell your child, "If you do that two more times you are going to have a time out," or, if you tell him, "If you do that one more time, you are going to have a time out," which warning would tend to reduce the likelihood of the child repeating the prohibited conduct? Every parent knows the answer.

And what would be the anticipated response of the academic community to this truism? They would be sure to say, as they so often do, no matter how clear the issue, "It's not that simple. Everything is not all black and white. Most big issues contain many shades of gray. The issue is far more complicated than that." And the true answer is: No, it is not more complicated than that. Not *every* public policy issue is that complicated. Drug users, most of whom really like taking drugs, given the choice, will choose two more chances over one more chance. And the drug user who knows there is no penalty for a second drug conviction is more likely to get arrested again for possessing illegal drugs than the drug offender who believes he may go to prison for his next drug conviction. And that is the reason the rearrest rates for those who enter the Prop 36 drug programs are so much higher than the rearrest rates for those who enter non-Prop 36 drug-treatment programs. I would think this logic would elicit a big, "duh" from just about everyone.

The promoters of Prop 36 want to expand Prop 36 to other so-called "nonviolent" crimes. In a *Los Angeles Times* story published April 13, 2006, titled "Drug Treatment Program [Prop 36] Lowers Jail Population," the co-author of a study of Prop 36 by the Justice Policy Institute, which even the *Times* describes as "left-leaning," said that "he and others believe that the next goal should be to expand the reach of Proposition 36 to include those arrested for nonviolent crimes related to drug abuse—such as theft to purchase drugs." If this goal is realized, I predict that thefts of all kinds, including car thefts and burglaries will increase substantially if, as in the case of Prop 36, there is no possibility of jail or prison time until after the third conviction. A large percentage of defendants steal and commit burglaries to buy drugs. In this *Times* story, there was no mention of the fact that 76% of the defendants who are ordered into Prop 36 treatment programs by judges fail to complete the programs.

In July 2006, the California legislature amended Prop 36. The sixteen-page amendment (SB 1137) recited the fact that 30 percent of convicted drug defendants ordered by the judge to participate in a Prop 36 treatment program had failed to show up for the programs.

Of those defendants who did show up, only 34 percent completed the treatment program. The legislature, to their credit, believed this record of failure was unacceptable. The amendment to Prop 36 was obviously a compromise. The amendment now provides that drug testing be included in Prop 36 court-ordered drug treatment programs. The new law also includes a modicum of an incentive to encourage the defendant to enter and complete the treatment program. The amendment authorizes the judge to impose a maximum 48 hours jail time if the defendant violates his probation by failing to enter the treatment program or, while in the program, "tests dirty" for a prohibited drug. If the defendant violates his probation a second time, the new law authorizes the judge to impose up to 120 hours of jail time. In reality, in Los Angeles County, this amounts to zero jail time because of the sheriff's policy of not holding defendants sentenced to less than three months in jail.

More significantly, the amendment to Prop 36 prohibits the California parole authorities from revoking the parole of a state prison parolee convicted of using or possessing a restricted drug while on parole—even though it was a condition of the inmate's release that he not use or possess restricted drugs.

31

STUDIES OF CAREER CRIMINALS AND SELF-ESTEEM

Numerous studies have been done of criminals and what makes them choose lives of crime. A study that impressed me greatly was a fifteen-year study of 255 criminal offenders, ages 15 to 55, at St. Elizabeth's Hospital in Washington, D.C. The study, which began in 1961 and ended in 1976, was conducted by Dr. Samuel Yochelson, a psychiatrist, and Stanton E. Samenow, a clinical psychologist. The results of the study were reported in a two-volume work titled *The Criminal Personality*.

In *The Criminal Personality*, Yochelson and Samenow concluded that there does exist a criminal personality which share certain traits in common. For example, the anger of criminals is pervasive; they suffer no guilt from injuring others; they break promises without thought; they lie incessantly even over the smallest issue. They crave excitement; they thirst for power. Dr. Samenow said that criminals believe they are superior to others and seek, through their activities to, "own the world." None of these traits is unique to the criminal, but the criminal shows them in the extreme, says Dr. Samenow.

The study found that these traits in the criminal emerge at an early age, as does criminal behavior. Some chronic offenders begin committing petty thefts as early as age four. The study concluded that there is no such thing as a "first offender." "The criminal gets away with far more than is ever known by anyone else. By the time he is apprehended, he has more than likely committed hundreds, if not thousands, of offenses."

The study also found that career criminals are not mentally ill, and they commit their crimes by free choice. Dr. Yochelson concluded from his work that such offenders, despite psychiatric diagnoses to the contrary, are sane and their crimes are the result of rational decisions. The study concluded that only about 20% of criminals could be taught new thinking patterns to help them control their criminality. Dr Samenow avoids the word "rehabilitation" and uses "habilitation" when describing the chronic offenders he worked with. "When you think of how these people react, how their patterns go back to the age three or four, there isn't anything to rehabilitate," he said. The study also concluded that there is only so much society can do, and that the true "habilitation" of the criminal personality must proceed from the criminal himself.

This study marked a departure from the conventional wisdom that society and its policies were ultimately responsible for the prevalence of crime. This study blamed the criminal for committing crime and corroborated my experience as a prosecutor. As a new prosecutor, I slowly became convinced that I was not dealing with people who were criminals because they were "sick" or suffering from low self-esteem, as I had been taught to believe by the media and the liberal establishment. In my old liberal days, by calling the criminals "sick," I could attempt to explain, and thereby excuse, even the most cruel, horrendous conduct.

One year after the Yochelson/Samenow study was published, the researchers at the Rand Corporation released their results of a study of 49 adult armed robbers, each with long criminal records, who were incarcerated in California prisons. The Rand study recommended longer prison sentences for the younger, more active criminal offenders. The Rand study, like the Yochelson/Samenow study, also found that criminal patterns become fixed early in life, rather than from their experiences in prison. The director of the Rand study, criminologist Dr. Joan Petersilia, stated, "Unfortunately, there is a poor correlation between a criminal's actual behavior and his arrest record. A meager arrest record often disguises a very active and dangerous criminal."

Dr. Petersilia reported that the 49 inmates studied had committed 10,500 crimes despite the fact that most had spent nearly half their criminal careers in prison. Of the offenses committed by the study subjects, only 12% resulted in arrest and about half of those led to a conviction, Dr. Petersilia said. This means that 94 times out of a hundred, the criminal committed a crime without being convicted. Pretty good odds in favor of the criminal! This is why, arguably, crime pays, at least for those who don't mind being arrested occasionally. The Rand study said of one of the felons: "Upon release from prison, he headed straight for his old neighborhood to rob a liquor store. 'I wanted to make sure I still had it in me. It's like getting back up on a horse after you've been thrown off. I wanted to show myself that I wasn't scared.'"

Within three to four months after release, a majority of the subjects were again involved in criminal conduct, according to the Rand study. The Rand study found that "For most [of the 49 felons studied] crime was the occupation of choice: 'I wasn't equipped to handle the outside world,' one felon explained. 'I always felt really uncomfortable with straight people. I remember working in a dry cleaners once. I had nothing in common with those people. I was anxious to get back with my own kind. I deliberately got myself busted when things got too bad. I'd go into the joint [prison]; I knew how to function there. Outside, I didn't know what my role was; I was a hustler, robber and junkie. Those things are lifestyles, not just a category that appears on a rap sheet.'"

From these two studies, we can safely assume that there are thousands of three-strikers out there who have not been arrested for their crimes. These two studies also lead us to the conclusion that career criminals commit crimes because it is their lifestyle, their chosen occupation. These criminals believe, based on their experience, that crime pays because they know the chances of getting caught and convicted are minimal. How can one argue that getting away with crime 94% of the time are not good odds in favor of the criminal?

Of course, the liberal media criticized the 15-year Samenow/Yochelson study that said only one out of five career criminals is capable of being reformed. What a coincidence! Only 21% of all inmates paroled from California prisons are able to successfully complete their paroles—one in five.

The Rand study stated, "A majority of habitual felons studied said that nothing—not harsher treatment in prison, the possibility of a longer sentence, stricter parole supervision, nor the certainty of being caught—would have prevented their return to crime."

Self-Esteem Study

Many liberals want us to believe that increasing self-esteem is the answer to many of our problems, including criminal behavior. My experience as a deputy DA has taught me this is not true. I have seen countless career criminals who, by any measure, had plenty of self-esteem. Many are very street smart, have leadership qualities and are great risk-takers. Sometimes they refuse to accept the public defender and choose to represent themselves even when charged with serious felonies. This is called "going pro per"—short for the Latin, "in propria persona." Less experienced DAs tend to underestimate these pro pers. They beat us more often than we like to admit.

My theory is that in some of these pro per cases, the jury assumes the pro per defendant cannot afford an attorney and they feel sorry for him. The jury is often not aware that the pro per defendant *chose* not to be represented by a free public defender. Also, at work is the David and Goliath phenomenon, the poor defendant alone, battling the police and the powerful DA's office. The twelve fair-minded jurors sense unfairness in the match-up and want to even the playing field. They, in effect, become the defendant's attorneys. The more the pro per screws up, the more the jury sympathizes with him. And sophisticated, career-criminal pro pers, who have been through the system repeatedly, are well aware of this and often do a good job of manipulating the jury.

One cause of having self-esteem could be genetic. Self-esteem is *not* achieved by using the liberal's approach: requiring inner-city kids to repeat out loud the mantra, "I am somebody" enough times in the hope that somehow self-esteem will be infused into their psyche by a kind of osmosis. Or another liberal favorite: for teachers to reward students with an A or a B grade when they deserve a D or an F. If someone does not already possess self-esteem, there is no short cut to getting it. It must be earned "the old-fashioned way"—by self discipline and hard work which produce a series of successes—not necessarily from law-abiding conduct. Of course, it would be nice if the child had nurturing, supportive parents who encourage the child to live a principled life. But there is no guarantee that a child who has high self-esteem will develop into a principled, responsible, law-abiding adult.

A December 2004 American Psychological Society study titled "Exploding the Self-Esteem Myth," published in *Scientific American*, concluded that the self-esteem movement was misguided. Roy F. Baumeister, a professor of psychology at Florida State University, wrote an op-ed piece for the *Los Angeles Times*, published January 25, 2005, titled "The Lowdown on High Self-Esteem." Professor Baumeister was part of the 2004 study which concluded, "High self-esteem in schoolchildren does not produce better grades." The professor said, "Kids with high self-esteem do have slightly better grades in most studies, but that's because getting good grades leads to higher self-esteem, not the other way around." The professor reported that "According to a study by Donald Forsyth at Virginia Commonwealth University, college students with mediocre grades, who got regular self-esteem strokes from their professors, ended up doing worse on final exams than students who were told to suck it up and try harder."

Professor Baumeister said, "It was widely believed that low self-esteem could be a cause of violence, but in reality violent individuals, groups and nations think very well of themselves. They turn violent toward others who fail to give them the inflated respect they think they deserve. Nor does high self-esteem deter people from becoming bullies, according to most of the studies that have been done; it is simply untrue that beneath the surface of every obnoxious bully is an unhappy, self-hating child in need of sympathy and praise."

The study also concluded that "High self-esteem doesn't prevent youngsters from cheating or stealing or experimenting with drugs and sex. (If anything, kids with high self-esteem may be more willing to try these things at a young age.)"

Professor Baumeister concludes by saying, "After all these years, I'm sorry to say, my recommendation is this: forget about self-esteem and concentrate more on self-control and self-discipline."

These recent conclusions of the American Psychological Society study reported by Professor Baumeister are consistent with both the Yochelson/Samenow study and the Rand study.

32

THE CHANCES OF GETTING CONVICTED? NOT MUCH

Over the years I've read many stories in the media about the lives of career criminals. Any honest portrait of a career criminal, whether he is a robber, burglar, rapist, child molester or thief, will show that he was never convicted for the great majority of crimes he committed. But the media likes to say that "He fell through the cracks of the criminal justice system." The media seems to be implying that it is unusual when the criminal is not held accountable for his crime. If "falling through the cracks" means not being held accountable in a court of law for a crime the criminal committed, then falling through the cracks is the rule—not the exception to the rule. The truth, as we have seen, is that the career criminal is held accountable for only a small fraction of the crimes he commits.

To understand the reason for this, one need only look at a few statistics. First, many thousands of serious crimes are not even reported to the police. The FBI announced that in 2004, only about half of all violent crime and less than 40% of property crimes were reported. Second, very few crimes that are reported are solved (cleared) by police (see Chapter 41), and third, the DA's high rejection rates. Considering all the crimes committed, it is relatively rare for the police to have such strong evidence against a suspect that they will arrest the suspect, and the DA will file the case believing all twelve jurors will conclude the defendant is guilty beyond a reasonable doubt. In May 2006, criminologist Joan Petersilia said the chances of a reported serious crime committed in California leading to a state prison sentence for the perpetrator is about 5%, which, she said, is about the national average.

Realizing how few crimes are ever solved, I have often thought that the criminal justice system serves little more than a symbolic function. Law-abiding parents teach their kids that crime doesn't pay. But those who have been committing crimes for years know how seldom they get caught for the crimes they commit. Oftentimes it is a fluke that snares a suspect—something the criminal could never have anticipated. But flukes, by definition, are a rarity.

To the career criminal, the relatively few times he is caught, convicted, and incarcerated, usually for a short time, is like overhead—the cost of doing business. For the career criminal, the risk of being caught is clearly outweighed by the lifestyle a life of crime affords. One of the things I learned as a deputy DA is that some criminals do a cost-benefit type of analysis.

I recall a case in which a defendant charged with a narcotics offense decided to cooperate with the prosecution and testify against his co-defendants. He told my I/O and me that up until a couple of years before, he and his gang had been heavily involved in the sale of the drug PCP, also known as angel dust. He told us that when a new law was passed which precluded probation for anyone convicted of selling any amount of PCP, and mandated a state prison sentence, he and his crime partners met and discussed the situation and decided to start selling cocaine instead. Probation and a small amount of county jail time (usually 60 days—but only six days real time, or less, in accordance with the L.A. County Sheriff's early-release policy) has, for many years, been the standard, first-offense sentence for one convicted of selling a small amount of cocaine in Los Angeles County.

33

IF YOU CAN EXPLAIN IT, YOU CAN EXCUSE IT

The late Reuven Frank was a former president of NBC News. In January 2004, he wrote an op-ed piece for the *Los Angeles Times*[8] dissecting the lack of shock or outrage over the frequent occurrence of the most horrendous acts, such as those committed by suicide bombers who have murdered so many innocent men, women, and children so often and for so many years. "Repeat an unimaginable brutish and outrageous phrase enough and it becomes common parlance," Frank said. He said, "There is an acceptance that there are such people as suicide bombers, just as there are grocery clerks, or children's dentists or ladies' tailors. One of the reasons suicide bombers have become accepted is because they can be explained. They live under such and such conditions of isolation, of poverty or disadvantage."

As Frank pointed out, "Whatever tragedy happens, however outrageous it may seem, there are always those whose reaction is to look for an explanation." He quotes a Frenchwoman, Madame de Stael, who, about 200 years ago, is supposed to have said, "Explaining everything excuses everything." As examples, Frank cited liberals Gore Vidal and Noam Chomsky who ascribed 9-11 to "an understandable reaction to American colonial imperialism." As Frank pointed out, people in the 1930s sought to explain the rise of Hitler and the Nazis by placing the blame on the Treaty of Versailles. Frank conceded this may be true, "but it does not explain Buchenwald. Some things defy explanation."

mankind is essentially good. After all, if mankind is essentially good, such widespread, apparently senseless violence, perpetrated by people who are not mentally ill, makes no sense to us. And therein lies our conundrum.

The real villain, it seems to me, is the underlying belief that mankind is essentially good. I concede it is an attractive, feel-good belief—but a myth nevertheless. We are taught to believe we are better people if we believe mankind is essentially good. The same goes for forgiveness. We are taught it is good for us to forgive. But whom should we forgive? The serial killer or the killer we believe has killed only once? Would it be a good thing for the career criminal to know that *all* his numerous victims have forgiven him—and that his future victims, as well as society, will forgive him too? Should there be *any* point when we should stop forgiving the career criminal for his continuing crimes?

An article published April 4, 2004, in the *Los Angeles Times Magazine* titled "The Ultimate Forgiveness," authored by Vince Beiser, explored the phenomenon of crime victims' next of kin forgiving and even befriending their loved one's killer in prison. Dr. Paul Berg, an Oakland, California psychologist, who testifies in death penalty cases, was quoted as saying, "Some psychiatrists will tell you forgiveness is healing. I don't believe it. I think it's overrated." I consulted Dr. Berg, who told me, "These befrienders [of the violent criminals] are not necessarily acting compassionately, but sometimes pathologically."

Of course, there are millions of good people in this world. But to embrace a philosophy which has as its main premise the essential goodness of mankind, contrary to a mountain of evidence suggesting otherwise, is simply foolhardy. If mankind were basically good, why have wars been fought throughout recorded history? Why do we need hundreds of laws that threaten people with punishment if they kill, hurt or steal from their fellow man, pollute the air and water, and manufacture unsafe products?

"Man's inhumanity to man" is as old as mankind itself and has been chronicled throughout the ages. If this is a fact, and the evidence for its truth is overwhelming, how can the liberals continue to believe that mankind is essentially good? Civility and "goodness" are not congenital. Civility, thin as it may be, must be instilled in our children by good parenting. And if one or both parents are absent or incapable of being good parents and fail to instill good values and habits and draw boundary lines, we can expect some of these children to enter the criminal justice system at an early age.

I do not mean to suggest that all criminals are the products of bad parenting. I know of cases in which the defendants had wonderful, loving parents and were raised in affluent areas. But as little boys or girls (most often boys) they were incorrigible and seemed to enjoy hurting other kids and animals. Their parents finally realized that all their love and nurturing was having no effect. Their crimes often escalated in seriousness and they sometimes ended up spending a good portion of their lives in prison. In these cases, causes can be difficult to ascertain.

35

IF YOU WAKE MY LITTLE SISTER, YOU WILL HAVE TO KILL HER TOO

Sometimes a case is so bizarre that even seasoned prosecutors, who think they have seen it all, are left bewildered. I know I was. The murder victim was an attractive woman, a successful record executive who lived in a nice neighborhood in a suburb of Los Angeles. She had a teenage daughter who had been a good student, but who rather suddenly started missing classes and getting poor grades. She then went to "continuation school," designed for kids having trouble in the mainstream schools. The girl's parents were the streets safe again. Critics of the planned research claimed this research was dangerous. The biggest fear was that the studies would be used to discriminate against blacks. That fear flowed from the fact that although blacks are only 12% of the population, they "account for 45% of all arrests for violent crimes such as homicide, rape and robbery," the story said.

But other scientists, among them Adrian Raine, a USC psychologist, countered that "It is irrefutably the case that biologic and genetic factors play a role. That is beyond scientific question. If we ignore that over the next few decades, then we will never rid society of violence."

The National Research Council (NRC), the research branch of the prestigious National Academy of Sciences, stepped into the fray on the side of Raine. The NRC brought together nineteen of America's most prominent academics to conduct biomedical research into violence. The scientists believed the human body may hold clues to what makes people violent, and scientists ought to pursue them. In a massive 464-page report titled "Understanding and Preventing Violence," these nineteen scientists recommended that, along with traditional research into the social causes of violence, biomedical research into violence should be increased.

Among the most vocal critics of genetic research into the causes of violence is Dr. Peter Breggin, founder of the Center for the Study of Psychiatry. Dr. Breggin has made a career of fighting medical approaches to social problems. He envisions a frightening scenario in which government-funded genetic screening programs will label inner-city youngsters at risk for becoming violent, and then dope them up in what he calls "a massive drugging of America's children." Dr. Breggin compares attempts to find genes for violence to the horrifying experiments that took place during the Nazi Holocaust.

Dr. Breggin is not alone in his criticism of this genetic research into the causes of violence. Ronald Walters, a political scientist at Howard University, poses this question: "Assume we find a genetic link to violence. The question I have always raised is how will this finding be used? There is a good case, on the basis of history, that it could be used in a racially oppressive way, which is to say you could mount drug programs in inner-city communities based on this identification of so-called genetic markers."

On the other side, Kenneth Kidd, a geneticist at Yale, said that "Violent behavior is a problem for society and there is growing evidence that some small component—I have no idea how big yet—of violent behavior has a genetic basis. So I think it is worth trying to understand what causes that and trying to understand how we can minimize it."

Dr. Frederick Goodwin, former director of the National Institute of Mental Health (NIMH), called upon government scientists to embark on a large-scale project called "The Violence Initiative" that would include biomedical research. But Goodwin was accused of using racist language when he suggested that studies involving monkeys might prove useful in understanding violence in humans. His comments caused such an uproar that The Violence Initiative was abandoned.

About a year later, David Wasserman, a lawyer and research scholar at a University of Maryland think tank, organized a conference on genetics and crime for October 1992. Although the National Institutes of Health (NIH) agreed to pay the $78,000 bill for the conference, it withdrew the funding after Dr. Breggin and others complained and Wasserman was forced to cancel the meeting. After a successful appeal, the conference was reinstated but, in view of all the criticism, the researchers were afraid to discuss their work and the agenda was watered down. Wasserman said, "I had scientists who were invited to the conference telling me they were going to tone down what they were going to say because they didn't want their funding to be placed in jeopardy."

In 1983, Sarnoff Mednick, a USC psychologist, proposed a biomedical study of juvenile delinquents in an attempt to predict who would become repeat offenders. Mednick's study received initial approval from the U.S. Department of Justice, which was to fund the study. But the funding was withdrawn after a Washington newspaper columnist compared his proposal to "something cooked up by the Nazis' Dr. Mengele." Mednick had to go to Australia to conduct the study where the political opposition was not as great. Mednick was not optimistic about the future of biomedical research into violence. "It's kind of hopeless," he said. "Nobody permits the studies to be done. Nobody permits the conferences to be held."

The late Dr. Markku Linnoila, formerly with NIH, also searched for many years for biomedical causes of violence. He told the *Los Angeles Times* he worried that anything he said would be misconstrued. He feared he would be branded as "one of those crazies," and he chose his words with caution. He was careful to say that, in his vision, drugs would be used to control violent behavior only as a last resort, after other programs had been tried and failed. And he offered—without being asked—that he did not consider his research an ethnic issue. But he believed fiercely that science may hold at least some clues to curing America's violence epidemic, and that his own research was crucial to the public health of a nation at risk. He told the *Times*, "Our critics paint these nightmare scenarios based on their own imaginations...that somewhere there is a bogyman who wants to immediately start drugging people, and I don't see that. I think we have a very significant problem with interpersonal violent behavior. And it behooves us, if we are serious about this, to try to understand how to prevent it."

In 2001, Cambridge University Press published *Genetics and Criminal Behavior*, by David Wasserman and Robert Wachbroit. The authors say, "The success of genetics in understanding human disease suggests that it could be a powerful tool in the scientific investigation of human behavior, including criminal behavior."

The authors say, "Currently there are a variety of research programs investigating the genetic influences on human behavior… Heritability studies seek to tease out genetic from environmental effects on human behavioral differences, largely by examining twins and adoptees; molecular researchers look for markers and, ultimately, genes associated with crime and violence."

The great irony of this controversy is that if the research were to confirm that genetics does play a role in predisposing a person to violent behavior, and further research were successful in formulating a treatment for the condition, thereby possibly preventing thousands of homicides and countless young men being imprisoned for much of their lives, my hunch is that the objectors to this research would prefer the status quo. They would rather not know the truth if they believe there is any possibility that the truth would invalidate their deeply held conviction that the main causes of crime are poverty, racism, and government indifference.

On November 2, 2004, Californians voted to expend $3 billion on stem-cell research—with no guarantees of success. We need the same kind of resolve and commitment to try to understand and reduce the epidemic of violence in this country.

It is a horrific statistic that the number one cause of death among young black men in this country is homicide. How can we call ourselves compassionate if we stand by, year after year, watching and lamenting this ongoing slaughter of young people while failing to explore every possible lead to determine the causes? The stakes are too high to be deterred by political correctness. We should be investigating all avenues that might bring us some answers, even if they turn out to be only partial answers. We just might be able to save thousands of young lives from death, injury and prison. What is there to lose? If the research leads nowhere, at least we tried. But if we succeed, the benefits cannot be overstated.

Winston Churchill said, "Truth is incontrovertible, ignorance can deride it, panic may resent it, malice may destroy it, but there it is." We should not be afraid to seek and discover the truth—wherever it leads us.

37

IF MANKIND IS NOT ESSENTIALLY GOOD, THEN WHAT?

The liberal media would have us believe that the cause of the career criminal's adult crimes is the fact he had spent so much of his life in prison—from adolescence. The media tell us that prisons are schools for crime. This is no doubt true. One does not meet many good, honest people in prison. In a story of the arrest of a suspect for a brutal murder, the liberal media asks, "What do you expect from a young man who has been in prison since childhood?"

But Dr. Petersilia, who conducted the above-mentioned Rand study (see Chapter 31) found that "Contrary to our expectations, we found that the sophisticated offenders developed their criminal skills quite early in their crime careers, rather than through their experiences in prison."[1] This finding is consistent with the findings of the Yochelson/Samenow study.

The liberal media does not tell us what should be done with a young, violent, incorrigible adolescent who continues to commit crimes, who has been placed on probation repeatedly, who has received counseling and been referred to program after program. What does a judge do with such a youth who has been given second, third and fourth chances? Many of the liberals I have known would be willing to give such an incorrigible youth or adult an endless number of chances to go to therapy and counseling rather than incarcerate him to spare his future victims. They believe that with enough therapy, the therapists will be able to reach the career criminal's inner core and liberate his essential goodness.

Our state and federal prisons are filled with people who knew the risks of committing crimes and yet took those risks. What do the liberals think would happen if we suddenly repealed all of our criminal laws, anti-pollution laws, and laws against the manufacture of unsafe products? Could any rational person deny that we would have a large increase in crime, pollution, and unsafe products? Why would this be true if mankind is essentially good— as McGovern and the liberals claim?

When I was a teenager delivering liquor on the Sunset Strip, my boss, the owner of the store, told me he had grown up in Germany during World War II. He told me he and everyone he knew loved Adolph Hitler, and that I should not believe anyone who tells me that the German people did not love Hitler. He said Hitler told the German people what they wanted to hear. That may be true, but could that explain their *love* of Hitler and their willingness to go along with his plan to eradicate millions of European Jews (I know, they say they didn't know) and to invade and conquer other European countries? If it is true that tens of millions of law-abiding Christian Germans did love Hitler and accepted his master-race theory, and his goal of dominating Europe, how can this be reconciled with the belief in the essential goodness of mankind?

The Roman Colosseum held about 50,000 spectators who delighted in watching lions eating Christians and gladiators fighting each other to the death of one of them. Was this Roman brand of entertainment consistent with the belief in the essential goodness of mankind? Has mankind become more civilized in the nearly 2,000 years since the lions fed on Christians in the Roman Colosseum? Hardly. Watching lions eating Christians was regular entertainment for Saddam Hussein and his inner circle. Reportedly, a UN inspector secretly filmed one of these spectacles.

No, mankind is not basically good. We are basically self-interested in our own happiness, welfare and survival. This can be witnessed from the time we are tiny tots. What happens when very young children are playing together in a sandbox and one child takes the little shovel or pail that belongs to the other? We are not surprised when the child whose shovel was taken bops the other child over the head. This trait of protecting what is ours is a fundamental character trait of not only human beings but dogs, monkeys, and other animals. Who has not seen two dogs fighting over a bone?

Even if those who believe in mankind's essential goodness were to concede that wars have occurred throughout recorded history, and that there would be large increases in crime, pollution, and unsafe products if the laws against them were repealed; that thousands of Romans enjoyed watching lions eat Christians; that millions of Germans adored Hitler and supported his conquests of other nations; and that recorded history is a chronicle of man's inhumanity to man, they would still stubbornly cling to the myth that mankind is essentially good.

If these believers in mankind's essential goodness would concede that if, for example, we repealed all laws against rape, that thousands more women would be raped by men who would have nothing to fear from the police, how could they maintain their belief that mankind is essentially good? If mankind is essentially good, why would rapes be sure to increase dramatically after the rape laws were repealed? Are these believers in our essential goodness claiming that mankind has a genetic predisposition for fairness and good morals as a foundation supporting our essential goodness, despite history's rebuttal of this notion? Isn't it clear that good morals and the Golden Rule must be taught and repeatedly reinforced—from the time of near infancy? And, even if such lessons are taught, there are still no guarantees.

We should not confuse "self-interest" with "selfishness." We can act in our own self-interest and yet not be selfish. Americans, for example, are arguably very unselfish. We give billions to charity every year. We respond to emergencies, catastrophes, and those in need all over the world. We insist there be a safety net for those who are less fortunate. But our unselfish acts do not rebut the fact that we, whether as nations or as individuals, can usually be depended on to act in our self-interest—to the disadvantage of others, if necessary.

Of course, there are true heroes. We have all read about acts of heroism and self-sacrifice—often by soldiers, firefighters, and police officers. But this is a departure from the norm. That is the reason truly altruistic acts are reported in the media, and the hero is given recognition in the form of a medal or reward. If saving another's life at great risk to oneself, for example, were the norm, we would not make such a big fuss over the hero.

It is difficult to pinpoint the first time I began to doubt my belief in mankind's essential goodness and, instead, began to embrace the idea of mankind's essential egoistic nature. It may have been during a college philosophy class. The professor asked the class this hypothetical question: "If you were given the power to choose between saving the lives of your immediate family or saving the lives of all the men, women and children living in South America, which would you choose?" The majority of students responded that they would allow the millions of South Americans to perish in order to save their own families. I was stunned by this. But I have asked this same question of others over the years and most have given the same answer. I invite the reader to ask this question of yourself and your friends.

How could this view, sacrificing the lives of millions of strangers to save the handful of people closest to us, possibly be consistent with the belief that mankind is essentially good? The Bible quotes Jesus repeatedly as telling us, "Thou shalt love thy neighbor as thyself." For all but the most saintly, this is an unattainable goal. The evidence is quite overwhelming that it is not in man's nature to love his neighbor as much as he loves himself. Could anyone seriously believe the day will come, short of heaven, when we love our neighbors as we love ourselves?

Liberals, always searching for an excuse for crime, are often heard to say that crime is committed because of poverty. But, there are thousands of well-educated, white-collar criminals who commit crimes who are not poor, who have never been poor, who steal simply for greed; millionaire CEOs who steal from their shareholders and employees; wealthy stockbrokers and attorneys who steal from their clients; politicians who trade their votes for campaign contributions; lawyers, doctors, hospitals, and chiropractors who defraud Medicare and insurance companies; and multimillionaire professional athletes who continue to commit violent crimes. We continue to pass more criminal laws and strengthen existing ones, either because the existing laws have too many loopholes or have been too weak to deter criminal conduct.

How many thousands of lawyers, both civil and criminal, would be looking for work if people could overcome their tendency to take unfair advantage of each other? Lawyers are the most unpopular professionals in the country. But, in my view, it is not because lawyers are any more dishonest, as a group, than other professionals. To some extent, it is because the public perceives that there are far too many frivolous lawsuits designed to strong-arm wealthy and corporate defendants into making settlements. Many see the lawyer as willing to represent the first person who comes up with his fee, regardless of the merits or morality of his cause. This strikes much of the public as inherently wrong. It doesn't help the lawyer's image that the public sees the criminal lawyer on TV-news shows protesting his client's innocence in just about every newsworthy criminal case. And then, oftentimes within a few weeks or months, the public sees this same client pleading guilty.

Of course, many lawsuits result from honest disputes. Obviously, the lawyer is an indispensable part of our justice system. We need lawyers to defend the rights of a person wrongfully sued. We need lawyers to enforce clean-air laws and product-safety laws. We need lawyers to seek justice in the case of the negligent doctor who removes the wrong kidney or leaves a surgical instrument in the patient during surgery. We certainly need lawyers as prosecutors to enforce our criminal laws. And yes, the most dangerous career criminal has a right to be represented by a competent lawyer. Lawyers often get a bad rap because much of the public does not fully understand how the justice system works. Many do not understand that a lawyer owes his full allegiance to his client—not to the public. As unpopular as lawyers currently are, they provide an important check on the wrongdoing and abuse of power of both the government and the private sector.

Our founding fathers who wrote our Constitution knew very well that too much power in one person or institution has a corrupting influence. They took great pains to write into our Constitution the concept of the separation of powers to avoid concentrating too much power in one person or one branch of government. They accepted as a fact that it is inherent in man's nature that "Power corrupts and absolute power corrupts absolutely." After all, they had come to America to escape the tyranny of the King of England.

38

THE STANFORD PRISON
EXPERIMENT

$\mathcal{DO}$ liberals not believe it is man's basic nature to abuse power if he has too much of it? Isn't the story of civilization ample corroboration that this is true? If this is true, can it be said that man's tendency to abuse power is consistent with the liberal belief in the essential goodness of mankind?

I recall several years ago reading about a psychology experiment called the Stanford Prison Experiment.[2] Stanford University psychologists conducting the experiment placed an ad in a local newspaper to recruit college students who were to be paid for participating in the experiment. More than seventy college students responded to the ad. They were given diagnostic interviews and personality tests to eliminate candidates with psychological problems, medical disabilities, or a history of crime or drug abuse.

Finally, the researchers were left with twenty-four of those considered the most normal, well-adjusted college students. Half of the students were randomly selected, by a coin flip, to act as prison guards. The other half were designated as the prison inmates. The "guards" were given law enforcement uniforms and badges. The "inmates" were given the drab clothing customarily worn by prisoners. The experiment actually took place in a jail-like setting on the Stanford campus in a building fitted with cells and bars.

The guards were responsible for feeding and otherwise caring for the inmates. The guards were given no specific training on how to be guards. They were free, within limits, to do whatever they thought was necessary to maintain law and order in the "prison" and to command the respect of the inmates. The guards were supervised by the "warden," a Stanford undergraduate. The experiment was videotaped.

As the days passed, the guards became increasingly belligerent and punitive toward the inmates. The guards forced the inmates to do pushups and would step on the backs of the inmates doing the pushups and forced other inmates to sit or step on the backs of their fellow inmates trying to do pushups. At one point in the experiment, the inmates rebelled against the treatment they were receiving from the guards. They barricaded themselves inside their cells by putting their beds against the cell doors. They taunted and cursed the guards. The guards responded by using fire extinguishers to shower the inmates with skin-chilling carbon dioxide. The guards then broke into each cell, stripped the prisoners naked, took the beds out and forced the ringleaders of the rebellion into solitary confinement, a small, dark closet, and began harassing and intimidating the prisoners.

Every aspect of the prisoners' behavior fell under the total and arbitrary control of the guards. Even going to the toilet became a privilege which a guard could grant or deny at his whim. After the 10:00 p.m. "lights out," prisoners were often forced to urinate or defecate in a bucket that was left in their cell. On occasion, the guards would not allow prisoners to empty these buckets, and the prison would smell of urine and feces.

Less than 36 hours into the experiment, one of the prisoners began suffering from acute emotional disturbance, disorganized thinking, uncontrollable crying and rage. The psychologists supervising the experiment thought, at first, he was faking, and it was not until quite awhile later, and after this prisoner went into a rage, screaming, cursing, and acting crazy, that the psychologists were convinced he was really suffering.

As the experiment continued, the guards escalated their level of harassment, increasing the humiliation they made the prisoners suffer, forcing them to do menial, repetitive work, even to clean out toilet bowls with their bare hands. The jailers became increasingly abusive towards the inmates, even, on at least one occasion, depriving an inmate of food. Another prisoner went on a hunger strike to protest his treatment. The guards responded by putting him in solitary confinement. The guards then told the other prisoners that if they agreed to give up their blankets, the prisoner in solitary confinement would be released; otherwise, the prisoner would have to remain in solitary confinement all night. Most of the prisoners elected to keep their blankets and allow their fellow prisoner to suffer in solitary confinement all night.

A review of the videotapes revealed the escalating abuse of the prisoners in the middle of the night when the guards thought no researchers were watching. The guards had been driven to ever more pornographic and degrading abuse of the prisoners.

The experiment was prematurely stopped at the end of six days when a Stanford Ph.D. came to the experiment to conduct interviews of the prisoners and guards. She was outraged when she observed prisoners being marched by the guards with bags over their heads, legs chained together, and hands on each other's shoulders.

How could this cruelty happen among apparently well-adjusted, intelligent college students chosen at random to play the role of guard and inmate? It is simply another example and further corroboration of the principle that power, not even official power in this case, has a corrupting influence. The "guards" became cruel to the "inmates" and treated them inhumanely because they could. They had the power and they used it. Again, is this ugly character trait we possess, this tendency to abuse power, consistent with the liberal dogma that mankind is essentially good?

This experiment provides additional corroboration, if any is needed, that our founding fathers were correct. Too much power in one person or institution or unsupervised group is corrupting and dangerous. Unsupervised, unchecked power will likely be abused. But society must give some segments of society extraordinary power over others—such as the police and prison guards. What are we to do? One answer is for us to understand that power is likely to be abused if it is not closely monitored. Another is for us to acknowledge that it is not man's nature to always treat others with kindness and respect, especially if we are free to treat each other in any way we desire without fear of sanctions. One might say it is a sad commentary, but how much proof do we need to accept this as truth?

Although the abuse of unchecked power is likely, it is not inevitable. Though difficult, each of us has the ability to resist abusing power—if we so desire. The first requirement is to acknowledge our innate tendency to abuse power. The second is to discipline ourselves to resist this powerful inclination by constant introspection. Successful resistance to our tendency to take unfair advantage of others requires strength of character while trying to live the Golden Rule.

My rejection of the myth of mankind's essential goodness, and my acknowledgement of man's tendency to abuse power, might suggest I have a negative outlook. Not true. It is simply a matter of accepting what, to me, is obvious. In fact, I am optimistic. It is not necessary to embrace myths to live a happy, healthy, principled, and fulfilling life. Albert Einstein said, "The foundation of morality should not be made dependent on myth, nor tied to any authority, lest doubt about the myth or about the legitimacy of the authority imperil the foundation of sound judgment and action."

39

POLICE AND THE COMMUNITY

The police will always be in an adversarial relationship with some of those in high-crime areas, because there is an inherent conflict between the actions of the police in suppressing crime in high-crime areas, on the one hand, and being loved and respected by the people of those communities on the other—even though the law-abiding citizens of those communities are more dependent upon the police than those in communities with less crime.

Many people have little idea of the kinds of people the police routinely encounter in high-crime areas. I have learned, for example, that police deal routinely with people who not only have no respect for the police, but also have no fear of the police. I have learned that hardened street criminals often seem to have little or no regard for their own safety and often take enormous and senseless risks. For example, before I became a deputy DA, I would not have believed anyone would charge at a police officer who was pointing a gun at him. I believe it now, and I am no longer surprised by it.

When I was growing up, I could not have imagined anyone throwing a punch at a police officer. The truth is that violence against police officers is not uncommon today, and police officers are frequently injured by suspects—especially in high-crime areas. These areas sometimes resemble war zones. Police officers are often apprehensive. They sometimes overreact. When they do overreact, for example by using force that is not justified under the circumstances, they, like anyone else who injures another without justification, must be held accountable.

I recall an incident when I was the Deputy in Charge of the Glendale Area DA's Office. Glendale is not a high-crime area. I had a new deputy DA assigned to me. One day he came into my office and told me he did not want to prosecute a defendant who was charged with drunk driving, resisting arrest, and striking a police officer. I asked him to tell me the facts. He related that a California Highway Patrol officer stopped the defendant for DUI. The defendant opened his car door hard, hitting the officer with the door. He then struck the officer with his fists, knocking the officer down. The officer was alone, but he was able to call for back-up. The defendant was trying to get the officer's gun out of its holster when back-up officers arrived. Using their police batons (billy clubs), they were able to rescue their fellow officer. The defendant had sustained some bruises in the scuffle, but no serious injuries. The new deputy DA believed the back-up officers should have *asked* the defendant to stop attacking the officer before using their batons on him.

When the new DA finished relating the story, my filing deputy, an experienced deputy DA, who overheard his story, walked into my office and asked the new deputy DA, very calmly, "John, do you know what a Sam Browne is?" John replied that he did not. My filing DA told the new deputy DA that a Sam Browne is that big, wide, black-leather belt police officers wear. He asked the new deputy DA, "Have you noticed that the Sam Browne belt has many little holes in it?" John, becoming visibly perturbed, said he hadn't noticed. My filing deputy told the new deputy DA, "The reason for all those holes is so the police officer can hang all kinds of police paraphernalia on that big belt, such as a baton, a gun, ammunition, handcuffs and mace. John, do you know why police officers hang all that stuff on their Sam Brownes?" "No, why," he asked. "To make sure it won't be a fair fight" he replied. He then walked back into his cubicle. I could not have said it better. When police are attacked by suspects they are arresting, the police are supposed to win. Police officers are supposed to go home uninjured to their families at the end of their watches (shifts). This defendant was convicted of all the charges. And yes, John tried the case.

I grew up at a time and in a neighborhood where nearly everyone respected police officers. I grew up at a time when we could go on a two-week vacation and think nothing of leaving our front door unlocked. When I was a new deputy city attorney, I remember going on a ride-along with a police sergeant in a high-crime area. We were stopped at a traffic light. The sergeant called my attention to a man sitting in a car next to us. He was looking at the police sergeant and giving him the finger. The sergeant told me that was not unusual. I told him I would not like working every night in an area where so many people disliked me and expressed contempt for me. The sergeant acknowledged it would make his job a lot easier if the police were respected and appreciated by the community.

40

THE HUSBAND AND WIFE
BURGLAR TEAM

I recall a case I had in the mid-1970s. It was an unusual case because it involved a husband and wife burglary team. They were each charged with the burglary of an upscale home in an affluent neighborhood. They were representing themselves, which is one of the rare occasions when the prosecutor is permitted to speak directly to a defendant. My investigating officer and I were discussing a plea bargain with this Mr. and Mrs. burglar team. They were very candid with us. They admitted proudly, "off the record," (see Chapter 41) that they had been committing burglaries for years and had never been caught. They only burglarized upscale homes that had no dogs or alarms. They explained that they would do no more jail time if they were arrested for burglarizing a high-end home in a good neighborhood than if they burglarized homes in poor neighborhoods. They told us they did not use drugs, did not pay taxes, slept late in the day and traveled frequently. Both had a good sense of humor.

They said they had made up their minds early in their burglary careers that if they were ever caught, they would quit doing burglaries. Inasmuch as neither of them had ever been convicted of any crime, they pled guilty and were sentenced as first offenders to probation, given credit for the few weeks they had already served in the county jail, and immediately released. My I/O said to me, "And they say that crime doesn't pay." I had never before encountered criminals who had made such well-thought-out, long-range plans. But then, this was one of those cases in which the defendants refused to accept the public defender, a free lawyer. Consequently, we had the privilege of being able to speak to them.

41

CRIME STATISTICS

"*Clearance* rate" is the term used by police departments to describe the percentage of crimes solved. Clearance rates are maintained separately for all the major felony offenses. Police departments consider a crime "solved" when an arrest is made regardless of whether the DA's office decides to file charges or reject the filing of charges.

For example, in Los Angeles, burglaries have about a 14% average clearance rate, which means that out of every one hundred burglaries committed, the police "solve" only 14. If the police department were to request the DA's office to file charges in these 14 cases, they would, on average, get charges filed in about nine or ten cases. Therefore, in about 90% of all burglaries, the burglar gets away with his crime without even being charged. In 2003, LAPD had a clearance rate of about 25% for robberies. The FBI reported that in 2004, nationwide only 46.3% of violent crimes, which were reported to the police, were solved. These violent crimes include murder, forcible rape, robbery, and aggravated assault. Only 16.5% of property crimes reported to the police were solved. These crimes include burglary, larceny, and auto theft. Only 17.1% of arsons were solved in 2004.

The highest clearance rate of the commonly committed felonies is for murder. Nationwide, in 2004, 62.6% of murders were solved. But in the big cities the clearance rate is usually less. For example, in 2000, the clearance rate for murder in the city of Los Angeles was only 44%. In 2001, LAPD was able to solve about half of all murders. But LAPD is making progress. In 2004, LAPD solved 62.5% of its murders. In 2004, the Los Angeles County Sheriff, which has a fine homicide department, solved only 33% of its homicides. Combining the homicides for both Los Angeles City and County, i.e. LAPD and the Sheriff, the overall clearance rate for homicide in 2004 was 51%. I expect homicide clearance rates to improve as the DNA data bank continues to grow—no thanks to the ACLU and the *Los Angeles Times*.

It must be emphasized that merely because the police "clear" a case does not mean the person responsible will ever be held accountable for that crime in a court of law. The reasons are many. Many cases are cleared by the police when the suspect admits "off the record," commonly referred to as "outside of Miranda," his responsibility for a particular crime. Before interrogating a suspect who has been arrested, the police must advise him of his Miranda rights, which are the right to remain silent, the right to a free attorney if he cannot afford one, and that anything he says will be used against him in court. If the suspect tells the police detective that he will not give up these Miranda rights, which is common, nothing he tells the police can be used against him in court. That means no jury will ever hear what the defendant told the police.

I know of many instances in which a burglary suspect, after making an "off the record" confession (i.e., a confession made after he refused to give up his Miranda rights), has ridden around with the police in a patrol car pointing out the numerous houses or businesses he has burglarized. Because his confessions were off the record, the burglar could not be prosecuted for any of these burglaries. The police department benefits because they get to "clear" (i.e. solve) numerous burglaries. If the police did not agree to the "off the record" arrangement, the burglar would not have confessed, and the burglaries would have remained unsolved.

As mentioned earlier, the Los Angeles County District Attorney's Office rejects 30% to 40% of the cases that the police believe are good, prosecutable cases and request a filing from the DA. In 2005, the L.A. County DA's Office rejected 35,387 felony filings—34% of all cases presented to the DA's office by police detectives seeking felony charges. In 2005, 68,597 felony complaints were filed. Less than three percent of the defendants, or 1,613 defendants, were tried by a jury. Of those defendants who had jury trials, juries returned guilty verdicts in about 68% of the cases. About 12% of the trials resulted in hung juries.

A great many people were upset over the acquittal of O.J. Simpson. Most of us dislike seeing justice fail. But we should see this case in perspective. Inasmuch as about 50% of all murders in Los Angeles County are never solved, O.J. is just one more of thousands of murderers who was either not caught or who "beat the rap."

I have kept excerpts from a speech given by my former boss, DA John Van de Kamp, in 1978.[3] In this speech, Van de Kamp outlined three major misconceptions of criminal behavior: that criminals will be caught, that crime doesn't pay, and that prisons fail to help the crime problem. Far from all criminals being caught, only 20% of all reported crimes result in arrest, Van de Kamp said. He said this arrest rate largely discredits the second myth that crime doesn't pay. He said that, with an 80% chance of success, criminals are only slightly deterred by the prospect of arrest. Van de Kamp told the audience of one burglar who committed two thousand burglaries before being caught. Van de Kamp said the third myth, that prisons do not help the crime problem, is accurate to the extent that prison rehabilitation is an unlikely prospect. However, he said that longer periods of incarceration would substantially cut down the number of crimes committed by taking the hard-core recidivists out of action. This goal was accomplished sixteen years after Van de Kamp's speech when the Three-Strikes initiative passed.

In February 2003, it was revealed that because of a lack of resources, the Los Angeles Police Department had fingerprints from more than 6,000 unsolved murders that had not been compared with fingerprints in the national computer database.[4] The LAPD cold-case unit is working on solving 9,000 unsolved murders from 1960 through 1997.[5] And these 9,000 unsolved murders are just in the *city* of Los Angeles. The city of Los Angeles is a much smaller area than the entire county of Los Angeles. On January 1, 2004, it was reported that in the city of Los Angeles there were 11,000 homicides between 1988 and 2003, and that no arrests have been made in nearly 6,000 of them, a clearance rate of about 45%.[6]

Nationally, between 1960 and 2002, there were approximately 200,000 unsolved murders, and this number grows by about 6,000 each year. Although more police departments are forming cold-case units, most of the nearly 18,000 police departments in this country still lack the manpower to investigate old murder cases.[7]

More people have been murdered in this country between 1960 and 2003 (approximately 780,000) than all the Americans killed in World War I (116,516), World War II (405,399), the Korean War (54,246), the Vietnam War (58,152), the Gulf War (529) and the wars in Afghanistan and Iraq combined.[8]

Although 9/11/01 is regarded as one of our worst national tragedies, with nearly 3,000 people killed by terrorists, the fact is that many more thousands of innocent victims are murdered in this country each year: 16,503 in 2003 and 16,137 in 2004, according to FBI statistics.

When I became a deputy DA, I was surprised to learn how few crimes are ever solved. When there are so many thousands of unsolved murders, which means there are thousands of uncaught murderers in the community, how does one explain the excitement and fear generated when one or two murderers escape from prison? The answer: the public is unaware of these statistics because the media rarely tell us.

42

CRIMINAL LAW ODDITIES

There are many apparent oddities in criminal law. For example, if the suspect stabs the victim, intending to kill him, but the knife misses a vital organ by a hair and the victim does not die, the sentence in California for the attempted murder is five, seven, or nine years—unless it is willful, deliberate, and premeditated—which is very difficult to prove. If he pleads guilty to the attempted murder charge, he will probably be sentenced to the low term of five years plus one year for the use of the knife—three years after 50% credits. However, if he had been slightly more accurate and the knife had hit its mark, he would be guilty of first- or second-degree murder and would be sentenced to either 25 years-to-life or 15 years-to-life. The question is, does it make sense that there should be such a disparity—from a low of three years in prison to a maximum of life in prison—when the perpetrator's intent was the same in both scenarios—to kill the victim? After all, it is pure luck that the knife missed the vital organ by a hair. Is the perpetrator any less dangerous? Does society need any less protection from him?

Similarly, if the perpetrator, with intent to kill, stabs the victim five times in the chest in an urban area and the ambulance responds quickly and saves the victim's life, the crime would be attempted murder and the perpetrator, if sentenced to prison, could serve as little as three years. But suppose the perpetrator stabs the victim only once, and the stabbing occurred in a rural area where emergency medical facilities were not close by, and he bleeds to death before help can arrive. In this case, the perpetrator is guilty of murder and is subject to a 25 years-to-life or 15 years-to-life sentence—only because of the longer time it took for the ambulance to arrive. Should such a fortuitous circumstance as the emergency response time play such an important role in how many years the perpetrator must spend in prison?

Another example: The suspect enters a market, says he has a gun in his pocket and tells the clerk, "This is a robbery, give me all the money." Instead of complying with the robber's demands, the clerk pulls out a gun and the robber runs from the store. Inasmuch as the robber did not get his hands on any of the store's money, he can only be convicted of attempted robbery. The sentence for robbery in California is two, three, or five years. The sentence for attempted robbery is one-half of that or one year, 18 months, or 30 months. If he is sentenced to the low term of one year, which would probably be the case if he pleaded guilty, after he gets his 50% good-time/work-time credits, he would actually serve only six months. It would have been a completed crime of robbery if the victim had given the robber even ten cents.

Should the robber be given so much less prison time solely because the intended victim pulled a gun which prevented the crime of robbery from being completed? Does this make any sense? Again, is the robber any less dangerous? Does society require any less protection from him because he received no money? Why should the robber benefit so greatly because the clerk pulled his own gun?

Until 1988, the sentence in California for asking someone to kill another person (the crime of solicitation of murder) was two, four or six years—actual time being one, two, or three years. Inasmuch as about 90% of defendants plead guilty, and defendants rarely plead guilty for the high term, the real sentence for soliciting someone's murder was either probation or one or two years. California legislators believed that sentence was too low, so in 1988 they upped the sentence to three, six or nine years—actual time being 18 months, 36 months or 54 months. In nearly every solicitation of murder case I've heard about, the DA's evidence was a tape recording of the defendant hiring someone he thought was a hit man, but who, in reality, was an undercover police officer. The DA must prove to the jury beyond a reasonable doubt that the defendant really intended the victim to be killed, or he cannot be convicted.

The sentence for this crime always struck me as unreasonably low. I never understood why a defendant who, for example, was convicted of hiring a person he believed was a hit man to kill his wife to collect on her life insurance, was eligible for probation or a sentence range in prison from 18 to 54 months, actual time. If a defendant is convicted of soliciting the murder of his wife, the conviction would not even constitute a strike, because the crime of solicitation of murder is not classified as either a violent or serious felony. If the person the defendant hired was a real hit man who killed the defendant's wife, the sentence could be LWOP or death.

Why should the fact that the "hit man" turned out to be an under-cover police officer benefit the defendant so greatly in terms of his sentence? He intended to kill his wife, and he thought he had hired someone to do the killing. He did everything he could do, often including paying the "hit man" for the killing. Is a sentence of probation or 18 months in prison an appropriate sentence for this man who tried to kill his wife to collect her life insurance? Is the defendant any less dangerous because the hit man he thought he hired was really a police officer?

If a husband offers someone money to kill his wife, whether or not the person solicited agrees to do the killing, the husband has committed the crime of solicitation of murder. But if the person solicited agrees to *help* the husband kill the wife *and* either of them does *any* "overt act" in furtherance of the plan to kill the wife— even, for example, just making a phone call to find the wife or buy the weapon, the crime becomes conspiracy to commit murder which calls for a sentence of 25 years-to-life (the same sentence for first degree murder) even though no attempt is ever made to kill the wife. Thus, there could be as little as 18 months in prison (or even probation with no jail or prison time) without the phone call, but 25 years-to-life if they agree to kill the wife and either of them makes the phone call.

The lesson from these examples is that the severity of the defendant's sentence is often determined by results or technicalities, not necessarily the perpetrator's intent or how dangerous he is. As far as I know, these rules are pretty much the same in every state. Our laws are written this way because this is the way our laws have always been written. The question is whether these laws, so dependent on fortuitous events and technicalities, make sense.

There are attitudes among Club members which always struck me as a bit odd. For example, when a defendant is charged with car theft, few Club members, judges and DAs included, consider the value of the car stolen in determining the sentence.

A defendant will not likely receive a stiffer sentence for stealing a $50,000 car than if he had stolen a $1,000 clunker. A GTA (grand theft auto) is a GTA is a GTA (my apologies to Gertrude Stein)—no matter the value of the car. The sentence range for a GTA is 16 months, two or three years—but really 8 months, 12 months or 18 months. But most defendants convicted of GTA are sentenced to probation with a few weeks or months in the county jail—unless he was already on felony probation or parole when he committed the GTA or is a second or third striker.

The same applies to a defendant charged with residential burglary. That is, if a defendant enters a $1,000,000 home to commit theft, he will not likely receive a greater sentence than if he had entered the victim's trailer-home to commit theft. The law does not generally discriminate based on the value of the victim's house. In reality, there is not a big difference between the minimum and maximum sentence for most crimes. In the case of residential burglary, for example (the sentence range being two, four or six years), the real minimum state prison sentence is one year and the maximum is three years—after good-time/work-time credits are awarded.

43

POLICE DEPARTMENT PRIORITIES

In some smaller police departments, murder investigations are sometimes conducted by police detectives who have had no training in homicide investigations. In one of the murder cases I handled, the investigation was especially poor. I asked my investigating officer how long he had been assigned to homicide. He admitted it was his first case. I asked him how much training he had had in homicide investigation or interrogation technique.

He said he hadn't had any. I asked him if he had ever worked with an experienced homicide investigator. He said he had not. He was just winging it. If solving murder cases was important to this police department, they would not assign a police officer with no homicide training or experience to be the investigating officer. This was not the Los Angeles Police Department or the Los Angeles County Sheriff's Department.

One might wonder how it is possible that the LAPD had fingerprints from more than 6,000 unsolved murders that had not been compared with the fingerprints in the national computer database. The reason is that only two people in the Los Angeles Police Department were assigned to enter cold-case finger-prints into the federal fingerprint database. Los Angeles City Councilman Jack Weiss said, "There is absolutely no excuse for failing to prioritize the necessary technology and resources in a modern department's budgets." One prosecutor described it as "cart and buggy stuff."

It is not uncommon for police departments to lose valuable evidence in criminal cases. In July 2002, it was reported that the LAPD had mistakenly destroyed DNA samples in 1,100 sexual assault cases. Detectives explained that they destroyed this crucial evidence because they were not aware that the statute of limitations had been extended in rape cases. The law does not require police departments to store evidence forever. Police departments routine-ly destroy evidence in completed cases. I once had evidence destroyed by the police in a case where an arrest warrant had been outstanding for many years. When the defendant was finally arrest-ed, I was informed that the police had mistakenly destroyed the evidence.

Space limitations for evidence storage is a big problem for many police departments. They must discard long-stored crime evidence periodically. I recommend that it should be the policy in every police department to check with their local DA's office before destroying evidence. And every DA's office should have someone assigned to approve or reject police requests for the destruction of evidence. In my judgment, the cursory, superficial way that murder cases and some other serious cases are sometimes handled can be attributed to three causes:

One reason is political. Homicide detectives, especially in the LAPD's high-crime divisions, have impossibly heavy case loads. I say this is political because it is the Los Angeles City Council who approves the police department's budget. The councilmen's constituents like to see police in uniform driving black and white police cars, and the councilmen, being politicians, like to accommodate their constituents. Consequently, the detective ranks, comprised of plainclothes officers in unmarked cars, have historically been shortchanged.

But the detectives play a major role in solving the robberies, rapes and murders. They are the ones who run down leads, conduct interviews, and put the cases together. It is the detective who presents the case to the DA for the filing of charges and who, at the request of the deputy DA, does additional follow-up investigation and sits in court with the DA during jury trials. Most of the homicide detectives I have worked with are excellent. They are conscientious and hard working. But because their case loads are so heavy, there is often not enough time for the detectives to conduct high quality, thorough investigations in the ordinary homicide case in high-crime areas. Los Angeles City Councilman Jack Weiss, a former federal prosecutor, told the *Los Angeles Times* (April 6, 2006) that "Each of these detectives is worth dozens [of uniformed patrol officers] on the streets. They and only they can get recidivist rapists or killers off the streets." Until recently, LAPD detectives only worked day shifts even though a large percentage of homicides and robberies occur at night. Homicide detectives are often called at home at night to respond to a homicide scene.

The second reason is that there is no pressure or incentive coming from anywhere to do things differently—except in the rare case of negative publicity. There are no lobbyists or campaign contributors trying to persuade councilmen to allocate more funds to beef up detective ranks. LAPD would not be 6,000 murder cases behind in entering fingerprints into the national database if there were a meaningful incentive that this be done.

The third reason is that there are insufficient sanctions, other than the possibility of bad publicity, for the police losing or accidentally destroying important evidence or assigning inexperienced officers to investigate murder cases or for stalling the investigation of 6,000 murder cases simply because of their failure to hire a few more clerks.

More consultation between the DA and the police would be helpful in a number of areas. For example, every DA who has extensive trial experience knows that the most important piece of evidence in nearly every case is the defendant's statement to the police—especially if it is tape-recorded. I am convinced many police departments don't fully understand this. I have heard countless tape recordings of conversations between homicide detectives and suspects in which I could make out only bits and pieces of the conversation. I had cases where the tape recorder's batteries died in the middle of the interrogation, where the tape ran out during the conversation, and where the detective's voice was clear but the suspect's was barely audible because the microphone had been placed closer to the detective than to the suspect. Often, there was so much background noise on the tape that the suspect's words could not be clearly heard. There is often a dispute at the trial with respect to what the defendant actually said. The clarity of police recordings of suspects has never been a high priority with many police departments. Of course, they will deny this, but the proof is there.

On June 12, 2005, the *Los Angeles Times* published a page-one story about a murder in the Southeast Division of LAPD—which has one of the highest murder rates in Los Angeles. The story revealed that when the LAPD recently renovated the Southeast Division police station, they neglected to include an interrogation room with taping equipment and a one-way mirror. The *Times* story said, "Detectives had to interview people in storerooms, at their desks or in a small windowless office with bad acoustics." The remodeling design of this police station surely would have included an interrogation room equipped with built-in taping capability if the LAPD had consulted the DA's office. The story was both complimentary and critical of the LAPD. It revealed the impossibly high case loads of its homicide detectives in the high-crime areas of the city. The story quoted a homicide detective who complained about the priorities of the LAPD, citing the policy of sending twice as many detectives to the scenes of dog shootings than to most homicide scenes.

Six months after this June 12, 2005, *L.A. Times* story, the LAPD, on December 30, 2005, reported impressive progress in another page one *L.A. Times* story titled "Police Make Presence Felt on South L.A. Homicides." The story said that the LAPD was in the process of nearly doubling the number of homicide detectives assigned to the high-crime areas of South Los Angeles. An LAPD deputy chief admitted that the high case loads of LAPD homicide officers in high-crime areas was "substandard." The deputy chief said that more homicides are being solved because, with more detectives, they can devote more time to each case. An LAPD commander admitted that one of the reasons for LAPD's decision to double the number of homicide detectives in the high-crime areas of Los Angeles was the June 12, 2005, story in the *Los Angeles Times*.

Had the LAPD been unaware that its homicide detectives in the high-crime areas of Los Angeles had unreasonably high case loads until it was spotlighted by the *Times* story? Of course not. But this press coverage exposing the high case loads, overworked detectives, and low homicide clearance rates embarrassed the LAPD and caused them to act. The publication of this story has resulted in a major policy change at the LAPD which will result in many more killers being caught and convicted. The *Times* story even resulted in giving homicide detectives in the Southeast Division equipment to record interrogations with suspects. Now that's progress! Kudos to the *Times* for performing this valuable lifesaving community service. I say "lifesaving" because the December 30th story quotes an LAPD Commander as saying that "Officials believe that many killers are multiple murderers. Catching them will prevent subsequent crimes." But this is something Club members already know.

Ever since I can remember, there has been conflict between the police and the residents of the high-crime communities they serve. Why is that? Do we continue to hire corrupt, cruel, violent-prone, prejudiced people as police officers decade after decade? Of course not. I know how closely they screen out police candidates who exhibit antisocial tendencies during their preemployment psychological test and interview—except when affirmative action plays a part in the hiring process.

According to a *Los Angeles Times* story on April 17, 2006 titled "The Changing Face of the LAPD," 12.7% of LAPD officers are black, which roughly reflects the percentage of blacks in the city of Los Angeles. Yet, according to this article, there has recently been a drop in black applicants to become police officers. As a result, there is a strong push to hire more black officers. I have no issue with the goal of having the ranks of LAPD officers reflect the diversity found in the general population of the community served by the officers. The problem is that when hiring standards are lowered to recruit black, Hispanic and other minority officers because of affirmative action, the results can be disastrous and costly.

On March 3, 2006, a *Los Angeles Times* story titled "3 More Arrested in Rogue Cop Robberies," told of one former LAPD officer who was indicted for several robberies and burglaries committed when he was employed as a police officer. Before being hired as a Los Angeles police officer in 1997, he had already accumulated five felony arrests and one conviction for attempted burglary. The five felony arrests did not prevent his hiring because none resulted in a conviction. And because the attempted burglary conviction was reduced to a misdemeanor, he was hired as a Los Angeles police officer. As a police officer, he continued to get into trouble, which, of course, should have been expected. The *Times* never mentioned whether this officer was given a preference in the hiring process because he was a minority, or whether lowered standards resulting from affirmative action policies played any part in his hiring.

According to a December 20, 2001 story in the *Los Angeles Times* titled "LAPD Pair Focus of Criminal Probe," this same LAPD officer was the subject of several misconduct investigations. On one occasion, investigators obtained a search warrant to search this officer's locker. The affidavit, filed with the court by the investigators to support their request for the search warrant, stated that this officer exhibited a "pattern of conduct that is consistent with criminal police misconduct during narcotics investigations. The misconduct includes manufacturing evidence and unreasonable and/or illegal entries into private residences." This 2001 *Times* story said that during the search of this officer's locker, investigators "found a replica handgun that, in the opinion of one detective, was most likely possessed [by this officer] to be used as planted evidence." In another incident, this officer shot at an alleged drug dealer and was accused by LAPD investigators of lying about the circumstances of the shooting. He was also accused of falsely arresting witnesses to the shooting on drug charges. The city of Los Angeles agreed to pay $1.7 million to settle a civil lawsuit filed by the man at whom this officer shot, as well as others who claimed they were tormented by this officer. This is just one incident showing the consequences of lowering hiring standards to achieve diversity. There are many more such stories.

In a June 2005 story published by the *American Enterprise Magazine* titled "How Racial P.C. Corrupted the LAPD," author Jan Golab wrote: "The LAPD was once known as 'the world's greatest police department' due largely to its stringent character screening. Back in the era of Sergeant Joe Friday [the fictional lead character of the 1950s TV show *Dragnet*], LAPD candidates were checked out as thoroughly as homicide suspects. Even a casual relationship with any known criminal excluded a candidate from being considered as a police officer."

Golab goes on to say that "All that is now history. In a bid to appease racial activists and meet federal decrees, strict screening and testing measures were dismantled. New black and Hispanic officer candidates were hustled into the ranks at any cost. What former, now retired, LAPD deputy chief Steve Downing called 'a quagmire of quota systems' was set up, and standards were lowered and merit took a back seat to the new political imperatives.'"

Golab interviewed retired LAPD training officer Jim Peasha who told Golab, "I had mediocre trainees, some just plain incompetent. They were giving us trash. I finally transferred out, because I didn't want to go out in the field with these kids anymore." When Peasha got a bad minority recruit, he could not drum him or her out, no matter what. "I had some fantastic minority recruits," Peasha told Golab. "One black kid was the best I ever had. But I also had one [black] guy who I knew was on drugs and I couldn't get him out. He wound up getting caught working as a guard at a rock [cocaine] house. An off-duty cop!" Retired LAPD deputy chief Downing told Golab and me, "Rampart wasn't about cops who became gangsters. It was about gangsters who became cops."

The *Los Angeles Times*, in an April 20, 2006 story titled "Case Not Closed Yet for LAPD," reminded its readers again of LAPD's Rampart disaster, which, the *Times* says, caused one hundred criminal convictions handled by corrupt officers to be overturned, a dozen LAPD officers to resign or be fired, and the city of Los Angeles "to pay $70 million to settle lawsuits by more than two hundred people, many of them suspected drug dealers and gang members who alleged that they were shot, beaten or framed." The story the *Times* has *not* told its readers is the story of the backgrounds of many of these corrupt cops, *before* they were hired by the LAPD and *why* they were hired. That story would clearly be in the public interest, and it might even result in raising the hiring standards for LAPD officers—even to the point of preventing police officer applicants with multiple felony arrests and criminal convictions from being hired.

I have been told by two LAPD officers that because of affirmative action requirements, and the pressure to hire more minority officers, minority LAPD police officer applicants can be hired with substantially lower written test grades than required for white applicants. Is it wise public policy to tell black and Hispanic applicants that they do not need to perform as well on the LAPD oral or written tests as white applicants? Is it good for a black or Hispanic police officer applicant's self-esteem to be told that he or she is not expected to make the same grade on the tests as white applicants? I don't think so.

Although the LAPD is operating under federal consent decrees requiring the department to hire more minorities, none of the consent decrees requires the department to hire unsavory characters having long arrest records or gang affiliations. LAPD must scour the country, if necessary, to recruit black, Hispanic, and other minority men and women of character and integrity. How can the LAPD justify hiring a police officer, who they knew when they hired him, had been arrested five times for felony crimes and convicted of attempted burglary? Diversity on the police department is a worthy goal, but not at the expense of having to hire police officer applicants who have a history of breaking the laws they are expected to enforce. We would not elect a politician who had been arrested five times for felony crimes and had been convicted of attempted burglary. We should demand no less of our police officers. The LAPD's motto is "To Protect and to Serve." The public has a right to insist that the men and women hired as police officers to protect us and to serve us must be of the highest moral character. This issue is too important to be compromised by political correctness or to achieve racial quotas. As the Rampart scandal has proven, we will continue to pay a big price if this ill-advised policy of lowered standards for minority applicants is allowed to continue.

44

STATEMENTS BY DEFENDANTS IN THE LOS ANGELES COUNTY JAIL

Perhaps my biggest disappointment with a law enforcement agency occurred in 1975 when I was in the middle of a trial in a three-defendant, murder-for-hire, death penalty case. Two brothers had hired a hit man to kill the victim. They first kidnapped him, threw him in the trunk of a car and drove him to a location in an alley where they opened the trunk and shot him in the face with a shotgun. Somehow, though severely injured, he was able to run between some houses and onto a major street in Los Angeles. The injured man saw a woman park in the street and get out of her car. Her little niece was getting out on the passenger side. The injured man, who was bleeding profusely, ran to the woman, who was still in the street, grabbed her and begged her to take him into her house. The woman, who was very heavy, lost her balance and fell in the street, pulling down the injured man. Just then, the car from which he had escaped was speeding up the street towards him. The car stopped next to the woman and the injured man. The shooter alighted from the car, pushed the woman out of the way and shot the injured man, who was still lying in the street.

The woman, a nurse, was later shown a six-pack of photos and positively identified the shooter. There was ample other evidence to prove he was the shooter. He was charged with a special circumstance, murder for hire, as were the two brothers who had hired him. This shooter had a prior murder conviction as a juvenile for which he had served 18 months in the California Youth Authority. I was asking for the death penalty on the shooter mainly because of his prior murder conviction. Because he was a juvenile when he committed the prior murder, the jury was not permitted to learn about the prior murder conviction even though he testified in the current murder case. When the nurse took the witness stand, she positively identified the shooter. After she testified, the judge called a recess.

Because there were three defendants, and because the Los Angeles County Sheriff had received word of a possible escape attempt, two plainclothes deputy sheriffs were assigned to sit in the courtroom during the entire trial which lasted about two months. The nurse had testified in the first week of the trial. After several more weeks into the trial, and after I had rested the People's case, the two plainclothes deputy sheriffs asked if they could speak with me. We went into a little attorney's room next to the courtroom. They asked me if I remembered a few weeks before when the nurse testified and identified the shooter. I said I did. They told me that immediately after she finished testifying, the judge called a recess and they assisted the two court bailiffs who took the three defendants back into the holding cell next to the courtroom. The two brothers went in first, followed by the smaller shooter. The two plainclothes sheriff's deputies said they were behind the shooter. As they were walking toward the holding cell, the shooter said to his two co-defendants, "I shoulda done blowed that fat bitch away too."

I asked them if they realized that they had heard what amounts to a confession in a death penalty case, and I had already rested my case. They understood that. I asked them why they didn't tell me what they had heard immediately after they heard it. They said it was because they heard it in the jail. I said, "So what"! They told me there was an unwritten sheriff's department policy that statements made by inmates inside the jail do not leave the jail. I told them I did not believe there could be such a rule. They told me that jail personnel frequently hear inmates say all kinds of incriminating things, and it would be impractical to make written reports of all these statements and then try to find out which DA is assigned to the case to send him the report of what was said. Also, they said it would disrupt shifts among the jail personnel if jailers were constantly being subpoenaed to court to testify to what they had overheard.

I was dumfounded and frankly demoralized. I had thought the police and the DA were on the same side. I told these two deputies that I had been preparing this case for several months, and they heard a confession and kept quiet about it. I told them I was going to ask the judge for permission to reopen my case and call them as witnesses. They warned me not to do it. They said they would get in trouble. I asked them how a deputy sheriff could possibly get into trouble for telling a prosecutor about a confession from a murderer—a murderer who had a prior murder conviction?

I went back into the courtroom and got all three defense attorneys together. I told them what the two deputies had told me, and that I was going to ask the judge for permission to reopen the People's case. The three attorneys asked the judge for a recess and went to the attorney room to speak to the two deputies. One of the attorneys returned to the courtroom in a few minutes with the proverbial Cheshire-cat grin on his face and told me that the two deputies told the three attorneys that they didn't remember who said what to whom. I decided not to ask the judge to reopen. I thought if I called the sheriff's deputies to the witness stand and they said they didn't remember who said what to whom, it could only hurt my case. In the end, it really didn't matter as all three defendants were convicted of murder and the shooter received a death sentence—which was later commuted to life in prison after the death penalty was declared unconstitutional in California. Although the death penalty was reinstated by Proposition 7, in 1978, this would not affect anyone who had had his death sentence commuted to life in prison.

After the trial, I made it my project to try to corroborate what the two sheriff's deputies had told me about the sheriff department's unwritten policy precluding sheriff's deputies from reporting to the DA an inmate's incriminating statements overheard by deputies in the Los Angeles County Jail.

I spoke to another deputy DA who told me he had a similar incident in a case he was trying. This deputy DA told me that while the defendant he was trying was in the court lockup, the bailiff, all of whom are deputy sheriffs, overheard the defendant make a threat against a prosecution witness. The bailiff told the deputy DA about the threat and the DA asked the defendant on cross-examination about the threat. The bailiff later told the deputy DA that he was sorry he had told him about the threat, because he could get suspended for revealing what was said by inmates in the jail.

But the third incident, which again corroborated the existence of this policy, was so startling that it caused me to write a memorandum on December 13, 1976 to the chief deputy district attorney. In that memorandum, I explained the facts of my case and the two others. The third incident eclipsed in importance the first two.

I spoke to a deputy sheriff who was in my office discussing a pending felony case. I asked him if he was aware of the unwritten policy of not reporting to the district attorney's office incriminating statements overheard by sheriff deputies in the jail. The deputy confirmed the existence of the policy. He then told me that he had been one of the sheriff's deputies assigned to guard Sirhan Sirhan who was in jail awaiting trial for the assassination of presidential candidate Robert Kennedy. The deputy told me that during one casual conversation with Sirhan, Sirhan asked him if he was a Republican or a Democrat. The deputy sheriff told Sirhan that he was a Republican. Sirhan reportedly replied, "I sure did you a favor, didn't I?" The deputy told me that although he knew he was not permitted to contact the DA, he made a written report of this conversation to his superiors. I have no knowledge whether or not this information ever reached the deputy DAs who prosecuted Sirhan. But I doubt the DAs ever heard about it, because the deputy sheriff was never called as a witness to testify to Sirhan's statement to the deputy. I do not recall receiving a response to my memorandum.

45

JUDGE EARL BROADY SR.

When I was preparing cases for trial, and during my trials, I invariably took my cases home and worked till late in the evening preparing my questions for each witness, my cross-examination of the defendant in the event he took the stand, my final argument, etc. One night shortly before the trial started in the aforementioned three-defendant, murder-for-hire case, I was sitting on our king-size bed with parts of my case covering the entire bed spread. My two kids were sitting on the floor in front of the bed watching TV. Their mother yelled to the kids that it was their bedtime. When the kids left the room, the TV show, *Police Story*, a weekly series in the 1970s, started—without being preceded by a commercial. I looked up and saw my case, which covered the bedspread, come alive on TV. I yelled to my wife to come in. I told her the murder case I was preparing was on *Police Story*. It was not difficult to conclude that someone very close to the case had to have written it, because there were almost no differences between the story on TV and the real case. It was later determined that the LAPD captain in the area where the murder occurred wrote television crime dramas under a pseudonym.

The next day, the three defense attorneys asked the judge to issue a subpoena to the *Police Story* producer in order to identify the writer. The judge asked the attorneys, "Suppose we learn who the writer is and it turns out he is a police officer, what then? Will you then ask that the case be dismissed? Or do you just want the court to satisfy your curiosity?" The attorneys had not thought ahead. They could not come up with a good reason to justify revealing the identity of the writer. The judge denied the request to subpoena the producer of *Police Story*. What the judge did do was to ask all prospective jurors, who numbered in the hundreds, to raise their hands if they had seen *any* episode of *Police Story* that year. All those who raised their hands were excused without further inquiry.

The judge who presided in this murder-for-hire case was the late Earl Broady Sr., a fine, classy, fair, common-sense judge who was respected by both sides. Before being appointed to the bench, he had been the first black man to rise to the level of chief deputy district attorney—the highest ranking lawyer in the office next to the district attorney. He once told me that he had seen the criminal justice system from every perspective: as a defense attorney, then as a prosecutor, and finally as a judge. He told me there was one job in the criminal justice system that was by far the best: a grade IV calendar deputy in the Los Angeles County DA's Office—which was my job. I asked him why he believed that. He told me that I was like a sole proprietor in that I had very little supervision. This was true. Grade IV DAs in L.A. County have a great deal of discretion in what kinds of plea bargains to strike and how to try their cases.

Nobody ever told me or even suggested to me how to try a case. I was limited only by the law, my imagination and the ethical rules which govern all prosecutors. The judge told me I was free to choose which cases I would try and which cases to assign to my subordinates to try. Also true. The judge said that as a DA, as contrasted with a defense attorney, I had the luxury of only seeking the truth and prosecuting those I felt were clearly guilty and whose guilt I believed could be proved to a jury beyond a reasonable doubt. Also true. As discussed earlier, for the most honorable defense attorney, the defendant's guilt or innocence is largely irrelevant inasmuch as defense attorneys must represent their clients whether or not they are guilty.

Judge Broady was a very compassionate man. After he sentenced the shooter to death, he told me how difficult it had been. He told me that the night before the sentencing hearing, he and his wife had been up much of the night praying. He was still upset after sentencing the shooter to death, even though he was aware of the shooter's prior murder conviction. Perhaps it would have made it easier for him if I had told him that the defendant had confessed to my investigating officer, off the record, to killing many more people; he had been a killer for hire. But I did not. Because it was "off the record," this statement by the defendant was never revealed inasmuch as the statement was given "outside of Miranda"—meaning the defendant had not waived his right to remain silent before making the statement to the police.

4 6

MY "TRICK-ROLL" CASE

The first few years I was a deputy DA, I was sometimes given "hand-offs" to try. A hand-off occurs when a senior DA gives a junior DA a file and tells him the case is set for trial that day or the next. Of course, the junior deputy DA receiving the hand-off file has never seen the case before and would sometimes have to read the file while walking to court to choose a jury. It is a frightening experience for the new trial lawyer to be afforded almost no time to prepare. I had my share of hand-offs.

One of my hand-off cases I will never forget. I was given the file by a supervisor and told to report to the courtroom immediately. Of course, I had never seen the file and had no idea what the case was about. I looked at the file cover and saw that three men were charged with a strong-arm robbery, i.e., a robbery where force, but no weapon, is used. It appeared that two of the defendants had already pled guilty and were sentenced to three years probation and a year in the county jail. I was reading the facts of the case as I entered the courtroom and saw the panel of jurors who were waiting to be selected.

I spoke to the defense attorney who was seated at the counsel table with his client. I asked him why his client didn't accept the one-year-county-jail deal his two crime partners accepted. The attorney explained that his client couldn't plead guilty to a felony, because he was in the U.S. Marines and would receive a dishonorable discharge if he was convicted of a felony.

I spent that first day picking a jury without reading the entire file and without interviewing any of my witnesses. I learned the facts of the case that night at home. The case involved a "trick roll," a not uncommon type of robbery in which the "trick," a man seeking the services of a prostitute, is robbed by the prostitute's crime partner, often a boyfriend or pimp. The trick roll is a relatively risk-free crime because very few customers of prostitutes report the robbery to the police—for obvious reasons.

In this case, the robbery victim was a bartender at a high-end restaurant in Beverly Hills. He was stopped at a stoplight in Hollywood when a young, attractive girl approached the passenger side of his car and asked for a ride for just a few blocks. She told him she was late for an appointment. The bartender agreed. Once inside the car, the girl offered sex for money. The bartender agreed. The girl directed him to an underground parking garage of a large apartment complex just a half block above Hollywood Blvd. They left the car and entered the elevator. The elevator doors opened at the first floor and three men rushed into the elevator and roughed up and robbed the bartender, taking his money and jewelry. The three men and the girl all ran away leaving the victim on the elevator floor.

Although many trick-roll robbery victims do not report the robbery to the police, this victim was different. He had no wife, girlfriend, or family who lived in the Los Angeles area. Therefore, he could report the crime without anyone close to him knowing what he was doing when he was robbed. He went to LAPD's Hollywood Division police station and made a formal police report of what had occurred. But, being a bartender, he was fairly streetwise and he did not expect the busy Hollywood Division police officers to go out searching for the robbers. He decided that the best way to catch the robbers was to find the girl.

After driving around the Hollywood area for awhile, he spotted the girl at a busy intersection. He called the police, explained to the dispatcher that he had made a robbery report a short time before, and that he had located the girl who had lured him to the robbers. A police car responded, the bartender pointed out the girl and explained to the police the entire robbery incident. The police officers arrested the girl. The patrol officers then called for plainclothes officers in an unmarked police car to meet them.

The girl immediately confessed her role in the robbery. She, along with the victim, led the officers in the unmarked police car back to the same underground garage where the girl had taken the victim. The police, the girl, and the bartender entered the elevator and went to the first floor. When the elevator doors opened, there stood the three robbers who were waiting for their next victim. The bartender identified them as the three men who had robbed him, and they were immediately arrested. The police recovered a piece of jewelry from one of the robbers that he had taken from the victim. Good case, right? Dead bang!

Inasmuch as the victim was not seriously injured, and no weapons were used, another DA had made reasonable offers to all three defendants: three years probation and a year in county jail, which, at that time, really meant eight months. When I arrived at the courtroom the next morning, I told the defense attorney that his client should have accepted the offer because, if he was convicted, he could be sentenced to prison instead of probation and county [jail] time. I told the defense attorney that I could not imagine what his defense could be. The defense attorney smiled and said, "You'll see." Defense attorneys rarely reveal their defense to the prosecutor.

After the jury was sworn, I called the Beverly Hills bartender to the stand who told the jury his story and identified the defendant. Then I called the young girl who had pled guilty and agreed to testify for the People. She explained to the jury the entire criminal plan. Then the police officers testified to the arrest. It was a great case!

The defense attorney only called one witness, the defendant. He sat straight in the witness chair dressed in his Marine uniform. He turned to face the jury and told them he did not deny being with the other two men who had earlier pled guilty. But he claimed he had a very hazy recollection of what had occurred. He told the jury that when he was in Vietnam fighting for his country, he got hooked on heroin. He explained that in Vietnam, it was so easy and so cheap to buy heroin that he built up a big dependency on the drug. When he returned to the U.S., he could not break his addiction. He testified that the Marine Corps sent him to a naval hospital where he was tied down and underwent detox, but after being released he soon returned to his heroin habit. Finally, he went AWOL from Camp Pendleton and came to Hollywood where he got mixed up with the wrong crowd. He testified that on the night of his arrest, he was so strung out on heroin that he didn't know what he was doing. He said he certainly had no intent to rob anyone. The defense rested.

In rebuttal, I called back to the stand the two police officers who arrested the defendant. They testified that they had plenty of opportunity to observe the defendant on the night they arrested him and he appeared sober. The defense attorney and I argued the case to the jury. The jury deliberated for two days and announced they were deadlocked. The judge declared a mistrial.

The defense attorney and I spoke to the jury in the hallway. They had deadlocked 11 to 1 in favor of *"not guilty."* They just did not want to believe that a U.S. Marine, who had recently fought in combat, would knowingly engage in a robbery. They believed his testimony that he was in a haze that night and did not know what he was doing. One little Hispanic guy who hung the jury didn't buy it. He told us that his son was a heroin addict, and his son could remember everything he did when he was high on heroin.

When the defense attorney and I re-entered the courtroom, the judge, Kathleen Parker, asked me, "Well, Mr. Lewis, you were only able to convince one out of twelve jurors. Do I hear a motion to dismiss?" I explained to the judge that this case was a hand-off and that I had had no time to investigate the defendant. I asked the judge to set the case for a retrial and allow me two weeks to check out the defendant's story. The judge agreed. I subpoenaed the defendant's service record from Camp Pendleton.

I learned from his service record that he had never left the United States, and there was nothing mentioned about a heroin habit, and there was no record of his undergoing detox. I verified all this with his commanding officer (CO) and subpoenaed the CO for the retrial. On the day the retrial was set, the defendant's commanding officer was sitting in the back of the courtroom, ramrod straight, in his Marine uniform. He was holding the defendant's service record on his lap.

When the defendant emerged from the lockup with the bailiff, he spotted his commanding officer. He immediately made a crisp military about face which left him facing the lockup door. The bailiff, not knowing what was happening, escorted the defendant back into the lockup. The defense attorney approached me and asked me what was happening. I told him that the well-dressed Marine sitting in the back of the courtroom was his client's commanding officer, and he had with him his client's service record.

The defense attorney hurriedly went back into the lockup to be with his client. After a few minutes, the defense attorney emerged from the lockup looking very serious. He told me that his client was furious with me and that he was going to get me when he got out. I asked him why he was so angry. The attorney told me I should not have brought the Marines in on this case, because it was none of their business. The defense attorney said the defendant now knew he would get a dishonorable discharge. I thanked him for the warning, but I told the defense attorney I needed to show the jury that the defendant perjured himself in the first trial, and the best way to do that was to subpoena the defendant's commanding officer and his service record.

making height estimates and did not want to guess. But again, the attorney pressed the clerk for his best estimate. Finally, the clerk replied, "5' 8" and a quarter." All of us, including the judge and jury, had a good laugh.

One of the "never ask" rules (i.e., rule-of thumb) of cross-examination is this: an attorney should never ask a witness a question unless the attorney has some idea what the answer will be. This rule of thumb was violated by the defense attorney in an armed robbery case I tried. The victim of the robbery was a liquor store clerk. My evidence consisted of "direct" evidence, which is eyewitness identification evidence, as well as other circumstantial evidence. On cross-examination, the defense attorney asked the clerk how he could be so sure that the man standing in front of him pointing a gun at him was his client.

The clerk responded that two or three months before the defendant robbed him, he was robbed for the first time in his life. Before he could continue his answer, the defense attorney objected on the ground that the witness's answer was non-responsive to the question. I countered that the witness was trying to answer the attorney's question, and he should be permitted to finish his answer. The judge overruled the defense attorney's objection. The witness testified that when he was robbed the first time, the police asked him numerous questions about the robber's height, weight, hair, tattoos, whether he wore glasses, description of clothing, etc. The witness testified that he told the police on the earlier occasion that he was so concerned about the gun being pointed at him that he forgot to look at the robber and could not answer any of their questions. He testified that he made up his mind right then that if he was ever robbed again, things would be different. The clerk looked straight at the defense attorney and testified: "Sir, when your client stood in front of me and pointed that sawed-off shotgun at me, I looked at him and took an inventory of his features. And sir, that's him sitting next to you."

I was as surprised by the clerk's bombshell answer as the defense attorney. The case was over. The jury took only a short time to return with a guilty verdict for armed robbery. The defense attorney learned this "never ask" rule the hard way.

An equally devastating response, resulting from a violation of this rule, occurred during a child molestation case. During my case preparation, when I interviewed witnesses before trial, I told them they were not here to help me; they were here to tell the truth as best as they could recall it. I told them not to worry about whether their answer would hurt or help the case. I told them if they tell the truth on the witness stand, they had no reason to fear being cross-examined by the defendant's lawyer.

In the child molestation case, on direct examination by me, the young victim testified to what the defendant did to him. On cross-examination, the defense attorney asked the little boy if he had talked to the prosecutor, Mr. Lewis, about this case. The little boy testified that he did talk to me. The defense attorney asked him if the prosecutor told him what to say in court. The little boy testified, "Mr. Lewis told me I was not here to help win the case but to just tell the truth." This is the type of answer in a jury trial that can make a defense attorney sick to his stomach—and worse. The jury found the child molester guilty.

48

IRVING KANAREK

From the late 1960s through part of the 1980s, defense attorney Irving Kanarek was a legend. Kanarek had a hide as thick as a rhino. He was a bull in the courtroom. *Time* Magazine said, in its November 30, 1970, issue, that Charles Manson hired Kanarek, "whom he regarded as the most obstructionist and time-consuming lawyer in Los Angeles, in hopes of badgering the judge into allowing him to defend himself. When the judge continued to refuse, Kanarek proceeded to exasperate even Manson with a blizzard of objections."

There are countless Kanarek stories. It was rumored among some DAs that Kanarek, supposedly a former mechanical engineer, lived in his car. He always appeared a bit unkempt. No judge could control his courtroom conduct. He did not seem fazed when judges threatened to hold him in contempt of court. I recall hearing about one incident in divorce court when both Kanarek and his client, the husband, were held in contempt of court, handcuffed together, and placed in the custody of the sheriff.

Judges sometimes became so frustrated with Kanarek that they said and did things that could constitute reversible error. This is an error that could result in the reversal of a conviction by an appellate court. I had several cases with Kanarek, both as a deputy city attorney in the 1960s and as a deputy DA in the 1970s. In one of these cases, I called a police officer to the witness stand. When the court clerk asked the officer to state his name, Kanarek objected on the grounds of hearsay. When the judge exclaimed, "Hearsay?" Kanarek replied, "Yes, his mother must have told him."

In another case, a judge became so fed up with Kanarek that she told him she did not want to hear one more objection from him. She said it will be presumed, for the remainder of the trial, that he has objected to every one of the prosecutor's questions on every possible statutory, case law and constitutional ground. Kanarek objected to my very next question.

I had a case with Kanarek in which I offered an exhibit into evidence. Kanarek objected. The judge asked Kanarek the basis for his objection. Kanarek replied that his objection was based on the Constitution. The judge, exasperated, asked Kanarek, "Which Constitution, the United States Constitution or the California Constitution?" Kanarek replied, "Ohio, your honor." I do not recall ever seeing Kanarek laugh or even smile.

49

THE ELDERLY SEX SOLICITOR

When I was a young deputy city attorney trying misdemeanor offenses in the 1960s, I was assigned a case in which the defendant, a very elderly, obese man, was charged with soliciting sex from another man in a public restroom in downtown Los Angeles. The problem for the defendant was that the man he solicited was an undercover LAPD vice cop who arrested him. When I arrived at the courtroom with the file, I saw the defendant sitting at counsel table. He had refused a public defender and insisted on representing himself. He wanted a jury trial. We really didn't want to take up the court's time in a jury trial. Nobody was interested in sending this old man to jail. I offered the defendant a suspended fine if he pled guilty. He finally agreed to "plead guilty with an explanation."

Sometimes defendants simply want to tell the judge what they believe are mitigating circumstances even though they know they are guilty of the crime. Before he pled guilty, the defendant told the judge that he believed the LAPD was very unfair in this case. The judge asked the defendant why he believed the police were unfair. The defendant explained that he had been arrested for this same type of offense many times before, but the LAPD had recently started assigning its "cutest" cops to patrol the men's room in Pershing Square in downtown Los Angeles. The defendant claimed the LAPD knows how difficult it is for people like him to resist someone as "cute" as the cop who arrested him. The defendant said he thought because the LAPD chose to assign such a good-looking, irresistible police officer to patrol this public restroom that it constituted "entrapment." The courtroom staff had a good laugh. The old man then pled guilty, was sentenced to a suspended fine and went on his way.

50

"DO YOU KNOW THE DANIELS CASE?"

In the days before a defendant in a criminal case had a constitutional right to represent himself, judges had to determine whether the defendant was sufficiently competent to act as his own attorney. To this end, judges were required to ask the defendant a long list of standard questions dealing with the extent of the defendant's education, knowledge of the law, mental competency and on and on. I recall a defendant I was prosecuting for kidnapping for purposes of robbery with bodily harm. This was a crime that could have resulted in a life sentence if the defendant was convicted. The defendant wanted to go "pro per." It was late in the day and everyone wanted to go home. The defendant answered the judge's numerous questions regarding his qualifications to act as his own attorney for perhaps fifteen minutes. The defendant was losing his patience.

An important California Supreme Court case, *People v Daniels*, dealing with the crime of kidnapping for robbery had recently been published. The judge asked the defendant if he *knew about* the *Daniels* case. The defendant, looking exasperated, responded, "Look judge, not only do I know *about* the *Daniels* case. I know Daniels." The courtroom staff burst into laughter. The judge permitted the defendant to represent himself. Today, the rule is very different. Unless the defendant is mentally incompetent, he has an almost absolute right to represent himself—even in a murder case.

51

THE ELDERLY, LONELY SHOPLIFTER

Being a deputy DA is not always about putting people in jail, although protecting the public by incarcerating the bad guys can be quite gratifying. From 1976 to 1980, I was the Deputy in Charge of the Glendale Area DA's Office. One of the Glendale cops brought me a petty theft case and asked me to file the charge. The suspect was a man in his 80s who stole some merchandise at a local store. The store clerk saw the theft, detained the old man, and called the police. The police officer asked the old man why he stole the item. He gave this bizarre story: He said that his wife had recently died and that he was very lonely. He said that he had never stolen anything in his life—which checked out. He said he wanted some excitement in his life and he decided to do something he had never done—shoplift. I rejected the case and called around town to see if I could find something for him to do. Finally, I arranged with the Salvation Army office in Glendale to allow him to work there as the greeter-receptionist. He took the job. I checked up on him occasionally. I think it was just what he needed—to feel useful again.

52

JUDGE NANCY WATSON AND THE ALPHABET BOMBER CASE

In 1980, I was the calendar deputy DA in the courtroom of Judge Nancy Watson. Judge Watson was a large, but well-proportioned woman. She had a reputation for fairness and toughness. She would not take any guff from the attorneys or the defendants. She also had a good sense of humor and was very bright. She knew the law, knew what she was doing, and was respected by everyone. As they like to say now, "She was comfortable in her own skin."

Judge Watson presided over the notorious case of Muharem Kurbegovic, dubbed by the press, "the Alphabet Bomber." He was charged with placing a bomb at Los Angeles International Airport that killed three people and injured thirty-six. In addition, he was charged with trying to bomb the main Greyhound bus depot in Los Angeles, as well as firebombing the homes of several local officials. Although his crimes occurred years before, he was not brought to trial until 1980, because he had earlier been found incompetent to stand trial and was hospitalized for a few years. Later, the psychiatrists said he was competent. The People were represented by one of our top trial lawyers, Deputy DA Dinko Bozanich.

Throughout the eight-month trial, the defendant was unpredictable. His attorney was not able to control him. He would frequently scream insults at Judge Watson in front of the jury. But each time he did, Judge Watson would calmly order the bailiffs to escort the defendant into the lockup, which adjoined the courtroom. While in the lockup, he could listen to his trial through built-in speakers. After awhile, Judge Watson would allow him to return to the courtroom after he promised to behave. But he did not behave. When Judge Watson would make a ruling with which he disagreed, he would scream insults at her. He would then again be escorted from the courtroom. This cycle was repeated numerous times throughout the trial.

Even though Judge Watson was presiding over this long jury trial, she was still handling a large daily calendar of cases. As calendar deputy, it was my job to represent the People on all these cases. The defense attorneys and I would go into Judge Watson's chambers every day in an attempt to agree on "dispositions" (i.e., plea bargains) on each of these cases—that is, to which charges the defendants would plead guilty and what their sentences would be. On one of these occasions, I saw a *Playboy* magazine on the Judge's desk. I said to her, rather sardonically, that I didn't realize she subscribed to *Playboy*. The Judge replied that that (bleep) Kurbegovic had subscribed to *Playboy* in her name and had it sent to the courthouse to embarrass her.

Kurbegovic was convicted of all charges. When the defendant had committed his crimes, there was no death penalty in California. When Kurbegovic stood before Judge Watson waiting for his sentence, he appeared to be staring at the symbol of the Great Seal of California that hung on the wall above the judge. Depicted in the seal, among other things, is a large bear. Judge Watson asked the defendant what he was looking at. Kurbegovic told her he was looking at the bear in the state seal. He told the judge he had been looking at that bear throughout his trial, and that big bear in the state seal reminded him of her. Then, after a pause, he said, "I love that bear."

Judge Watson sentenced Muharem Kurbegovic to life in prison *with* the possibility of parole, the maximum sentence at the time he committed the murders years before. I am writing this after just having read Judge Nancy Watson's obituary. She was 77.

53

THE "BUSING JUDGE" LOSES TO KENNEDY

Early in my career, a superior court judge in Los Angeles, Alfred Gitelson, presided over a civil trial that led him to conclude there was de facto school segregation in Los Angeles. Judge Gitelson became known as "the busing judge," because it was thought his judicial opinion would lead to wide-spread busing of school children throughout Los Angeles. The "busing judge" was challenged in the next judicial election, November 1970, by an attorney named William Kennedy. Kennedy had had little or no courtroom experience. It had only been a little over two years since Bobby Kennedy had been assassinated and "Kennedy" was still a powerful name. Kennedy won. I was assigned to Judge Kennedy's court. The first day we met, he told me that he had no criminal law experience, and he would be relying on me. He told me not to ever mislead him. I assured him I would never mislead him.

Defense attorneys sometimes ask the judge for an indicated sentence if the defendant should plead guilty. As mentioned, in most felony cases, the law gives judges a wide range of sentencing options. With this new judge, I sometimes felt compelled to act as both prosecutor and defense attorney. On occasion, Judge Kennedy gave the defense attorney an indicated sentence I believed was too harsh. On these occasions, I would tell the defense attorney that I wanted to approach the bench without him to explain to the judge, without embarrassing him in front of the defense attorney, that under the circumstances of the case, and the defendant's record, his indicated sentence was too heavy. The defense attorneys were always appreciative and gladly agreed to this procedure.

I remember one case in which a young man was stopped for a traffic violation, and the officer saw a few amphetamine tablets (not *meth*amphetamine) on the front seat. The young man, who had no record, explained that he went to school and worked two jobs and needed the "uppers" to stay awake. The defendant was charged with felony drug possession. The defense attorney asked Judge Kennedy for an indicated sentence if he pled guilty. Judge Kennedy said he would commit the defendant to the California Youth Authority [CYA]. The defense attorney turned to me in disbelief. I signaled him to stay where he was as I approached the bench to advise the judge that this was a probation case, it was not a CYA case. The judge then said the defendant had a choice: either CYA or one year in the county jail. I told the judge both alternatives were too harsh for a defendant with no record, who was in college, and worked two jobs. But the judge would not budge. It was too late for the attorney to file an "affidavit of prejudice" against the judge which, in California, permits both sides one opportunity in each case to disqualify a particular judge without stating a specific reason. The attorney chose the Youth Authority option, which was an indeterminate sentence. I wrote to the Youth Authority explaining the situation and requested the earliest possible release date for the defendant.

54

THE GYPSY CASE

That anecdote from Judge Kennedy's court was the downside. But there was also an upside. I had a case in Judge Kennedy's court that involved a gypsy woman who told an elderly lady that for $10,000 she would allow her to speak with her dead son. The intended victim told a friend who called the police. The police

agree to be transferred to the "short-cause court." In the gypsy case, I would not agree, because I had no doubt the short-cause judge would give this gypsy fraudster straight probation, a small fine and no jail time.

The defense attorney announced he would seek an emergency writ from an appellate court to force Judge Kennedy to honor his affidavit of prejudice and to prevent Judge Kennedy from proceeding with the trial. The judge said that was fine, but if the writ was denied, he should be ready to start the jury trial or have his client plead guilty— *after lunch*. But after lunch, the attorney failed to appear in court. I called the appellate court and discovered they had summarily denied his request for an emergency writ. The judge had not faced this situation before and asked what he should do. I asked him to issue a body attachment for the attorney (similar to an arrest warrant) and then hold it, that is don't issue it, and I would try to contact the attorney.

A few minutes later I received a call from the secretary of one of the top supervisors in the DA's office who told me to report to his office. When I arrived, this supervisor told me the defense attorney had complained to him that I was being unreasonable in refusing to allow the case to be transferred to the short-cause court and too rigid in sticking to my demand for 60 days county jail for his client. I explained to my supervisor my position. He asked me if getting 60 days jail time for this gypsy woman was that important to me. I said it was. My supervisor then smiled and told me to remain in Judge Kennedy's court, stick to my 60-day offer, and he would back me up.

Shortly thereafter, the defense attorney called me. He asked me if I was now agreeable to the case being transferred to the short-cause court. I told him I would not agree. He asked me whether I had spoken with my supervisor about it. I said that I had. The attorney asked, "Didn't he order you to go to short cause?" I said that he did not. "He is backing me up on my demand for 60 days county jail for your client in Judge Kennedy's court." The attorney told me if his client does one day in the county jail, he will lose all his gypsy clients. I expressed my condolences. That was it. Again, checkmate. The defense attorney, in reporting me to my supervisor, had made his final move to save his gypsy business, which I am certain was very lucrative. He had no alternative but to plead his client guilty to the felony charge of attempted grand theft. After her guilty plea, the judge remanded her to custody to serve her 60-day sentence. I have had many murder and death penalty cases. Yet, getting this 60-day sentence for this defendant I count as one of my important victories.

But it was not over yet. About one week after the gypsy woman was remanded to the custody of the sheriff to serve her 60-day sentence, another political heavyweight attorney appeared. He had with him a report from a psychiatrist which said that confinement in the county jail was causing the gypsy woman to have a nervous breakdown. The psychiatrist claimed that to preserve her mental health, she should be released immediately. The case went to the master calendar court, because a few days earlier Judge Kennedy had been permanently transferred to handle only civil cases.

One of the functions of the master calendar judge is to assign cases to available courtrooms. The new attorney asked the master calendar judge to hear his request to release the defendant. I objected and the judge refused. I requested the case be heard by Judge Kennedy, because he was familiar with the case and, for that reason, was the logical judge to hear the defense attorney's request—even though Judge Kennedy was no longer in the same courthouse. Over the new attorney's strenuous objection, the judge sent the case back to Judge Kennedy who was now in the civil courthouse located about a block away. Judge Kennedy quickly denied the new attorney's request to release the gypsy woman and that was the end of it.

Many years passed before I again saw the first defense attorney. He told me he had not represented a gypsy since his gypsy client was sentenced to 60 days. He good-naturedly blamed me for the loss of his entire gypsy clientele. He reminded me again, with a smile, that gypsies can't do jail time. We were both able to laugh during our reminiscences.

55

ILLEGAL IMMIGRANTS AND CRIMINAL JUSTICE

One of the frustrating facts of life about the criminal justice system is that if an illegal immigrant from Mexico murders someone in the United States, all he must do to escape justice in this country is to cross the border back to Mexico. In fact, numerous victims in the United States have been murdered by Mexican nationals who fled back to Mexico. Since 1978, the Mexican government has refused to extradite Mexican nationals wanted for murder in the United States if the murderer could face the death penalty. In 2001, Mexico extended this extradition ban to any person wanted for murder in the U.S. who could be sentenced to life in prison.[1] Thus, Mexico has become a sanctuary for Mexican citizens who are wanted for murder in the United States.

It is not uncommon for a Mexican citizen to enter the United States illegally, commit crimes, return to Mexico, be convicted in Mexico for the crime committed in the U.S., and then later have the sentence drastically reduced. It was reported in January 2003 that a Mexican citizen, who came to the U.S. and killed a 17-year-old boy in Los Angeles, was convicted of the crime in Mexico, sentenced to eight years in prison by the Mexican judge, and was released from the Mexican prison after serving only two years. He then returned to Southern California.[2]

Why isn't there a public outcry over this continuing injustice? This situation has been reported in the media but few people, other than frustrated police, prosecutors, and the murder victims' families, seem very upset. Why hasn't the media editorialized about the shamefully easy way Mexican citizens who kill in the United States get away with murder by simply crossing the border back to Mexico?

Why don't we hear from the politicians? Is it because Mexicans are regarded as a minority (even though Hispanics in L.A. County now outnumber whites), and it would be politically incorrect to even publicly discuss the issue? Is it because of fear of losing the Hispanic vote? I doubt there are many Hispanic voters in this state who want illegal immigrants from Mexico, who kill in this country, to escape justice by simply crossing the border back to Mexico. Where is the outrage?

The liberal media often imply that politicians who speak out against crime or illegal immigration have some ulterior motive, such as pandering to those voters who believe crime and illegal immigration are important issues. I don't deny this may be the case with some politicians. But there are other politicians, such as former Governors Pete Wilson and George Deukmejian, who believe that public safety and illegal immigration are real problems that require substantive solutions. I doubt the *Los Angeles Times* would ever suggest that a liberal politician who advocates higher welfare benefits was doing so only to pander to low-income voters.

Our government has frequent dealings with the Mexican government regarding a host of issues. Why does our government not insist that the Mexican government allow the return of Mexican citizens who are wanted for committing murder in this country? How can our government justify its continued acceptance of this unjust Mexican policy? Los Angeles County District Attorney Steve Cooley estimates that, nationally, about 3,000 murder suspects, who are Mexican nationals, have fled to Mexico.[3]

But there is hope. On November 30, 2005, the *Los Angeles Times*, in a story titled "Mexico to Extradite More Suspects to U.S.," reported that by a six to five vote, the Mexican Supreme Court decided it would begin to extradite Mexican citizens wanted in the U.S. for murder—even when they could face life in prison if convicted. The extradition ban still applies if the DA in the U.S. is seeking the death penalty. It may be a coincidence, but this change of heart by the Mexican Supreme Court was announced a few weeks after the U.S. Congress approved legislation denying some foreign aid to countries that block extraditions. It remains to be seen whether Mexico will allow the extradition of thousands of its citizens wanted for murder in the United States—even if we promise Mexico the defendant will not be subject to the death penalty.

But we have reason to be optimistic. On January 10, 2007, the *L.A. Times* reported that Jorge Arroyo Garcia was extradited from Mexico to L.A. County to be prosecuted for the murder of Deputy Sheriff David March in 2002. Deputy March was killed during a traffic stop. Garcia, an illegal immigrant, fled to Mexico where he was arrested February 2006. Even though DA Steve Cooley agreed not to seek the death penalty, Garcia fought extradition for eleven months. Cooley said that 200 murder suspects from L.A. County have fled to Mexico. In 2006, eleven murder suspects were extradited from Mexico.

It was announced in January 2004 that 95% of all the then-outstanding arrest warrants for homicide in Los Angeles, which at that time totaled more than 1,200, were for illegal aliens. Up to two-thirds of all fugitive felony warrants, which total 17,000 (27,664 in March 2007), are for illegal aliens.[4] In 2006, the Los Angeles County jail processed about 170,000 inmates. Federal officials and the Los Angeles County Sheriff estimate that one-fourth of them are illegal immigrants, costing the county $80 million a year.

An LAPD policy, which started in 1979, known as Special Order 40, prohibits LAPD officers from arresting someone solely for an immigration violation or from even notifying the immigration service about an illegal alien. This rule even applies to prevent an LAPD officer from arresting a known illegal alien when the police are aware that he had been deported earlier following a criminal offense, and then returned to this country illegally.[5] It was reported in the *Los Angeles Times* on April 9, 2005, that LAPD planned to modify this policy to authorize its officers to check the immigration status of deported felons whom they believe have returned to this country illegally. Several immigrant rights activists protested the proposed new policy, claiming that illegal aliens may be stopped and deported for minor offenses.

The sentencing of illegal aliens presents a special situation. I've heard both liberal and conservative radio and TV commentators suggest that illegal aliens who are convicted of felonies in the U.S. be summarily deported to their home country—that is, instead of sentencing them to jail or prison. What are these talk-show hosts thinking? Illegal immigrants would like nothing better than to escape punishment for their crimes and simply be sent home. I cannot imagine a greater incentive for illegal aliens to come to this country to commit crimes if all they have to fear is being sent home. They know they can return to the U.S. illegally anytime they desire.

I have actually witnessed this situation in court—before the Three-Strikes law. At a sentencing for a residential burglar, the judge gave the illegal alien a choice between a sentence to state prison or a grant of probation with a recommendation of immediate deportation. Of course, the defendant, who had a prior conviction for residential burglary, chose probation and deportation—that is, being sent home to his family in Mexico. I doubt that any illegal alien, given the choice between prison and being sent home to Mexico, would choose prison. Today, the Three-Strikes law prohibits a judge from granting probation to a defendant after he is convicted of his second residential burglary.

Another suggestion I've heard is to send illegal aliens, who are arrested for felonies in this country, back to their own country immediately without even charging them with the crime they committed here. This suggestion is even worse than the first ill-advised suggestion. At least, if the illegal alien is charged and convicted in this country, we will have a record of his felony convictions. If we simply send him back to his home country after each arrest, his "rap sheet" will show all the arrests but no convictions.

To DAs, defense attorneys and judges, "arrests" on a rap sheet mean almost nothing. Why? Because every arrested person is presumed innocent until proven guilty. I have never seen a judge sentence a defendant more harshly because of his long "arrest" record. Club members, therefore, pay little attention to prior arrests. When Club members say a defendant has a long record, we mean a record of *convictions*. To those who say, let the illegal alien who committed crimes in the U.S. be prosecuted in Mexico, I say their naiveté is limitless. We have seen that the Mexican government cannot be trusted to prosecute and incarcerate Mexicans who commit crimes in this country.

The *Los Angeles Times* published a story June 15, 2006, titled "Immigrant Sweep Snares 36 Molesters." Immigration officials told the *Times* that "Illegal immigrants who commit crimes in the United States are supposed to be deported once they finish their jail or prison terms. Instead, many remain in this country because jailers don't process them through the federal deportation system." The story told of 36 illegal aliens who had been convicted of molesting children and who were simply released back into the community (Orange County, California) after serving their sentences instead of being deported. Immigration officials told the *Times* that about 630,000 illegal aliens enter the nation's jails and prisons each year. California prisons alone, not counting county jails, house about 40,000 illegal aliens.

On September 12, 2004, the *Los Angeles Times*, in a story titled "Deportation of Sex Offenders Opposed," a deputy public defender was seeking to have his client deported to Canada because he was illegally in the U.S. What a twist, the defendant's attorney wants the judge to kick his client out of the country! The defendant had just completed his prison term for sexual assault on a child. He had a history of rape convictions. The deputy DA opposed the PD's request for deportation and requested that the defendant be hospitalized under California's Sexually Violent Predator Act. If we had secure borders, I have little doubt that the DA would simply allow the defendant to be deported to Canada. We would tell Canada that this sexual predator was their problem. But our borders are not secure, and the DA, the PD and the defendant all knew that if the defendant was deported to Canada, he could be back in this country within a few days. The DA's duty to protect the public from this repeat sexual predator left him with no choice but to oppose deportation.

In March 2006, a Pew Hispanic Study Center found that 850,000 immigrants enter the U.S. illegally each year and that an estimated 11.5 to 12 million illegal immigrants now live in the United States—up from 8.5 million in 2000. We should understand and accept the fact that this country is not going to get serious about stopping illegal immigration from Mexico and Central America—even when the issue of terrorism is the predominant issue confronting us—unless there is a vociferous, continuing public outcry.

We should understand this, because neither Republican nor Democratic administrations has done much of substance to stop it. Why? The answer is two-fold: Business requires a surplus of cheap labor to keep labor costs from rising. Legislators of both parties are reluctant to vote against the nation's business interests—the source of so much campaign cash. In addition, inasmuch as most Hispanics register as Democrats, Democrats should not be expected to vote for any meaningful solution to stop illegal immigration from Mexico and Central America–unless they feel compelled to do so by public opinion polls. They do not want to appear anti-Hispanic.

Republicans also do not want to open themselves up for attack by appearing anti-Hispanic. Former California Governor Pete Wilson taught them that. Both parties are competing furiously for the Hispanic vote. Hence, the current stalemate.

In these dangerous times, we must fortify and protect our borders—both the Mexican and the Canadian— which will require a great deal of money and personnel. However, we need to allow sufficient numbers of immigrants to enter the U.S. to satisfy our need for cheap labor, but we must know who they are. They must all be photographed, fingerprinted, and ordered to report to the immigration authorities periodically. The alternative is the present, unacceptable situation: a porous, poorly regulated border. The present chaotic situation should not be acceptable. If an illegal alien commits a felony in this country, he should be charged, convicted, and sentenced appropriately. *After completing his sentence*, he should then be deported and thereafter not be permitted to re-enter this country—which is much more likely if our borders were substantially tightened. Today, an illegal alien who is deported knows he can return whenever he desires.

56

WHAT THE JURY GETS TO SEE

I am very fortunate. I had a career where I actually liked going to "work." It was so much more than a job that gave me a paycheck every two weeks. In my long career, I worked countless hours of overtime for which I rarely sought overtime pay. I know—to many liberals, that would indicate I was probably an overzealous prosecutor. Would they feel the same way about a defense attorney who worked many hours without pay on behalf of a criminal defendant? Of course not—that would be admirable. To have a job in which the objective is to reveal the truth in a jury trial is such a great luxury for a lawyer. In fact, it can be said that the job description of a deputy DA is to use the law, our justice system, to reveal the truth. No other kind of attorney can make that statement.

On the other hand, one of the criminal defense attorney's most important objectives in trial is to keep any evidence from the jury that might hurt his client. For example, if the defendant is a gang member and has gang tattoos all over his neck and body, the defense attorney will have the defendant dressed in such a way that it will hide these gang tattoos from the jury—unless the DA can convince the judge that the gang tattoos are somehow relevant to some issue in the case.

If the police possess a tape recording of the defendant making incriminating statements, the DA would want the jury to hear the tape. The defense attorney, of course, would want the judge to prevent the jury from hearing the tape recording.

There are many rules of evidence that, for reasons of policy, prevent the truth from being revealed. For example, if a serial murderer were to confess his guilt to his wife, his attorney or his priest, the jury will never hear that confession because such confessions are "privileged," and the law protects defendants by preventing such confessions from being revealed.

If a police officer fails to correctly advise the murder suspect of his Miranda rights, the murderer's confession may never be heard by the jury—even if it is tape-recorded, voluntarily given, and there is no dispute about what the defendant said. If a police officer finds the murder weapon in a search without a search warrant, and the judge concludes that the search was illegal, the weapon will be suppressed and the jury will never know the murder weapon was found.

Our rules of evidence prevent the deputy DA, with some exceptions, from informing the jury of the defendant's prior felony convictions, unless the defendant decides to testify. One of the reasons so many defendants choose not to testify is that they do not want the jury to learn of their prior felony convictions. The other main reason defendants do not testify is that they do not want to be cross-examined by the DA.

If, during a criminal trial, a person were to go to the defense attorney's office and tell the defense attorney that he saw his client, the defendant, kill the victim, the most ethical defense attorney is under no obligation to tell the police or the DA of the existence of this witness. In fact, if the defense attorney told the police or the DA about this eyewitness, he could be disciplined by the state bar. Remember, the mission of the most honorable defense attorney is to get his client off—or the best plea bargain possible. He has no obligation to seek the truth or reveal it—if it would hurt his client's case.

If, on the other hand, someone called the police or the DA's office and told the police or the DA that he saw somebody *other* than the defendant kill the victim, the DA has an ethical obligation to immediately notify the defense attorney of the name and whereabouts of this witness. If the DA failed to do this, he could be fired by the DA's office and disciplined by the state bar.

If the DA has a written report from the coroner or a psychiatrist or from an expert witness specializing, for example, in DNA, ballistics, fingerprints or shoeprints, and the expert's testimony will help the People's case, the defense attorney will want to find his own expert who will testify in opposition to the DA's expert. The defense attorney can interview many experts until he finds one who agrees to testify in opposition to the DA's expert, and the defense attorney has no ethical or legal obligation to tell the DA the names of the experts whom he contacted who refused to testify in the manner desired by the defense attorney. However, if the DA contacts an expert witness whose testimony would help the defendant's case, the DA has an ethical obligation to inform the defense attorney of this expert.

I have no quarrel with any of these rules of evidence. As DAs, we accept these rules. I mention them only to describe the kinds of issues deputy DAs deal with frequently and to point out how extensively the system protects defendants charged with crimes. The media cannot be depended upon to accurately inform the public how the system really works. And inasmuch as the public's knowledge of the criminal justice system comes mainly from newspapers, television and the movies, this explains the public's lack of understanding of the system.

There are numerous other rules of evidence that will prevent the jury from hearing certain kinds of evidence. For example, if the defendant consents to take a polygraph test (i.e., a lie detector test), and the test results show the defendant was lying when he said he had nothing to do with the victim's murder, the jury will never hear that evidence, because appellate courts have ruled that polygraph evidence is not sufficiently reliable to be admitted as evidence in court. This is a good rule. If polygraph evidence were admitted in court, I have no doubt it would become common for defense attorneys to hire private polygraph operators who, for a nice fee, would testify that they administered a polygraph test which indicated the defendant gave completely truthful answers to all questions. The outcome of the trial might come down to which polygraph operator the jury liked better, the DA's (who is paid a salary by the county) or the one hired by the defense attorney.

5 7

FAD DEFENSES

As with women's clothes, automobile styles, and popular music, defenses used by criminal defense attorneys come in, flourish for awhile and disappear—just like any other fad. For example, for the last several years, one of the "in" defenses in criminal cases has been the "I was molested as a child" defense. This defense is sometimes used in an attempt to reduce a murder to manslaughter or as a bid for sympathy or to explain deviant conduct in hopes of reducing the severity of a sentence. Twenty or thirty years ago, I had never heard of this ploy. Only in the last ten years or so of my career did I see it raised in trial or mentioned in probation reports. In the famous Menendez case, in which two brothers killed their wealthy Beverly Hills parents, the "we were molested" defense almost worked in the first trial, which ended with a hung jury. Once this defense hits the saturation point and becomes old hat, like fins on cars or skinny (or wide) ties, I predict that it too will disappear.

Another defense in murder cases I saw fairly often in the 1970s and 1980s was designed to reduce a murder charge to manslaughter, a less serious homicide than murder. The defendant would testify that the victim, allegedly a homosexual, made a pass at him, and he became so enraged he beat the victim to death. Some men on the jury might think, "Yeah, what would I do if some queer put his hand on my leg?" This strategy is not a complete defense, like self-defense, but it sometimes achieved its objective of reducing the murder to manslaughter or hanging the jury.

Some defense attorneys who represent defendants charged with violent crimes are currently attempting to use the so-called "organic brain syndrome" defense. The defense attorney will order a brain scan of his client's brain in hopes of identifying defects in the prefrontal lobe of the brain. If an alleged defect is found, the defense attorney will then call a doctor to the stand who will testify that the defendant suffers from an "organic brain defect" which caused his judgment to be impaired, thus preventing him from forming the required criminal intent to commit the crime.

It remains to be seen whether this defense "has legs" and will be successful. If it is, I predict we will see a substantial increase in the number of defendants who allegedly have organic brain syndrome. There is currently no agreement among the majority of neurologists and the brain-imaging community that a causal link has been established between alleged frontal lobe abnormalities and the defendant's ability to form the intent to commit a crime.

It is difficult to predict the next fad defense or when it will strike. But I will venture a guess. In the not too distant future, DAs might start seeing the "genetic predisposition" defense. It might go something like this: The defense attorney in a murder case, if permitted by the judge, will call a geneticist to the witness stand who will testify that he examined the defendant and, after an analysis of the defendant's blood or saliva, he concluded that the defendant possessed a gene which predisposes the defendant to violent or antisocial behavior. The defense attorney might then argue to the jury that it would be unfair to hold the defendant accountable for murder when he is predisposed to violence because of his genetic make-up. After all, he might argue, it's not his fault that he inherited these genes from his parents. I predict that defense attorneys might also try to use the genetic predisposition tactic in an attempt to reduce the severity of the defendant's sentence.

58

CONVICTING CELEBRITIES

I learned early in my career how difficult it is to persuade twelve people to convict a celebrity. We have all seen many well-known personalities acquitted over the years, including O.J. Simpson, Robert Blake and Michael Jackson. Early on, I developed my own theories for the causes. First, I believe most jurors are conscientious and want to do the right thing. However, they really do not want to bear the heavy responsibility of hurting anyone's career. I have seen several dead-bang cases involving celebrity defendants result in acquittals. Jurors do not want to hurt any defendant who they believe has some value. Based on what I've seen over many years as a DA, a jury would have had a tough time convicting actor Robert Blake, even if the evidence showed Blake had solicited three, four or five people to kill his wife instead of only the two who testified. The same goes for Jackson. The DA was permitted to call witnesses whom Jackson had allegedly molested years before. But it didn't matter. In reality, jurors use a different standard for judging celebrities.

Following Jackson's acquittal, eight of his jurors appeared together on the *Larry King Show*. King asked the jurors for their reaction to Jackson coming to court wearing pajama bottoms. One woman juror said that at the time she saw Jackson in his pajama bottoms, she wrote a note about it. Her note read, "Michael looks sick today. I hope he's okay." I feel quite positive that no jurors on any of my child molestation cases were ever so concerned about the defendant's well being. Another woman juror told Larry King she was impressed that Jackson's mother attended every court session. The juror said, "She never missed a day. She always looked lovely—and sat there with such dignity." Yet, all the jurors denied that Jackson's celebrity status affected their verdict. As mentioned, it didn't help the prosecution that the media falsely told the public repeatedly that if convicted, Jackson faced 20 years in prison and would be housed with Charles Manson.

Another reason it is difficult to convict celebrities is that jurors, who have seen the celebrity on television or in the movies, believe they know him or her. It is more difficult for a juror to convict someone they *know*—or think they know.

I have an additional theory to explain why it is so difficult to convict celebrities. I believe that jurors, either consciously or unconsciously, would like the celebrity to feel indebted to them— hoping (or fantasizing) that if they acquitted the celebrity, perhaps they would receive a dinner invitation or a thank-you note from the celebrity which they could cherish forever. I cannot prove this is true, and I have never heard of any studies on the subject.

59

THE CROSS-DRESSING DEFENSE

During the early 1990s, before the Three-Strikes law was enacted, I worked with a deputy public defender who had a great personality, a terrific sense of humor and was an excellent trial lawyer. I recall an occasion when I was about to go on vacation. This PD was representing a defendant who was charged with a residential burglary and had a prior conviction for residential burglary. The sentence range for residential burglary is two, four or six years. The prior conviction for residential burglary constitutes a "serious felony" and adds five years to the sentence. On the day before I left for vacation, I told the PD that if the defendant pleaded guilty, I would accept the low term of two years plus the five-year prior for a total sentence of seven years. The PD spoke with the defendant who rejected my offer. He countered by offering to plead guilty to the burglary for the low term of two years and wanted me to strike (dismiss) the five-year prior. I rejected the defendant's counter offer and the judge set the case for trial—meaning a date was chosen for trial.

I felt the burglary case was very strong. The homeowner had returned to her home in the afternoon to find the defendant in her bedroom wearing white socks on his hands going through her drawers. Of course, the purpose of the socks was to prevent leaving fingerprints. The woman screamed, and the man ran from the house. He had not had time to take anything. The woman ran after him and saw him get into the back seat of a car driven by someone else. She was able to get the license number and called 911.

Within a few minutes, the police were at her door and told her the car she described had been stopped a few blocks away. The police officer asked her to accompany him in the police car to see if she could identify the man she saw in her bedroom. When she arrived at the location where the car was stopped, she noticed it was the same car she saw the intruder enter a few minutes before. The officer escorted the woman to the detained car. She identified the man in the back seat as the man she saw in her bedroom. Next to him in the back seat was a pair of white socks. Pretty good case?

To prove the crime of burglary, the DA must prove to the twelve jurors beyond a reasonable doubt that the defendant entered the house with the intent to commit a felony or a theft inside the house. The crime of burglary has been committed when the defendant enters the house with the required intent. That's it. It is not necessary for the DA to prove that the burglar took anything. I felt this was another dead-bang case that, for a repeat burglar, was worth seven years, which, of course, is really 3 $\frac{1}{2}$ years.

When I returned from vacation I asked the PD what had happened on the burglary case. I expected him to tell me that after the defendant thought over my seven-year offer, he had reconsidered and had decided to accept it. He was facing a possible maximum of eleven years, high term of six years for the burglary plus the five-year prior, if he had been convicted by a jury. But that is not what happened. The PD told me the jury had found his client "not guilty." I asked how that was possible. I asked him what his defense was. He said the defendant told the jury that he did not enter the house to commit a felony or to steal. He testified that he was a cross-dresser, and he entered the house to simply try on the female victim's clothes. If true, this would not constitute a burglary. I congratulated the PD on his creativity and his victory. Our DA who tried the case could not disprove the defendant's bizarre story. My educated guess is that this case is another example in which the jury probably did not believe the defendant was innocent, but had a reasonable doubt that the DA had proved he entered the house for the purpose of committing a felony or a theft. Therefore, the jury believed it had no choice but to acquit.

60

THE SCARF—
A WHO-DUNNIT MURDER

One of the more interesting and tragic cases of my career involved the case of Robert Butler. Robbie, as he was called, was a 22-year-old college student. Robbie was tall and handsome. He was a nationally ranked college track star and had his sights set on the 1988 Olympics. He had no criminal record and had been a police cadet. His college major was police science and his goal was to become a deputy sheriff. While Robbie was still in high school, he was befriended by his 47-year-old high school social studies teacher, Robert Jones. Eventually, Robbie moved into the teacher's house. Mr. Jones helped Robbie with his studies and Robbie's grades improved. Robbie had real affection for the teacher who Robbie looked upon as a father figure, teacher and tutor, but also as his friend and benefactor. Mr. Jones even gave Robbie one of his cars to drive.

When Robbie moved from Mr. Jones' house to attend a nearby Christian college, Mr. Jones maintained Robbie's room adorned with Robbie's track trophies and plaques. Mr. Jones continued to call and write to Robbie at college and would even send him cookies. But suddenly the calls, letters and cookies stopped. This was very hurtful to Robbie.

On December 12, 1985, Mr. Jones failed to show up at the high school and had not called in sick. Mr. Jones had taught at that high school for 22 years and had always been very reliable. The principal was notified and two school-security people were sent to Mr. Jones' house to check on him. They saw that his car was still in his garage. They called the police. The police entered the house and found Ronald McClendon, a 17-year-old high school athlete dead on the couch in the living room. He had been shot twice in the head. The police entered the bedroom and found Mr. Jones in bed with the covers pulled up neatly to his neck. He had also been shot twice, once in the head and once in the lower back. He was also dead.

There had been no break in. Nothing appeared to be missing. There was nothing out of place—except for one thing: there was a plaid scarf lying on the kitchen floor. Given the fact that the house was otherwise immaculate, the homicide detectives concluded that there was no way Mr. Jones had gone to bed with that scarf lying on the kitchen floor. They concluded that the killer must have been allowed to enter the house or he had a key. The detectives also concluded that the killer must have dropped the scarf. After interviewing numerous people, including Robbie Butler, the detectives were baffled. Neither Mr. Jones nor Ronald McClendon appeared to have any enemies. The detectives showed the scarf to all those they interviewed, including Robbie and Robbie's uncle, who owned a sporting goods store. Nobody said they recognized the scarf.

The police discovered that the owner of a women's clothing store, located next to the uncle's sporting goods store, had purchased 16 scarves from the uncle's partner, Mr. Bhatia, who had an office in the rear of the uncle's store. Mr. Bhatia had purchased the scarves from a street merchant while on a trip to Korea. The scarves in the women's clothing store, which the police took for evidence, were similar in appearance and material to the scarf found on Mr. Jones' kitchen floor. Mr. Bhatia was interviewed and told the police that Robbie's uncle told him that he had given one of the scarves to Robbie the night of the murder. Mr. Bhatia gave the police all of his remaining scarves.

The police reinterviewed Robbie Butler. They asked Robbie if he still had the scarf his uncle gave him the night Mr. Jones was murdered. He told police that the scarf was in his car which was in the possession of his girlfriend. In a subsequent interview, Robbie gave the police a scarf which he said was the scarf his uncle had given him. The police now had all the scarves from Mr. Bhatia and the women's clothing store, as well as the scarf from Mr. Jones' kitchen floor and the scarf recovered from Robbie Butler. The police delivered all the scarves to the crime lab for analysis. The crime lab determined that all the scarves, except the scarf given to the police by Robbie Butler, were similar in several characteristics, including type of thread, weave, dyes used, etc. The scarf given to the police by Robbie Butler, although it looked similar to the other scarves, was different in all these characteristics. In addition, the criminalist found embedded in the weave of the scarf that Robbie gave to the police a small plastic "T" that holds a price tag. None of the scarves purchased by Mr. Bhatia in Korea had price tags or the plastic "T" that holds the price tag.

Robbie Butler was arrested for both murders based solely on the lab analyses of the several scarves. During his police interrogation, he denied having anything to do with the murders of Mr. Jones and Ronald McClendon. He said he didn't even know McClendon. It was after midnight. The police were getting nowhere in the interrogation. The Pasadena police detectives then called in one of the best interrogators I have known, Detective Don Gallon.

Gallon's interrogation technique was very low key. Gallon had also been an athlete, a professional baseball player. He could see that Robbie Butler was not the typical hard-core criminal he was accustomed to dealing with. He sensed that Robbie was carrying a tremendous burden and told him so. Detective Gallon genuinely sympathized with Robbie Butler. After awhile Robbie broke. He told Detective Gallon that he thought he had had a very close father-son type of relationship with Mr. Jones, and when Mr. Jones stopped calling and writing and failed to return his calls, he tried to find out what was wrong. He said he went to Mr. Jones' house to talk to him. He saw the other kid sleeping on the couch. He went into Mr. Jones' bedroom and found him sleeping. He woke him up to try to talk to him, but Mr. Jones ignored him, rolled over and went back to sleep. At that point, Robbie said he remembered that Mr. Jones kept a loaded gun in an ice bucket in a kitchen cabinet. He retrieved the gun, walked back into Mr. Jones' bedroom and shot him twice. He then walked into the living room and shot the boy on the couch. He could give no reason for shooting the boy. He told Detective Gallon that he wasn't even certain who the boy was. He said he shot him "because he was there." Robbie told Detective Gallon that he had not taken any alcohol or drugs, and he realized what he did was wrong.

Even though Robbie Butler's crimes made him eligible for the death penalty because of the special circumstance allegation of multiple murders, our office did not seek the death penalty. But because he killed two people, the "multiple-murder" special circumstance applied, and he faced life in prison without the possibility of parole. After several discussions with his attorney, we failed to reach a settlement in the case. The defense attorney and I started the voir dire process of selecting the prospective jurors. During the voir dire, the defendant's attorney walked over to me and asked if my plea offer was still open. I said it was. The defense lawyer then discussed my offer with his client who agreed to plead guilty to two counts of first-degree murder if we struck (dismissed) the special circumstance allegation. In June 1986, the judge sentenced the defendant to 27 years-to-life in prison on each murder count. The sentences were ordered to run concurrently—instead of consecutively.

The probation officer who interviewed the defendant wrote: "Nowhere during the interview [with Robbie Butler] is there even a suggestion of remorse. But there is an undercurrent of indignation that fills the defendant's remarks. The defendant refers to this double murder as a *mistake,* and he is upset that people consider him a "bad guy" when he has only made this mistake once in his life."

61

THE LOIS HARO MURDER CASE

I had another murder case in which the mother of one of the defendants described what her son did as a "mistake." On October 18, 1988, Lois Haro, a 26-year-old woman, left a note for her husband Tony saying she had gone to the Pasadena Plaza to buy a gift for a baby shower she planned to attend the following day.

The note said she would be back at 8:00 p.m. The note was signed "Lois 7:15 p.m."

Lois went to the mall, bought the gift at J.C. Penny's and then took the escalator down to the underground parking area. At the same time, Ronald Anthony Jones and George Marvin Trone were on the way up the adjacent escalator. Trone and Jones saw Lois and decided they would follow her to her car. Once she arrived at her car, the two men forced her at gunpoint to get inside. Jones got into the drivers' seat and Trone got into the back seat. Lois was ordered to sit in the front seat with Jones.

Jones drove the car out of the mall and onto the freeway. While driving, Jones and Trone took Lois' wedding ring, watch, wallet, and her credit cards. They did not take her bracelet or her rosebud earrings. Jones eventually drove down into the Arroyo near the Pasadena Rose Bowl where Trone and Jones took turns forcing Lois to orally copulate them and then raping her. Lois was then ordered out of the car and told to lie in the dirt. Trone had a 38-caliber revolver. Trone pointed it at Lois' head and was listening to Lois beg them not to kill her when Jones took the gun from Trone and shot Lois in the head.

Jones and Trone then left Lois dying in the dirt under a bridge known in the area as the Suicide Bridge. Jones drove Lois' car. He dropped Trone off near his house and then drove home.

Lois' husband, Tony, arrived home at 9:45 p.m. and read Lois' note. He was concerned that Lois was still not home. He thought she may have gone over to her parents' house. At about 10:30 p.m. Tony called Lois' parents, Herb and Elsie Purnell. Herb was a university professor of linguistics. He is also an ordained minister. Both Herb and Elsie were missionaries who had spent many years in Southeast Asia. I later learned that Herb was regarded as a hero in parts of Southeast Asia where he was instrumental in developing a common language enabling people to communicate who have never been able to understand each other's language. Herb has been working on a dictionary for this language for many years.

Lois was not at her parent's house. Herb and Elsie drove over to Tony's house to wait for Lois. After the three of them waited for some time, Tony drove to the Pasadena Plaza looking for Lois or her car, but the Plaza was closed. Finally, Elsie called the Pasadena police to report Lois missing. But the Pasadena police, like most police departments, refuse to take a missing-person report until the person has been missing for 72 hours. The police advised Elsie to check with the area hospitals, which she did. She first called Huntington Hospital in Pasadena and was told that Lois was not there. In fact, at that time Lois was there, but she was dead. Elsie again called the police. This time she insisted they take a missing-person report. The police officer told her to hold on. When he returned to the phone, he asked if Lois had been wearing rosebud earrings and a white bracelet. Elsie relayed the question to Tony and Tony said, "Yes." The Investigating Officer, Brian Schirka, took the two pieces of jewelry to Tony's house where Tony positively identified them as belonging to Lois.

Trone, after he was dropped off by Jones, gave Lois' watch to his girlfriend's mother and Lois' rings to his girlfriend. But the rings did not fit and the girlfriend returned them to Trone. The rings were sold to a Pasadena jewelry store. They were recovered by the police and identified by Tony Haro.

On October 18, 1988, at 9:03 p.m. a police officer was answering a burglary call in the Arroyo near the Rose Bowl. As he rounded a curve, his headlights shone on a body lying in the dirt several feet from the roadway. The officer stopped to investigate. Lois was just taking her final breaths. There was no identification. She had on no shoes or underwear. She was wearing a jumpsuit with several buttons missing.

At 7:30 a.m. the next morning, at "roll call," all Pasadena police officers on that watch (shift) were given a description and license number of Lois' car. A young police cadet, Larry Zimmerman, later to become a deputy sheriff, was permitted to take an unmarked Pasadena police car and drive around Pasadena looking for Lois' car. He drove into Pasadena's high-crime area. At approximately 8:30 a.m., he spotted what he thought was Lois' car coming toward him. After the car passed, he made a U-turn and followed it. He got close enough to see the license number. It was Lois' car. The driver drove into a residential neighborhood and parked. Zimmerman saw Jones exit the car, go to the rear of the car and remove the license plate, which he threw in the trunk. Jones then disappeared into the apartment complex.

Zimmerman called for back-up on his police radio. Numerous police officers responded. Zimmerman accompanied the officers as they went from door to door in the apartment complex. The plan was for Zimmerman to tell the officers if the man he saw driving Lois' car came to the door. After knocking on several doors with no luck, Jones opened his apartment door. Zimmerman said, "That's him" and Jones was arrested.

Officers saw a J.C. Penny's bag inside the car Jones was driving. It still contained the gift for the baby shower as well as the J.C. Penny receipt. The officers obtained a search warrant for Jones' apartment. They found Lois' wallet in Jones' kitchen trash can.

Jones was transported to the Pasadena police station where he was booked and searched. During the search, Detective Schirka removed Lois' car key from Jones' pocket. Schirka also removed from Jones' pocket a Wells Fargo ATM withdrawal receipt dated 10/18/88 at 9:48 p.m. Detective Schirka ordered Jones to remove his clothes. After handing Detective Schirka his shirt, shoes and socks, Jones attempted to take off his pants and underpants at the same time. Schirka told Jones to remove his pants first, then his underpants. Jones seemed to be extra careful when taking down his pants. While Jones was slowly pulling down his underpants, Lois Haro's J.C. Penny credit card, her Wells Fargo ATM card, and other credit cards in Lois' name fell out.

One thing we could not figure out. The ATM withdrawal receipt was not from Lois' Wells Fargo account, but it bore the date and time 45 minutes after Lois was found by the police. Thus, it was pretty good evidence that Jones had been at the Wells Fargo ATM either at 9:48 p.m. or sometime thereafter. But why would he have this ATM receipt that indicated a withdrawal—but not from Lois' account? Lois' Wells Fargo ATM card that fell from Jones' underpants, and the ATM receipt that was removed from Jones' pocket, did not become important in the case until over two years later when Jones took the stand and denied trying to access Lois' bank account.

Jones was interrogated at the police station by Detectives Don Gallon and Brian Schirka. Jones implicated Trone and claimed that Trone shot Lois. The interrogation of Jones was tape-recorded. Trone was arrested later that same day. Trone initially gave the arresting officer, Al Peinado, a false name and tried to resist being arrested but Officer Peinado is 6'3", 260 pounds. The scuffle was brief. After Trone was handcuffed, he told Officer Peinado his true name.

Trone was interrogated and claimed that Jones shot Lois. That was, for a time, the only issue in this case, i.e., which one was the shooter. There was DNA evidence that semen from both defendants was found in Lois' vagina proving that Lois was raped by both Trone and Jones. I had tape-recorded confessions from both Trone and Jones to either committing the charged crimes or to facts that constitute aiding and abetting each other in the commission of these crimes.

In a subsequent tape-recorded statement, Jones admitted that although the gun belonged to Trone and that Trone was pointing his gun at Lois as she lay on the ground, that he, Jones, grabbed the gun from Trone and shot Lois. Trone and Jones both told the detectives that they had not had any alcohol or drugs on the day Lois was murdered.

The trial judge was Charles C. Lee, an excellent judge. Jones was represented by Deputy Public Defender Bill McCallister, a fine lawyer who was handicapped by having to defend his client against a very strong prosecution case. We were seeking the death penalty for both defendants.

During the trial, in an attempt to save himself from the death penalty, Jones testified that Trone was the shooter and that his tape-recorded confession that he was the shooter was a false confession. Jones also testified on cross-examination that he never used Lois Haro's Wells Fargo ATM card in an attempt to withdraw money from her account. I then called a witness from Wells Fargo whom we flew down from their main office in San Francisco. She testified that on the morning of October 19, 1988, between 6:00 a.m. and 6:30 a.m., someone used Lois Haro's ATM card five times in an attempt to access Lois' account. But the person was unable to get any money from the account because he didn't know Lois' PIN number.

Jones was caught in a lie. Using Lois Haro's ATM card might not seem like an important issue, when Jones admitted from the witness stand to kidnapping, robbing and raping Lois Haro. But it was an important lie, because it wasn't just a lie to the police. That is expected. This was a lie Jones told to the jury—a senseless lie, a seemingly inconsequential lie. But I know that jurors, who are always searching for something good to say about defendants, do not like to be lied to by defendants. Don't misunderstand me. There is no question that defendants charged with serious crimes commonly lie on the witness stand. It is even a joke among DAs who say, tongue in cheek, that defendants have a constitutional right to lie. But these commonly told lies are most often the kinds of lies that are difficult for the DA to prove clearly to the jury to be lies. It is often one person's word against another. But Jones' lie was different. When Jones looked at the jury and testified that he never used Lois' ATM card, which fell out of his underpants, to access Lois' account, and then a Wells Fargo representative comes to court with the records showing otherwise, this was very damaging evidence which made it difficult for Bill McCallister to argue to the jury that they should believe his client in other respects.

On cross-examination, I asked Jones what he did after he left Lois Haro dying in the dirt. He testified that after he dropped off Trone he drove home in Lois' car. I asked Jones what he did when he arrived home. He said he was hungry. I asked him whether he had something to eat. Jones testified that he made himself a hamburger. I asked if he ate it. He said he did. I asked him if he watched television while he ate his hamburger. He said he did. I asked him if he remembered what he watched. He testified that he watched an old rerun of the Honeymooners with Jackie Gleason. I asked him if it was a pretty funny show that night. He said it was. I asked him if he laughed a lot. He said he did.

Each defendant was tried separately. Jones was found guilty of first-degree murder, kidnapping, robbery, rape in concert, and forcible oral copulation. Four special circumstance allegations, which made Jones eligible for the death penalty, were also found true; that is, that the murder was committed during the commission of the same four felonies, robbery, rape, kidnapping, and oral copulation.

We had a separate trial, called the penalty trial, on the issue of whether Jones should be sentenced to death or to life in prison without the possibility of parole. Jones' attorney called several witnesses including his mother and a school teacher to testify for Jones. Jones' teacher testified that Jones was a smart student and a good writer. She testified that she assigned him to tutor other students. The teacher described Jones as witty and likeable. Jones' mother testified and used the word, "mistake" to describe what Jones did to Lois Haro. She asked the jury, "If God saw fit to forgive us for the *mistakes* that we made in life, why can't we forgive him for the mistakes that he made?"

Lois' father, a professor of linguistics, confided to me that he was amazed that of all the words available to describe what her son did to his daughter, Jones' mother chose the word "`mistake" to characterize the kidnapping, robbery, rape in concert, and execution-style murder of his daughter. Jones just made a mistake. On May 7, 1991, the jury recommended the death penalty for Jones. The case was continued to June 4, 1991 for formal sentencing by Judge Lee.

California law, thanks to Proposition 8, now permits the family of a murder victim to make a statement to the judge prior to sentencing. I include here excerpts from statements to Judge Lee on June 4, 1991 from Lois' husband, Tony Haro, Lois' mom, Elsie, and Lois' dad, Professor Herb Purnell. Tony went first:

> Your honor, I am the surviving husband of Lois Anne Haro. At this time I would like to express some personal remarks and feelings reflecting on this trial and how it has affected my life during the two and one-half years of waiting patiently, in great humility, for this day.
>
> For myself and the family, this has been the most horrifying and agonizing time of our lives. No words can fully construe the pain and stress we have all experienced in these last two and one-half years.
>
> To sit and face the murderer of my precious wife, knowing he has no feeling of regret for what he has done, brings my whole being to burn with

unyielding anger and disgust. However, I live in the hope that my God will not leave me a victim for the rest of my life. And I know Lois felt the same way. For she lived her life to the fullest, unselfishly and joyfully. She encouraged me, loved me, inspired me and supported me in so many areas of my life, and I can rest assured she knew of my love and devotion to her.

I can only relate to the loss as a violent, unexpected amputation from my life which will forever leave a tender scar in my heart. Lois was not only dear to me but to her family, my family, and hundreds of friends who attended her funeral service, and those who gave their condolences through letter, card and phone. The loss has been felt by many.

And it hurts to know that there are other innocent victims who have experienced the same torment we have felt. This whole ordeal seems so senseless for those who value life. We have been violated and raped of the right to live in peace, not once, but many times over by this process of justice.

The tears have been countless and the heartache horrendous. We are all trying at our own pace to go on with life, but it is hard to avoid reality, especially the hard, cold reality of what Lois went through. ...She cared about people and had no enemies, only the enemy of evil, which obviously manifested itself in the ruthless actions of Jones and his partner. They apparently have no value for life and should never be allowed to be set free in society again.

Then Lois' mother , Elsie, spoke:

Your honor, on October 18, 1988, our lives were forever changed. We can never be the same people we were before that night of horror. How can we possibly put into words what we have experienced as a family and as individuals? Our greatest earthly treasure was torn from us in a fashion beyond imagination.

Surely a woman can shop in the early hours of the evening. But this innocent woman never came home. She was taken captive at gunpoint by two despicable men. What happened after that we have all heard in this courtroom, a story so horrible one could not even have imagined it.

Two totally selfish men, without morals and without conscience, treated her as a piece of trash. They tortured her and humiliated her beyond belief, then shot her execution style as she lay in the dirt on a desolate hillside.

Mr. Jones did this without a twinge of conscience and to this day seems to show no signs of remorse. Indeed, he has entered this courtroom repeatedly with a grin on his face. He has tried to make an impression by wearing a crucifix around his neck and carrying a new testament into court. We have not been fooled by these ludicrous actions nor by the words of his lawyer when he said, 'He loves God.'

How has his heinous crime affected us? The toll has been great, physically and emotionally. We all lost weight, made many trips to the doctor, have undergone medical tests, gone for therapy and spent many hours in convulsive crying. Not only were we affected but our relatives and friends also suffered and continue to suffer greatly.

Two of our parents became ill following Lois' death and neither recovered, and we had to bury them. Mr. Jones has brought death and destruction into the very heart of our families. But greater than all this is the unspeakable loss. Never again will we be able to hear her laugh or enjoy her frequent chats. We will never hear her play the piano, organ or keyboard. We won't have the joy of hearing her sing or play a duet with her father or sister. We won't see her graduate from college with a degree in anthropology or see her fulfill her dream as a cross-cultural marriage and family counselor. We will never hold her baby in our arms. All we have left are some photographs, some precious things that she made for us over the years, our memories and a grave to visit. We cannot hug a grave. I not only lost a daughter. I lost one of my closest friends.

Last to speak was Herb Purnell, Lois' father:

Thank you your honor for the way that this trial has been conducted. We all are grateful that the perpetrators of these terrible acts against Lois were apprehended and that one of them has been found guilty at such a level as to receive the death penalty, and yet all of us share such deep sorrow that even sending a justly-convicted rapist and murderer off to prison will not relieve it.

This man kidnapped my daughter and held her hostage; he robbed her, raped her, and aided and abetted outrageous sexual assaults against her; and in the end he murdered her.

I feel as though I, too, have been held hostage by this man; that already nearly three years of my life have been spent either in court or on legal proceedings, and a final disposition is not yet in sight.

I have been robbed, as well, robbed of a daughter I loved deeply. Lois and I shared many things—reading, academic interests, music and much more. But on October 18, 1988, this man forever robbed me of the special joys that Lois brought into my life.

He also robbed Tony and his family and ours of the joys we had anticipated, such as the joy of seeing Lois receive her bachelor's degree last year the joy of holding the children she might have borne, and the joy of seeing her develop her many God-given talents. Of these, and much more, we have been robbed by this cruel man.

And, of course, he has killed a part of us too. As surviving husband, mother, father, siblings, we will never fully recover from his violent, murderous acts.

For more than two and a half years, our hearts have been pierced with a jagged grief on every remembrance of what Lois had to endure at the hands of Ronald Anthony Jones; a piercing grief when we see her pictures and come across—sometimes quite by accident—another memento which reminds us of our loss. A jagged grief, especially when we stand and weep by her grave.

But this personal and family sorrow is as nothing when compared to the agony that my lovely daughter suffered at this man's hands during the last hour of her life. The defense attorney did not want anyone to imagine what Lois might have been saying during the hour in which his client terrorized her. But any person with the least bit of common sense and any feeling for a suffering human being can readily imagine what she may well have said after Jones and his partner refused to release her and began to abuse her.

Your honor, the jury in the penalty phase found this man's crimes to be of such magnitude that he deserves to receive the death penalty. I fully agree with their finding but without any personal feeling of vengeance. It is simply that these crimes against an innocent, lovely woman, who was in a public shopping center on an errand of kindness, merit the strongest penalty allowed by the law.

Jones was then given the opportunity to speak before sentencing. Jones said, "You guys call me a murderer. I call you guys murderers. You guys want my murder. You all have the law behind you all. It makes it legal for you guys to kill. I see no difference in it—no difference at all."

Judge Lee then proceeded to sentence Jones to death. Then began the appeals process. In California, the appeal is automatic in death penalty cases, and unlike other appeals in criminal cases, an appeal from a death verdict goes directly to the California Supreme Court, skipping over the first level of appeal, the state Court of Appeal. We would have to wait until 1997 for the California Supreme Court to uphold the jury's guilty verdicts and the death penalty verdict. The ruling was unanimous, 7 to 0. The opinion was written by the late Justice Stanley Mosk, arguably, at that time, the most liberal member of the court.

After the supreme court ruling, Jones filed a writ of habeas corpus in the federal court, which is what virtually all death penalty defendants do. The case has remained in the United States District Court in Los Angeles since that time and is still ongoing. At this writing, Jones has been appealing his murder conviction and death penalty sentence for about 16 years. It could be many more years before his appeals are exhausted.

As mentioned, Trone was tried separately. He was represented by Charles Dickerson, a private attorney appointed by the court, because the Public Defender's Office is permitted to represent only one defendant in a multiple-defendant case. Trone's trial was more difficult on the issue of the special circumstance allegations. The law at that time required the DA to prove, in the case of a defendant who is convicted of first-degree murder but was not the actual killer, that at the time the victim was killed by the crime partner, the defendant also had the intent to kill. I had to prove beyond a reasonable doubt that at the moment Jones pulled the trigger, Trone shared Jones' intent to kill Lois.

In Trone's first trial, he was convicted of first-degree murder and all the other charged crimes. As to the special circumstance allegations, the jurors could not agree whether Trone also intended to kill Lois when Jones took the gun from him and shot her. I retried the case on the special circumstance issue alone. The second jury found all four special circumstance allegations to be true. Trone faced a penalty trial. At that point we agreed with Trone's attorney that if Trone made a full confession under oath from the witness stand and waived his right to appeal (which the law permits), he could be sentenced to life in prison without parole. And that is what happened. Lois' family supported this disposition.

Herb, Elsie and I remained friends. Elsie became the chairperson of the local chapter of POMC, Parents of Murdered

Children. At Elsie's invitation, I have spoken at a few of the POMC meetings. The stories these parents tell are heartbreaking. At one of the meetings I attended, a woman told about the day when several members of her family were murdered, and the emotional pain she had been through since that day.

Many of the parents were upset with the police because they hadn't arrested their child's killer. Some were upset over the multitude of rights the defendant has. To the murder victims' families, it often appears that the defendants and their lawyers are calling the shots, and the deputy DA has to jump through hoops for years of pretrial hearings. Some get frustrated with the slow pace of the criminal justice system.

In the Trone and Jones case, for example, the two killers were arrested on October 19, 1988. Jones was sentenced in June 1991. There were numerous court appearances for each defendant in that $2^{1}/_{2}$ year period and Lois' parents tried to attend every one of them. The system is very hard on the families of murder victims. They feel guilty if they miss the proceedings. Yet, they are devastated when they hear the gruesome details of how their son or daughter was murdered.

After the Jones trial, as I mentioned earlier, Herb and Elsie confided in me that they could not understand how I could be so friendly with the defense attorney, the man who was doing his best, in their eyes, to attack our witnesses and to obstruct the search for truth. I tried to explain to them that he was a competent defense attorney who was only doing his job—which did not include the search for truth. I even gave them a copy of the United States Supreme Court opinion, *U.S. v Wade*, from which I have quoted earlier, which explains the role of the criminal defense attorney. It did not seem to help.

Elsie passed away on June 25, 2005, from cancer.

6 2

INMATE-ARTIST IS EXECUTED
IN TEXAS

I have no doubt that if the day should ever come when Jones' execution is imminent, the *L.A. Times* will write stories which laud him as a talented writer who may not be guilty of these horrible crimes. The same group of Hollywood stars, who we have heard from so many times, will allege that the wrong man was convicted or that he received poor representation or that racism played a part in his conviction or death sentence. Jones, like others before him, will become a sort of folk hero. I have seen it before.

I saw it in the case of liberal author Norman Mailer, who was so impressed by the writing talent of a man imprisoned for murder that he started a campaign among his liberal, allegedly compassionate, friends to get him released. And it worked. Mailer persuaded the parole board to release Jack Henry Abbott. Abbott had been serving time for killing a fellow inmate, as well as armed robbery. He was a career criminal who had spent nearly his entire life in prison. Shortly after Abbott's release, he was interviewed on ABC's *Good Morning America*, profiled in *People Magazine* and was guest of honor at a testimonial dinner. Within six weeks of being released he got into an argument with a waiter at a Manhattan restaurant, because the waiter refused to allow Abbott to use the employees' restroom. Abbott pulled out his knife and murdered the 22-year-old waiter, an aspiring actor.

What is it that draws the liberal elite to champion the causes of such brutal murderers as Jack Henry Abbott, cop killer Mamia Abu Jamal and most recently, Kevin Cooper, on California's death row for twenty three years for killing four people, including two children? These champions of the downtrodden, as they see themselves, like to say that death is so permanent that they must be sure. But I don't believe that is the only reason. If they were to see Kevin Cooper, a prison escapee, on videotape killing those four innocent people, I believe their sympathy for the killer would still eclipse any sympathy they felt for the families of the innocent murder victims. For these people, there would always be (to quote Reuven Frank, see Chapter 33) an explanation and therefore an excuse: a bad childhood, a broken home, racism, slavery, molestation, a low IQ, poverty, an unfair criminal justice system, etc. I believe I can speak with some authority on this point because this was how I was raised and these were my strong feelings until I was in my thirties. My liberal friends and I would give each other mutual support and reaffirmation of the correctness of our views. We felt so good about our "progressive" views, so superior—so special!

Have you noticed how many murderers on death row have lost the "murderer" or "killer" label and have taken on the title "artist" or "writer," as in the case of Jack Henry Abbott who was paroled because, according to Mailer, he was such a fine writer? Abbott certainly would not have been paroled when he was if he had not attracted the attention of Mailer.

Stanley "Tookie" Williams, the co-founder of the notorious Crips street gang, was sentenced to death for four murders in Los Angeles. Williams murdered a 7-Eleven clerk, Albert Owens, during a robbery by shooting him in the head with a sawed-off shotgun. Williams and his three crime partners split $120 taken from the cash register. A witness at Williams' trial testified that Williams told his brother about the robbery. "You should have heard the way he sounded when I shot him," Williams bragged. Williams then made a growling noise and laughed. In another robbery of a motel clerk, Williams murdered Robert Yang, Yang's wife and daughter.

Williams' gang, the Crips, are responsible for countless murders and incomprehensible heartache among the families of their murder victims. While on death row, Williams allegedly began co-authoring several children's books warning youths of the perils of gang life, according to the *Los Angeles Times*. In 2000, Mario Fehr, a member of the Swiss parliament, nominated Stanley "Tookie" Williams for the Nobel Peace Prize.[1] As his execution approached, Williams was described in the media as "Author of children's books" and "Nobel Peace Prize nominee." In the weeks leading up to his execution, the Tookie Williams case, and the question whether Governor Schwarzenegger would grant clemency, dominated the media, including newspapers, radio and television. On December 12, 2005, the governor denied clemency and Williams was executed December 13, 2005 by lethal injection.

On August 27, 2004, The *Los Angeles Times* reported the execution in Texas of James Allridge III, who murdered a convenience store clerk. The *Times'* headline read: "Inmate-Artist is Executed in Texas." Not "Convicted Murderer Executed," but "Inmate Artist Executed." The story went on to say that celebrity death penalty opponent, Susan Sarandon, had corresponded with Allridge for years and had purchased some of his paintings.

I have little doubt that if these same people, who think of themselves as good, compassionate people, who are chronically drawn to support violent murderers, had seen as many devastated families as I have seen; if they had seen as many smirking, remorseless, conscienceless, violent career criminals as I have seen over so many years, they too would not be so consumed by their emotional commitment to the killers. If they had seen what I have seen, from an early enough age (it may be too late if the chronic defender of killers is in his or her 50s or 60s) they too, at some point, would have had a sort of epiphany and wake up to the realization, as I did, that their compassion had been misplaced. No matter what their background, no matter how poor they were while growing up, no matter what color they are, the career criminals who hurt people repeatedly, and like the excitement of it, are not the good guys. "Oh, but I've never said they were the *good* guys. I just want them to get a fair trial; I want to be sure of their guilt," they will argue. My reply is to ask these perennial defenders of the killers to look in the mirror and repeat ten times, "To thine own self be true."

I was a proud member of the ACLU in my twenties. I thought then that their mission was to protect First Amendment rights. If that really had been their sole mission, I might still be a member. Over time, I learned that this was not their only mission. They also seem to be against any measure that would increase sentences for violent or career criminals or any measure that would make it easier to apprehend or prosecute criminals.

Why, for example, would the ACLU oppose legislation that would simply require arrested felons to submit a DNA sample so that California would have a larger DNA database, which all agree would result in the apprehension of more rapists, murderers, and other career criminals? Is it really because of their fear that the arrested felon's DNA information would be sold to others, including insurance companies, or that it is too difficult for a defendant, who has been exonerated, to remove his DNA from the database, as they claim? I feel certain that no amount of safeguards would satisfy the ACLU, the *Los Angeles Times* or the other liberal groups who consistently sympathize with the plight of the criminal, and who do not want a larger DNA database, even though DNA evidence has been credited with the release of some innocent defendants who have been wrongly convicted.

I believe the same holds true for the Three-Strikes law. These same groups would oppose *any* law mandating longer sentences for career criminals—even if the criminal were allowed four, five or six strikes. It is just not "cool" in the liberal community to be in favor of laws that protect victims by seeking longer prison terms for the career criminals who repeatedly hurt them. They would not feel good about themselves.

A very liberal relative and friend who lives in Berkeley, California, a very liberal area, once told me, in all seriousness, that he believed the TV show, *America's Most Wanted*, was unfair. I asked him how it was unfair. He told me that once the criminal's face is shown nationwide, he had very little chance of getting away. I looked for the twinkle in his eye, but I saw none. He told me he could never sit on any jury, no matter what the charges, because he could never vote to convict anyone—regardless of the strength of the evidence.

I recall an occasion shortly after I became a deputy DA, still too naïve to be a full-fledged member of The Club. I was speaking to a court clerk. She was bragging how smart her judge was, a judge known to be in the liberal, pro-defense camp. She told me he had never been reversed on appeal. I was duly impressed. After I became more experienced, I realized that all a judge needs to do to make sure he is not reversed on appeal is to rule in favor of the defense. The People's right to appeal is very limited. For example, if we are in the midst of a jury trial, and the DA offers an item into evidence, if the judge erroneously rules that the item of evidence is not admissible, meaning the jury doesn't get to see it, and the defendant is acquitted, that's it—it's over. The DA cannot appeal from a not guilty verdict. Therefore, the judge could not be reversed for making an erroneous ruling against the DA, thus depriving the jury of considering relevant evidence and perhaps depriving the People of a fair trial.

But assume that the defense attorney had offered an item into evidence, and the judge erroneously ruled the defense evidence was inadmissible, thus not allowing the jury to consider it, and the defendant is found guilty. The defendant, of course, has the right to appeal. If the appellate court determines that the judge was in error in denying admissibility of the item of evidence offered by the defense attorney, the conviction will be reversed if the error is deemed to have deprived the defendant of a fair trial

I have no quarrel with these rules. The point is that if a judge wants to play it safe during a trial, in close questions he can simply rule in favor of the defense. He could thus maintain a perfect record of never being reversed by an appellate court for erroneous rulings during trial.

6 3

"WHITE-COLLAR" CRIMES

Murder cases, of course, are devastating to the victims' families, but fraud cases can be heartbreaking as well. I've seen many habitual criminals who don't hurt anyone physically, but who have ruined many lives. I've seen elderly people lose their life savings to con men. I've seen con men forge deeds and the elderly victims lose their homes. The elderly are the main targets because they tend to be more trusting. The consequences of the con man's deceit of the elderly can be life shattering, but very few of these heartbreaking stories are ever reported in the media. These "white-collar," "nonviolent" criminals, as they are called, for all the tragic consequences of their deceit, serve very little prison time.

The range of sentences for grand theft, which is what these fraud defendants are charged with, is 16 months, two or three years. Remember, with good-time/work-time credits the real sentence is 8 months, 12 months or 18 months. Yet, the media seem to believe that even these sentences are too long for white-collar criminals. I have read many editorials which urge that *any* incarceration should be used sparingly except for violent crime.

On August 30, 2004, in an editorial titled "Governor's Reform Option," the *Los Angeles Times*, in their continuing campaign to release more prisoners, asked the Governor to "take some nonviolent inmates out of costly prison cells and subject them to 'alternative sanctions' in the community." This may sound good and compassionate, but allowing these white-collar criminals to commit their crimes repeatedly, with little fear of meaningful incarceration, is the opposite of compassion. It is unjust and cruel to the many victims of these "nonviolent" con men who have little to fear from the criminal justice system.

In spite of the slap-on-the-wrist sentences often meted out to those convicted of fraud, I have had real gratification in seeing juries bring fraud defendants to justice—especially in those cases in which a truly vulnerable person has been the victim. I have found that the "fraudsters" as I call them, often do not do well in jury trials. The reason is, they are "not playing in their own ballpark." Fraudsters usually have a great deal of street smarts and are often very likable. They often make the victim feel important. They gain the victim's confidence, which is where the expression, "confidence man" or "con man" comes from. DAs simply call them "cons."

We have all encountered these kinds of people. They come in both genders. They have big egos. When charged with a crime, they often refuse to plead guilty and insist on a jury trial, because they see the twelve jurors as their next challenge to con. They almost always take the witness stand, often against their attorney's advice. But these fraudsters often have a difficult time on cross-examination by a competent deputy DA. They are great on direct examination when their lawyer is asking the questions, which they are expecting and have rehearsed answering. They often turn in the witness chair to face the jury and make eye contact with individual jurors. They sometimes make the jury laugh. They are often very charming.

But on cross-examination they are forced to do something they never had to do outside of the courtroom: answer a specific question. Cons usually can dodge and weave and avoid answering specific questions from their victims while committing their frauds. But on the witness stand, if the DA is persistent, the defendant can be compelled to answer a specific question he would rather not answer. It is similar, in a way, to riding a bucking bronco. The DA must stay on him. If the defendant will not answer a difficult question directly, the DA can ask the judge to order the defendant to answer the question. If the defendant still will not respond to the question directly, the DA should object to the defendant's answer as nonresponsive and again ask the judge to order the defendant to answer the question. I have done this a number of times. The jury soon begins to see through the defendant's charming facade.

But sometimes a defendant is just too good a salesman and too convincing for the DA to persuade the twelve jurors to convict. I recall such a case in our office. Our deputy DA was no match for him. The defendant was charged with bilking numerous people out of many thousands of dollars by conning them to invest in his "new invention," a perpetual motion machine, not a new scam. After the many victims testified how the defendant took their money under false pretenses, the defendant took the stand and insisted that his machine really worked. The DA's evidence in such cases is nearly always an expert witness who testifies that the machine is a scam. But the defendant was able to con the twelve people on the jury, because they found him not guilty.

What makes this case so bizarre is that after the defendant was acquitted, he met with the jurors and thanked them. When the DA and defense attorney spoke to the jurors in the hallway outside the courtroom, the defendant was pitching the jurors to invest in his invention. The DA told a colleague that some of the jurors really seemed interested. Some con men are so glib, so talented at their craft of defrauding people, it is difficult for victims or jurors to believe that anyone seemingly "so nice" and "so sincere" could be so corrupt.

64

THE AUTO-BROKER CASE

I once prosecuted an auto broker charged with fifteen felony counts of grand theft. In California, auto brokers are licensed car dealers. The defendant's scheme was remarkably simple, yet quite sophisticated. The defendant lived in an affluent neighborhood, was a Little League soccer coach, attended church regularly and was a good con. He lived very well and filed bankruptcy every six years, which federal law then permitted (every eight years from 2006), discharging large amounts of debt he incurred during the previous six years. Many Little League parents and the defendant's fellow church parishioners ordered high-end cars from the defendant. When a customer buys a car through an auto broker, the customer tells the auto broker what kind of car he wants, the specific model, color, interior, etc. The auto broker searches all the dealerships until he locates the car his customer has ordered. The broker pays the dealer the wholesale price and then sells the car to his customer at an appropriate markup.

In the case of this defendant, that was the procedure that was followed, but there was a glitch. The check the defendant gave to the dealer was either returned, nonsufficient funds, or the defendant stopped payment. In either case, the angry dealer called the defendant broker to demand an explanation why his check bounced or payment was stopped. And this is where the con comes in. The defendant told the dealer how sorry he was; he told the dealer that one of his employees had embezzled money from him, and he had to close one of his bank accounts or transfer money between accounts. He always told the dealer to redeposit the check and to please accept his apologies for any inconvenience he had caused. The dealer then redeposited the check and it bounced again. The dealer called the broker again. He is now angrier than the first time. The broker made his apologies again and told the dealer that he was also a victim because the embezzler ran off with a great deal of money. This M.O. was repeated by my defendant with many auto dealers.

One might think the dealer could have repossessed the car if the broker didn't pay him. But that was not possible in this case, because the dealer sold the car to the broker who paid in full—but with a bad check. The broker, in turn, immediately sold the car to his customer, who paid the broker in full with a cashier's check. There was no conditional sales contract between the dealer and the broker or the broker's customer giving the dealer a right to repossess the car for nonpayment. The car dealer was out his car and his money.

But the reason this scheme is so sophisticated is that it looks like a civil case. That is, suppose the dealer who lost his car in this scheme calls the police. Almost any police detective working fraud cases would tell the dealer that this was not a criminal case, but simply a business dispute. The detective would tell the dealer to call his attorney and sue the auto broker. The detective would not even take this case to the DA's office because he knows it would be rejected.

Of course, this is exactly what the defendant anticipated. He knew he would never pay the dealer for the car. He did not mind being sued, because he knew he would be filing bankruptcy and any money the dealer would win in a lawsuit would be discharged in bankruptcy. Although proving that a debt was incurred by fraud prevents the discharge of that debt in bankruptcy, proving fraud in bankruptcy court is not easy.

The result was that the auto broker walked away with what his customer paid him by cashier's check. In one count, involving a Mercedes, it was over $52,000. In another count, it was over $55,000 for another Mercedes; almost $49,000 for a Jaguar, etc. Not a bad day's work. And the bankruptcy trustee would never get his hands on all that cash because the defendant was not a typical debtor. He was a wily crook.

The only reason I filed this case was that a Department of Motor Vehicles (DMV) investigator came to the DA's office to file a misdemeanor charge against the broker for operating as an auto broker while his license was suspended. I read the report which included one transaction of the type described above. I suspected there might be many more. I asked the DMV investigator to do something a bit unusual: to go to the court clerk's civil index and find out how many times the defendant had been sued civilly, and get me the names and addresses of the plaintiffs (the people suing him) and the phone numbers of their attorneys. Understandably, he balked. He told me he only came to the DA's office to file a misdemeanor and why was I making such a big deal out of it. He agreed to do this however, after I told him I would make the same request of his supervisor.

As you may have guessed, many dealers all over Los Angeles County had sued him, alleging the same M.O. Checking the civil index in the County Clerk's office was the only way this could have been discovered. It turned out that many auto dealers had called their local police departments. But Los Angeles County is very large, having within its borders 88 cities. The auto dealers were spread all over the county, and no one police agency was aware that auto dealers in other areas of the county had also called their local police departments. After collecting all the names of the various dealers who were suing the broker, I sent the investigator out to interview each of them. That is how we built our 15-count fraud case.

The defendant had no criminal record. He had been too clever to be caught. Being the great con that he was, he chose to have a jury trial. He was very good on direct examination; he was good-looking and charming. But like so many fraud defendants, he fell apart on cross-examination.

I had an idea for closing argument that I admit was quite unorthodox and a bit risqué for a court of law. I remembered seeing a movie in the 1960s where the wife leaves home for several days to visit her family, leaving her husband home alone. The wife returned home a day early and upon opening the door to their bedroom saw her husband in bed with another woman. The wife screamed at her husband, "What are you doing in our bed with that woman?" The husband sat up, looked up at his wife and said, "What woman?" The wife screamed, "What do you mean, what woman?—the woman lying right there beside you." The husband responded, "You know, I'm really getting tired of all your suspicions and accusations. You need to get some help."

After reciting this movie scene to the jury, I told them that just like the cheating husband proclaiming, "What woman?" this defendant, also faced with overwhelming evidence of grand theft from many victims, has the gall to look you in the face and say, "Where is the evidence?" The defendant was convicted of all counts and was sentenced to prison where he served a little over one year.

A person can live very well on other people's money if he is willing to hold off creditors and file bankruptcy every eight years. This defendant had filed bankruptcy just before the start of the criminal case. I spoke to the bankruptcy trustee. She told me they were going to get all the defendant's cars that were in his name. I told her I doubted that but I wished her luck trying to find them. She told me, "You don't understand. I have a court order for him to surrender his cars." I told her, as politely as I could, that *she* did not understand. She was not dealing with a debtor who simply got in over his head in debt. She was dealing with a crook.

Months later, I spoke to the trustee and asked her if she had recovered the broker's cars. She had not. She told me the defendant had been served with a court order to deliver his cars to the bankruptcy trustee but had not complied. I told her that people like the defendant don't care about court orders. To the defendant, as with other crooks, a court order is just a piece of paper. I told her that people like the defendant will not comply with a court order unless his incarceration is imminent—like, within three minutes. It was obvious that she had not been accustomed to dealing with people like the defendant.

6 5

THE MAIL-ROOM CAPER

My first white-collar case occurred when I had only been a DA for a few months—still believing that criminals suffered from low self-esteem. The defendant's rap sheet showed many convictions for grand theft and forgery. Although many of his prior convictions involved schemes to con money from victims, the several grand theft and forgery charges against him in my case were different and more straightforward. When the defendant committed the crimes in my case, he was on federal parole for mail theft. His parole officer was successful in finding him a job with Los Angeles County. Where do you think they assigned him? The mail room for the Department of Public Social Services—DPSS. This is the agency that sends out the welfare checks.

When the welfare recipients died or moved without a forwarding address, the mail was returned to the DPSS mail room. The defendant was given a key to the mail room. He opened the mail room very early in the morning, before anyone else arrived for work. He had even been commended for starting work earlier than his scheduled shift. While alone in the mail room, he would open the envelopes containing the returned welfare checks, forge the signature of the recipient on the backs of the checks, then go to the Department of Motor Vehicles and apply for a temporary driver's license in the name of the welfare recipient. He would then cash the check using the temporary driver's license as ID. He did this numerous times over many months, pocketing many thousands of dollars before he was caught.

I told his attorney the defendant could plead guilty to a number of grand theft and forgery counts, and the prison sentence could run concurrently with the time he would serve for his federal parole violation. The defendant, a very friendly and charming man, rejected my offer. He wanted his jury trial. But I had a very strong case, and the jury rejected his perjured denials that he had stolen any money.

At the time of sentencing, which, in Los Angeles criminal courts, is called "Probation & Sentence" or more commonly, P&S, the defense attorney made a pitch to the judge for probation. When it came my turn to respond, the defendant did something so unusual that I never saw it happen again. He walked over to me and implored me in a very kindly, obsequious manner to tell the judge that I did not object to the defendant receiving probation. What chutzpah! Here I had offered this career-criminal thief, who was on federal parole for mail theft, a disposition (plea bargain) allowing him to serve his sentence for his current crimes concurrently with his federal parole violation instead of consecutively. He rejected my offer, lost his jury trial, and now asks me to join with his attorney in asking the judge for probation. This is *not* an indication of low self-esteem.

Of course, I rejected the defendant's request and asked for the maximum state prison sentence—which the judge gave him. I have little doubt the defendant actually served any more than a year or so in prison.

66

THE JAMAICAN SWITCH

In the early 1980s, I tried a defendant for grand theft who cheated a man who had just received his check at the unemployment office. The fraudster and his crime partner accompanied the victim to the bank where he cashed his check and gave the defendant his money. The defendant and his accomplice were able to pull off the theft by using an age-old con game called the Jamaican switch. There are many variations of this scam, but all involve the crooks ending up with the victim's money and the victim ending up holding a bag of play money or shredded paper. The defendant took the witness stand and exhibited a strong, clipped Jamaican accent. The defendant was hilarious, a natural comedian. He had the jury bent over with laughter. I thought for sure I had lost the case. I was upset that this charming con man was able to entertain the jury so well. I felt that not only had he conned my victim; now he had conned my jury.

In my argument to the jury, feeling righteously indignant and believing I had nothing to lose, I abandoned decorum. With stinging sarcasm, I told the jury I was glad they were entertained by this con man and that they all had a good laugh. But I reminded them that the victim's wife and kids were not laughing when the victim returned home without his unemployment check. I reminded them that because of the defendant's scam, these victims had no money to pay for food or rent. The jury must have been brought back to reality because they found the defendant guilty of grand theft. It was not a big case, but for me it was a big, come-from-behind victory.

67

INSURANCE FRAUD

Many people make a good living committing insurance fraud. It is very lucrative and the insurance proceeds are tax free. I once prosecuted a defendant for a type of insurance fraud I had not seen. He had homeowner policies on two homes with two insurance companies. He used a different name on each policy. The defendant reported burglaries in each house and submitted the same list of stolen property to each insurance company. It was a fluke that the two insurance companies discovered that they were both insuring the same man using different names as to each house. When the two companies compared the lists of allegedly stolen items submitted to each insurance company, they called the police.

But the defendant was very streetwise. He claimed racism was the reason that the insurance companies were harassing him—not anything he had done. He knew what a powerful label that is, and that he could intimidate insurance companies into not taking any action against him by threatening to call the media and claiming the companies were hassling him because he was black. But it didn't work this time. The jury convicted him and, because he had a prior felony conviction, probation was denied, and he was sentenced to state prison.

My last two years in the DA's office were spent in the Auto Insurance Fraud unit. The amount of auto insurance fraud in Southern California is staggering. Auto insurance fraud costs Californians at least $3 billion per year. The average household pays hundreds of dollars in additional auto insurance premiums each year due to auto insurance fraud. On November 24, 2005, the *Los Angeles Times* ran a story titled "Lawyer Held in Car Crash

Fraud." The story was about an attorney arrested for hiring 29 people to participate in the staging of more than 60 car crashes on Los Angeles freeways. The attorney is alleged to have collected millions of dollars in fraudulent insurance claims arising out of the bogus accidents. Former California Insurance Commissioner John Garamendi said, "Everybody who purchases auto insurance is paying for the fraudulent costs." Garamendi estimated that 25% of our insurance costs go to fraud. It is estimated that as many as 67% of auto accidents in Los Angeles County involve some sort of fraud. That is well above the 45% estimated fraud rate for the rest of California. It is estimated that there are about one hundred organized crime auto insurance fraud rings in the Los Angeles area that stage as many as 7,000 collisions each year. The Insurance Research Council says that every dollar spent fighting fraud nets $10.00 in gains.[2]

Auto insurance fraud takes many forms. Staged auto accidents are very popular in California. Each car is filled with people, all of whom claim whiplash injuries which do not show up on X-rays and therefore cannot be verified. The "patients" all go to a crooked lawyer, who, in turn, refers the allegedly injured people to a medical clinic. The doctor at the medical clinic, usually a chiropractic office, is part of the scam. The medical clinic often has the patients sign in on twenty-five or thirty different dates, often in different colored ink, indicating the patient received medical or chiropractic treatment for his "injuries" twenty-five or thirty times. The medical clinic then sends a bill, in the thousands of dollars for each "patient," to the attorney who forwards the bill to the insurance company. The crooked lawyer and doctor are paid the bulk of the proceeds of the insurance settlement. If there are four or five people in each car, the insurance payout can amount to a good deal of money. And this is just for one alleged accident. It is very risky for the insurance company not to pay the claims. If a jury were to believe the allegedly injured plaintiffs, it could cost the insurance company much more.

The California Department of Insurance receives nearly 15,000 suspected fraudulent auto insurance claims each year. But due to limited investigative resources, the fraud division only investigates about 300 to 500 new cases each year. In the 1997-98 fiscal year, when I was assigned to our Auto Insurance Fraud unit, only 412 arrests were made in the entire state for auto insurance fraud.[3] In the 2000-2001 fiscal year, the state fraud unit of the Department of Insurance (DOI) made only 244 arrests statewide.[4] The fraud division within the California DOI only has enough investigators to scratch the surface of this massive scam. To make a meaningful impact, the legislature would need to significantly increase funding of the fraud division. Why wouldn't the legislature increase the funding of the fraud division so we could be more effective in fighting auto insurance fraud—especially if the Insurance Research Council is correct when it says that every dollar spent fighting fraud nets $10.00 in gains?

The reasons for the underfunding of the fraud division are, first, the public is largely unaware of the extent of the problem, because the media rarely report on the subject of auto insurance fraud. Second, the average auto insurance consumer believes, to the extent he is even aware auto insurance fraud is a problem, that it is the insurance companies who are the victims of insurance fraud. The consumers do not seem to realize that the insurance companies pass on to their customers their losses due to fraud, and that a significant portion of their insurance premiums are going into the pockets of the crooked doctors and lawyers. Because the consumer fails to see himself as the victim, there is little public pressure on the legislators to adequately fund the fraud division of the Department of Insurance. And frankly, from what I discovered during my time as a supervisor in the DA's Auto Insurance Fraud unit, the insurance companies are not pushing vigorously for more state fraud investigators, because they can so easily pass on their losses to their policyholders by simply raising their premiums.

Even in the unlikely event that a crooked doctor, lawyer, or chiropractor is arrested and convicted, because auto insurance fraud is classified as a white-collar, nonviolent crime, the sentences tend to be quite low and therefore an insufficient deterrent to discourage these crooked professionals from engaging in this very lucrative scam. I do not recall ever seeing any media editorials seeking longer prison sentences for these "nonviolent" fraudsters.

But as much as auto insurance fraud costs all of us, it is dwarfed by what we all pay for medical fraud. The total cost of healthcare in the U.S. in 2003 was $1.7 trillion. Estimates of healthcare fraud vary from a low of three percent to a high of 10% of total costs.[5] Assuming the lowest estimate, three percent of $1.7 trillion is $51 billion. This is about $1 billion per week in 2003 lost to healthcare fraud. But Byron Hollis, Blue Cross and Blue Shield Association's national anti-fraud director, says that according to conservative industry experts, as much as $85 billion was lost to fraud in 2003.

It was reported on March 12, 2005, in the *Los Angeles Daily News*, that Blue Shield and Blue Cross, working with the FBI, had broken up an elaborate insurance-scam ring in which doctors filed more than *$1 billion* in fraudulent insurance claims. Thousands of "patients" from 47 states were sent to California doctors for unnecessary surgery. Recruiters of the surgery candidates were paid $2,000 to $4,000 for each "patient" who received a medical procedure. Each patient received from $200 to $2,000 in cash, a free trip to California and free lodging in a beach city. The Orange County District Attorney said that more than 5,000 people had unnecessary surgeries. Just one clinic in Orange County, which adjoins Los Angeles County, billed insurers for almost $97 million. The suspicious claims were first noticed in 1999. The recruiters were so brazen that flyers were distributed to factories offering $4,000 to $5,000 cash to any employee who was insured by Blue Cross, Aetna, Cigna, or any PPO medical insurance plan. The flyer said, "NO WORK INVOLVED."[6] And this was just one fraud ring!

Why is medical fraud so pervasive? Because the money to be made is enormous and the chances of getting caught are slim. Even if the fraudster is caught, the likelihood of his serving significant prison time, at least in state court (contrasted with federal court), is even slimmer. The main problem is that there are very few fraud investigators in comparison to the immensity of the problem. This shortage of fraud investigators applies to both medical fraud and other kinds of insurance fraud.

How high do the losses from fraud need to climb before the media and the politicians recognize the seriousness of the problem and bring it to the attention of the public? I would hope that if the people become informed of this huge drain on our economy, they will get angry enough that the politicians will act. It is the responsibility of the media to bring the scope of the fraud crisis to the attention of the public. Most of us only know what we learn from the media.

In spite of the generally bleak outlook for any progress in attacking this medical fraud crisis, there is some hope—at least in Los Angeles County. Los Angeles County District Attorney Steve Cooley has recently begun a unique pilot program to deal with healthcare fraud. The program is the brainchild of deputy DA extraordinaire Al MacKenzie who heads the program. In a story published in the *Los Angeles Daily Journal* March 1, 2006, MacKenzie said, "The gross amount of fraud [he is currently investigating] is over $200 million. ...You have one doctor alone who got $23 million in five years from the workers'comp. system," MacKenzie said.

MacKenzie's idea is simple enough and promises to be very effective. Many of the crooked lawyers, doctors, and chiropractors do not file state income tax returns. When MacKenzie identifies a medical fraud suspect, he sends an e-mail to numerous insurance companies, self-insured cities and counties, Medi-Cal and Medicare requesting each of these payers to send to his office the gross amount of money they have paid the suspect each year for the previous six years. MacKenzie then tallies the amounts paid and contacts the California State Franchise Tax Board, the agency that collects state income taxes, to determine if the suspect has filed a tax return. MacKenzie is discovering that many of these crooked healthcare fraudsters have either not filed state income tax returns or they have grossly underreported their income. It is a felony in California to fail to file a state income tax return or to underreport income. Many will recall that this is how the federal government was finally able to convict the legendary mobster of the 1920s, Al Capone. In 1931, this mobster, who had terrorized Chicago, was convicted of income tax evasion and sentenced to federal prison.

Prosecuting a crooked doctor or lawyer for failing to file a state income tax return, or underreporting income on a state tax return, is far easier than investigating and prosecuting a complicated fraud case.   MacKenzie hopes to persuade other prosecutorial offices nationwide (in states that have a state income tax) to adopt this approach. If he is successful, many crooked doctors and lawyers involved in insurance fraud nationwide will be convicted of tax fraud. If that should occur, medical fraud should decline significantly, perhaps saving billions of dollars. Kudos to District Attorney Cooley for giving DA MacKenzie the green light for this innovative project.

A few years ago, at a DA's retirement luncheon, I was seated at a table with an FBI agent. We started talking about our respective jobs. He told me he had been assigned to the Department of Agriculture working food stamp fraud. I told him that in the area where I lived, a nice area, food stamp fraud was rampant. I told him a story of being in a check-out line at my local supermarket. The lady in front of me paid with food stamps. When I walked out to the parking lot, I saw her placing her grocery bags in the trunk of a new BMW. The next time I was in the supermarket, I told the checker what I had seen. She said the box boys who help people with their groceries see that frequently and that it is a hot topic of conversation.

The FBI agent then told me something that stunned me. He said there was *nobody* in the FBI who was assigned to verify applications for food stamps. He said there were very large food stamp scams that he was assigned to investigate, but, to his knowledge, there were no attempts to verify the truthfulness of statements made in individual food stamp applications, by any state or federal agency. That is, there is no attempt to verify that the applicant qualifies for food stamps—even on a random basis.

There are not many taxpayers who would deny food stamps to someone too poor to buy food. On the other hand, taxpayers should not be buying food for people who can afford to purchase new BMWs. The issue is whether *some* investigative agency should be checking for fraud, or whether we should continue to operate on the honor system with taxpayer dollars?

I have no doubt that if the number of fraud investigators were substantially increased, and the sentences for fraud significantly increased, medical fraud, auto insurance fraud, and food stamp fraud would decline sharply. If the government substantially increased the resources devoted to investigating fraud, we would save many billions of dollars now going into the pockets of crooks. This money would then be available for other worthwhile projects, such as improving our overcrowded schools, roads and freeways.

But the liberal media would surely howl in protest claiming the government was harassing poor people or "nonviolent" people. The media would find a crooked lawyer or doctor who would claim that he had been unfairly harassed by fraud investigators. I am not optimistic that we will do anything of substance to reduce fraud—at least not until the public sees themselves as the real victims and demands reform. But who is going to tell them? Who is going to spur our legislators into action? Don't wait for the media.

68

IDENTITY THEFT

Identity theft is one of the fastest growing crimes in the country. It was reported in 2005 that identity theft has been the Federal Trade Commission's number one consumer complaint for five years in a row. In 2004, an estimated nine million people were identity theft victims, including one million in California. On February 1, 2006, the *Los Angeles Times* reported that U.S. consumers lost nearly $57 billion in 2005 to identity thieves—over $1 billion each week. Identity thieves steal our Social Security, driver's license, and credit card numbers. Victims often spend years trying to clear their names and rebuild their credit.

Senate Bill 830, the Identity Theft Trackers Act, was introduced in the California State Senate to toughen the sentences for identity thieves. The bill would have increased the penalty from a misdemeanor calling for a maximum of one year in a county jail (which, in Los Angeles County, currently means about 30 days actual time served—or less) to an alternate felony/misdemeanor called a "wobbler" by Club members. A wobbler allows the judge the option of sentencing the defendant to either a misdemeanor or a felony sentence. The felony sentence in Senate Bill 830 would have a range of 16 months, two or three years (actual time being either 8, 12 or 18 months) in state prison. On March 29, 2005, the bill was killed in the Public Safety Committee of the California State Senate. The Committee was comprised of seven senators, only two of whom were Republicans. To pass the bill out of Committee required four votes. Both Republicans and one Democrat voted for the bill. Four Democrats either voted "no" or failed to vote (abstained) and the bill died.

Why can't these Democrats sympathize with the victims of identity theft? Why are they so resistant to make it just a bit tougher for identity thieves and other criminals? The excuse offered by the Democrats for killing this bill was that it would be unfair to a defendant who already has two strikes. For example, if a convicted identity thief has a prior conviction for a violent or serious felony, the conviction for identity theft would make him a two striker which means that the usual felony sentence of 16 months, two or three years would be doubled to 32 months, four years or six years with only 20% good-time/work-time credits instead of the usual 50%. If the convicted identity thief has two prior violent or serious felonies, a conviction for identity theft makes him a third striker and thus eligible for a 25-year-to-life sentence.

My answer to the Democrats is twofold: first, the defendant who is convicted of identity theft, who has one or two prior strikes, could have chosen not to commit another felony—in this case a felony that requires a good deal of planning. He knew if he committed another felony, and got caught and convicted, he would be a two- or three-strike candidate, but he chose to commit the felony anyway. Second, DAs in many California counties, including Los Angeles and San Francisco, would not normally charge an identity thief as a third striker even though he is a third-strike candidate under the Three-Strikes law.

The truth is that liberal Democrats will always come up with some rationale to spare the criminals. If it is not the Three-Strikes law, which served as the excuse in this case, there would be some other excuse to go easy on the criminals. The Democrats' killing of the identity theft bill was not even reported in the *Los Angeles Times*.

69

CROOKED LAWYERS

In 1986, I filed 28 felony counts of grand theft and forgery against a prominent attorney. I say prominent, because he had been the president of his local bar association and had been named the local Chamber of Commerce Man of the Year. But for five years, from 1981 to 1986, he had cheated a dozen clients out of nearly $250,000. All the while, he appeared to live the good life. He owned or leased a Porsche, a BMW and a Mercedes, all at the same time. He dined at expensive restaurants and took expensive vacations.

The defendant (the attorney) even stole from his own bookkeeper and her brother. What a twist, the boss steals from his bookkeeper! The bookkeeper's 70-year-old mother had been raped and murdered. Because the bookkeeper worked for the defendant, she and her brother retained the defendant to handle their mother's estate. The defendant conned them out of $10,827 by telling them that the probate clerk demanded that a deposit in that amount be held in trust by the probate court pending the close of probate. The brother gave the defendant his check for the $10,827 which was deposited in the defendant's bank account. The probate clerk had never made such a demand. The defendant simply pocketed the money.

One of the saddest thefts by this attorney from his clients involved a mother and her young son. The mother retained the attorney to handle the estate of her husband who had been robbed and murdered. The mother received a check from her insurance company for $62,957.58. She gave the check to the defendant to invest for her. She agreed to pay him $10,000 for his fee. The life insurance company sent another check to be placed in trust for her son in the amount of $66,968.70. This check was sent by the insurance company directly to the defendant. The defendant lied to his widowed client telling her that the insurance check for her son was for only $30,000 and that he had set up a trust for her son at a savings and loan. The truth is, the defendant never set up a trust for the son. This widow and her son ended up losing nearly $100,000 as a result of the attorney's theft. These victims lost a husband and father, and then their attorney stole most of the insurance proceeds. The mother had to get a job as a waitress to provide for her son.

Although this attorney stole from ten more clients, I will only mention one more, an elderly husband and wife. They retained the defendant to handle a lawsuit arising out of injuries they sustained in a car-wash accident. The defendant, without their knowledge, settled their claim and the insurance company sent the defendant a check for $29,000 payable to the defendant and his clients—which is customary. The defendant forged both clients' signatures on the check and deposited the $29,000 check into his own bank account. He never informed his clients that he had settled their case.

What made this offense especially ugly is that about $1\frac{1}{2}$ years later, the defendant contacted his clients and told them he needed another $5,000 for expert witness fees in his civil suit against the car wash. The couple managed to get the money together by using all the money they had been saving for Christmas presents. This was simply an outright theft of $34,000 from a totally innocent elderly couple. Of course, there were no expert witness fees required in this case, because the attorney had settled the case $1\frac{1}{2}$ years earlier.

The defendant tried to blame alcohol for his problem, but the defendant's own law partner wrote a letter to the probation officer saying the defendant had no alcohol or drug problem. In this same letter, the partner stated that the only aberration of the defendant of which he was aware was a seemingly absolute lack of social conscience.

Perhaps the defendant's biggest mistake was that he lied to the judge—and got caught. Remember what I said earlier about the jury catching a defendant lying—*to them*! Well, when a defendant, who happens to be an attorney, gets caught lying to the judge, he is usually in a real pickle.

Here is what happened: The defendant's attorney called me the day before the defendant was to appear in court. He told me the defendant would be asking for a continuance because his (the defendant's) dad was having surgery, and he had to remain home to care for his mother while his dad was in the hospital. I said I would not oppose the continuance, but that I needed a letter from the defendant's doctor saying he would be performing surgery on the defendant's father. The defense attorney, who is a very nice guy and an excellent lawyer, said he would tell his client to get a letter from the doctor.

The following morning the attorney came to court with his client. I asked him if he had the letter from the doctor. He gave me a copy. I left the courtroom and took the letter to my office and read it. It was on the doctor's letterhead and purportedly signed by the doctor, but knowing the defendant's proclivity for deception, I suspected the letter was a phony. I called the doctor's office and identified myself as a deputy district attorney. That was the only way his receptionist would allow me to talk to him. I told the doctor I had a letter from him dated the day before and read it to him. I asked him if it was true that he was going to perform surgery on the defendant's father. He said it was true the defendant's father was his patient, but there was no surgery planned. I asked him if he had written the letter I had just read to him. He said he signed a blank page on his letterhead as a favor for the defendant, but he did not write the letter. I asked him to write me a letter telling me he did not write the letter and that no surgery on the defendant's father was planned. He said he would and he did.

I then went back to the courtroom where the defendant and his attorney were waiting. The judge called the case and the defense attorney asked for a continuance and submitted the doctor's letter to the judge. The judge was about to grant the defendant's request for the continuance and asked me if the People objected. I told the judge I had informed the defendant's attorney the day before that because the defendant had to care for his mother while his father was in surgery, I would not object to a continuance. I told the judge I just talked to the doctor and the letter he allegedly wrote was phony. It was not written by the doctor and the defendant's father is not scheduled to have surgery. The judge looked at the defendant and asked him if this was true. The defendant's attorney did not permit his client to answer.

The defendant had been out on bail. The judge immediately remanded the defendant to the custody of the sheriff. I'm sure it never occurred to the defendant that I would call the doctor to verify the story about his father's surgery. But frankly, when the defense attorney first told me the reason for the continuance, I would have bet my car that it was baloney.

Because I had such a dead-bang case against this attorney for stealing from twelve of his clients, there was virtually no defense story that could have made any sense. He had no alternative but to plead guilty. I accepted a guilty plea to twelve of the 28 felony counts, one count for each of his victims.

The probation officer wrote a report in which he stated his opinion that the motive for the defendant's conduct was greed and personal ambition. He noted that the defendant expressed no remorse, and he did not seem to appreciate the magnitude of his crimes. He said the defendant's illegal conduct appeared to have been premeditated, protracted, and betrayed a position of trust and confidence. The judge sentenced the defendant to four years in the state prison. He was released in less than two years. Instead of waiting to be disbarred, the defendant voluntarily resigned from the California State Bar. I know how tough it was getting through law school and the bar exam. I cannot imagine why any attorney would throw away everything he had worked so hard to attain.

70

REMORSE?—NOT LIKELY

What kind of person can steal almost $100,000 from a widow and her little boy, whose husband and father had just been murdered, and show no remorse? The answer: a sociopath, a person who has no conscience and does not have the capacity to feel empathy or guilt. They don't even understand what all the fuss is about. That is the reason for the probation officer's statement that this attorney, convicted of stealing nearly a quarter million dollars from twelve of his clients, did not appreciate the magnitude of the crimes he committed. Sure, he had the intellectual capacity to appreciate what he did was wrong, but it just doesn't bother a sociopath.

The truth is, like so many criminals I have prosecuted, he had no guilt or remorse for what he did and the pain he caused. Sociopaths are not bothered in the least by their victim's pain. That is why Ronald Anthony Jones, a good student, according to his teacher, could eat a hamburger and laugh at Jackie Gleason in the *Honeymooners* shortly after kidnapping, raping, and murdering an innocent woman. Sociopaths are not sick—at least not in the way we think about those who are mentally ill. Sociopaths are often very successful in their chosen occupations. Some may be CEOs of major corporations.

That is why it is so frustrating when I hear jurors, who have just convicted a violent or career criminal, say such things as, "He will have to live with what he did for the rest of his life." I want to tell them (but I don't) that he won't think about what he did for a minute. He will only think about the mistakes he made, or the stroke of bad luck (usually a fluke) that resulted in his being caught.

The juror who believes that the violent or career criminal feels remorse for his crime does not understand that the defendant she just voted to convict is not like her. If the typical juror killed someone, even accidentally, I have no doubt it would haunt her for the rest of her life. The average person cannot imagine that anyone who intentionally kills an innocent person would not be tormented by the memory and the guilt forever.

I believe the reason for this naiveté is our failure to acknowledge and accept the fact that there are such people as sociopaths. And the reason for our failure, I believe, can be attributed to the myth that we are all basically good. Those who believe that "goodness" is an inherent characteristic of mankind want desperately to believe that a murderer and other violent criminals are "sick," or, if not sick, would at some point feel terrible about killing an innocent person or knocking down an old lady to steal her purse. These believers in our essential goodness assume that although the criminal's "goodness" may not be apparent, it is still there, hiding beneath the surface, and all that is needed to find and release his essential goodness, i.e. to rehabilitate him, is a good psychologist, psychiatrist, or rehab program.

But the evidence is overwhelming that this is not the case with the great majority of killers, robbers, rapists, and career criminals. This was corroborated by the findings of the 15-year Yochelson/Samenow study of 255 criminals and the subsequent Rand study of 49 felons who had committed 10,500 crimes. For me, it is corroborated by 32 years of experience as a deputy DA watching the demeanor of violent and career criminals and reading probation officer's reports, which state with remarkable consistency that the defendants neither exhibited nor expressed remorse for the crimes they committed.

But I have seen a few killers who experienced remorse. It was usually a defendant who had no criminal record who, while intoxicated on drugs or alcohol, killed a loved one in a fit of rage or jealousy. This type of person, who often does not present a danger to the public, may become suicidal after committing the homicide. But this kind of case is relatively rare as compared to the violent criminals who commit the rapes, assaults, armed robberies and drive-by killings, and the white-collar criminals who make their living by conning others out of their money. In these kinds of cases, true remorse is rare. These kinds of defendants often "perform" poorly on the witness stand under cross-examination or at their sentencing hearing if they try to cry or pretend to have remorse.

71

THE DOROTHY MAE
APARTMENT FIRE

The biggest murder case I prosecuted, in terms of body count, was the Dorothy Mae Apartment fire case. Humberto de la Torre was charged with twenty-five counts of murder resulting from a fire he intentionally set on September 4, 1982. His motive for throwing gasoline in the apartment building, and then lighting it, was to retaliate against his uncle who was the manager of the building. Earlier in the day, his uncle told him to stop writing graffiti on the building. This angered De la Torre who returned that night and set the fire. The twenty-five people who died included four men, seven women, thirteen children, and an unborn fetus.

After setting the fire, De la Torre fled to Mexico. When LAPD detectives learned of his location, they went to Mexico and brought him back. After De la Torre was arrested, he was very cooperative with the LAPD detectives. He made a videotaped confession and even gave the detectives a videotaped tour of what was left of the Dorothy Mae Apartments, a four-story apartment building located on Sunset Blvd., a few blocks north of the Los Angeles Civic Center.

At the time he set the fire, De la Torre was 19 and had never been arrested. I did not believe the defendant intended to kill anyone when he threw the gasoline into a hallway of the building and then lit it. Of course, anyone should realize that throwing gasoline in the hallway of an apartment building in the middle of the night, and then igniting it, risks the lives of the inhabitants. California law says that because he committed arson, and deaths occurred as a direct result of the arson, the perpetrator is guilty of first-degree murder. Two special circumstances, multiple murders and murder during a burglary, made De la Torre eligible for the death penalty or life without parole (L-WOP). Remember, the crime of burglary is committed if a person enters a building with intent to steal or commit a felony. In this case, the defendant entered the building to commit a felony—arson.

I took a position that I believed would be very unpopular with the LAPD and with my boss, District Attorney Ira Reiner. I would not recommend the death penalty for De la Torre. My reasons were his age, his lack of any arrest record, and the fact that I was convinced he didn't intend to kill anyone. Most of the people died when they could not escape the building because the exit doors in the hallways opened in instead of out. The gruesome photos showed bodies piled high at the exit doors.

I wanted the LAPD on my side in my opposition to the death penalty. But considering that 25 innocent people had lost their lives as a result of De la Torres' arson, I expected to have an uphill fight trying to convince my LAPD investigating officers to join me in my opposition to seeking the death penalty.

Because of the numerous victims in this case, the LAPD assigned several investigating officers to the case. These were LAPD's most experienced homicide detectives. I asked my main I/O, Frank Garcia, if I could meet with all my I/Os in a conference room at Parker Center, the LAPD's headquarters. Garcia agreed. At the meeting, I asked these seasoned homicide detectives for a show of hands of those who favored seeking the death penalty for De la Torre. Not one hand was raised. I was surprised. I was prepared to make my pitch for L-WOP. Perhaps it was the lawyer in me that caused me to play devil's advocate: "This guy killed 25 people! He had to be aware that he was endangering the life of every occupant of that apartment building when he poured that can of gas in the hallway and lit it," I said.

One of the detectives who had seen it all and was close to retirement looked at me and said, "Look, this guy is a jerk, we all know that. But he has never been arrested, he was 19, and he really didn't intend to kill anyone. This isn't a death penalty case even if there are 25 dead people." I then told the assembled detectives that I had come to the same conclusion, but it might be a hard sell to the District Attorney who, after all, has to run for election. The detectives told me I could assure the DA they would make certain the police chief would not oppose a sentence of L-WOP.

Walking back to the DA's office from the police department, I thought about these veteran homicide detectives and their unanimous opposition to the death penalty in this case. I came to a conclusion: It comes down to the truism that the closer one gets to a subject, the more distinctions one sees. In the same way that Eskimos have many words to distinguish many different types of snow because they live in snow, and artists can distinguish subtle hues of different colors because they live with colors, highly experienced homicide detectives in big-city police departments, who have seen countless different kinds of murderers, see significant distinctions in these murderers a lay person would not see.

Detective Garcia suggested that he accompany me to a meeting with the District Attorney, Ira Reiner. I thought that would be a good idea. I needed all the help I could get. When we first told Reiner of our recommendation of L-WOP, he objected. "This guy killed 25 people! If this isn't a death penalty case, what is?" But we must have made a good pitch because we were able to turn him around. The DA approved L-WOP.

The defense attorney was the late Earl Hanson, one of the best attorneys in the business. After the preliminary hearing, which lasted two days, Hanson acknowledged this was not a triable case from his perspective. Because of his client's videotaped confession and lack of any mental problems, he knew he had no chance of prevailing in trial. He had no choice but to plead guilty. But Hanson didn't want to plead guilty to L-WOP. He wanted his client to have some hope of some day being paroled. He made this offer: If I would strike the two special circumstance allegations, (which *required* a sentence of L-WOP) he would plead guilty "straight up" to all 25 counts of first-degree murder. The term "straight up" means the defendant would plead guilty without first getting an indicated sentence from the judge. Straight-up guilty pleas are very rare because the defense attorney is gambling big. Defendants almost never plead guilty without knowing what their sentence will be.

A plea to one count of first-degree murder calls for a sentence of 25 years-to-life. Two counts, 50-to-life, three counts, 75-to-life, etc. However, the judge could run the sentences on some or all 25 counts of murder concurrently—which means, if the sentences on all counts were run concurrently, the sentence would be 25-to-life. Or, for example, he could run four of the 25 counts consecutively which would mean a sentence of 100 years-to-life. I spoke to my I/Os about the offer. I explained to them the judge's many sentencing options. They all agreed that I should accept Hanson's offer. The reason my I/Os were unanimous had nothing to do with the difficulty of proving the case. They simply believed that a plea of guilty to 25 counts of first-degree murder was a reasonable disposition.

Again, Detective Frank Garcia and I met with the District Attorney. Reiner initially expressed disbelief at our willingness to strike the special circumstance allegations in such a dead-bang case involving so many victims. But again, we prevailed. I called Earl Hanson and told him we accepted his offer.

On the day of sentencing, the judge asked if anyone would like to be heard before the defendant was sentenced. An elderly Hispanic man slowly rose from his seat in the audience and approached counsel table. He spoke in very broken English. He said he had lost eleven family members in the fire, including three of his daughters, one of whom was pregnant, his son, his son's wife, and their four children. He told the judge he was from Mexico and was not familiar with our laws. He then paused, pointed at the defendant and asked the judge, "Why is he still alive?" He then turned slowly and walked back to his seat. The courtroom was packed, yet eerily silent. The judge broke the silence with a question to me: "What is the People's position?" "Your honor, the defendant deserves the maximum possible sentence for the murders of twenty-five innocent people."

The judge's reading of the sentence took a long time, because he had to pronounce a sentence of 25 years-to-life on each of the 25 counts of murder. The big news would come at the end. How many murder counts would the judge run consecutively to each other—if any? The answer: all 25. The final tally was 625 years-to-life (25 x 25)—the longest sentence, at that time, in California history—other than L-WOP. The dark humor that permeates the DA's office prompted a colleague to say with a straight face that with 50% off for good-time/work-time credits, he would be eligible for parole in 312 $^1/_2$ years.

72

JIM ROGAN

I met many interesting and unforgettable people during my years in the Criminal Justice Club. One of the most interesting and talented people I met was Jim Rogan. I was his first supervisor in the DA's office. Although Jim had little experience as an attorney, having only passed the California bar exam less than a year before, he showed exceptional talent as a trial lawyer. As his immediate supervisor, I wrote his first evaluation in August 1985—a 90-day progress report. In it I stated, "This deputy has shown exceptional sophistication as a trial lawyer, considering his limited experience." I also commented on his good sense of humor. It was not long before I realized that Jim Rogan was gifted—in many ways. I had never met anyone like him. He is a political memorabilia junkie. Packages would arrive at the Pasadena DA's office every few days from around the country. He took a trip to Plains, Georgia and returned with Jimmy Carter's pre-presidential diary he got from the president's brother, Billy.

When he was a small boy, he somehow got into a chamber of commerce meeting where California Governor Ronald Reagan was speaking. After Reagan finished speaking, little Jimmy Rogan ran up to the lectern and told the governor how much he would appreciate Reagan giving him his speech notes. The governor handed them to Jim and they are now framed on one of Jim's very crowded memorabilia walls. After Reagan's term as president ended in 1989, Jim, still a deputy DA, visited with him. Later, Jim received a very complimentary, handwritten letter from Reagan.

I remember once waiting for Jim to go to lunch. He was on the phone. I was in my pacing mode, because I had to be back in court shortly. When he got off the phone he apologized. He said he had been talking to Cary Grant. "Cary Grant!" I said. How could this new, green deputy DA be talking to movie star (of the 1940s, '50s and '60s) Cary Grant? I soon came to learn how Harry Truman had helped him with his homework, that he had been pals with Hubert Humphrey, and on and on. I knew Jim would not remain a career deputy DA as I had, and I was right. He was named to the bench in 1990, becoming California's youngest judge at age 33.

There are many humorous Jim Rogan stories, but I will limit myself to one. It occurred a few days after he became a judge in Glendale. Someone had given Jim a pair of roller skates. He wanted to try them out, but as a new judge he did not want to go skating down the street in front of his house. Jim always gets up around 4:00 a.m. Before dawn, he took his new skates to the top of the multilevel parking structure of the Glendale Galleria shopping center. Of course, the structure was empty. Jim parked his car, put on his skates and began skating.

A Glendale police car was patrolling the parking structure and pulled up alongside Jim, who was wearing sweats. The officer asked Rogan for ID. Jim displayed his new judge's badge. The cop asked Jim where he got the badge. Jim explained that he is a judge in Glendale. The cop told Jim that he is in the Glendale court all the time, and he had never seen nor heard of a Judge Rogan. Jim said the governor had only appointed him a few days before. The cop was very skeptical of Jim's story, but inasmuch as Jim wasn't breaking any laws, the cop returned Jim's badge and drove off.

Later that day, Jim was on the bench (the place where the judge sits in every courtroom) in the Glendale courthouse. His clerk interrupted the proceedings to tell Jim that the Glendale police chief was on the phone. Jim left the bench and took the call in his chambers (the judge's office). The chief asked Jim if he had lost his judge's badge. Jim said he had not. The chief told Jim that one of his patrol officers was patrolling the Galleria parking structure before dawn and stopped some guy roller skating, and when asked by the officer to produce ID, he produced a judge's badge with Rogan's name on it. Jim said, "That was me." After a long pause, the chief said, "Damn, I just lost $20.00."

As I had predicted, Jim gave up his judicial robes after only four years to run for a seat in the California State Assembly. He won the election and rose to become the Majority Leader in a short time. During Jim's time as Majority Leader, I wrote two criminal justice bills. One bill required all felony defendants to be fingerprinted at their arraignment.[7] The fingerprint became a part of the superior court file. Thereafter, when a person is picked up on an arrest warrant for failing to appear in court and claims he is the wrong person, his prints can be quickly compared in court. Before this new law, the wrong man, who had the same name as the fugitive defendant, sometimes sat in jail for days waiting for the sheriff to locate and compare his prints to the fugitive's.

The other bill I authored prohibits granting probation to a defendant convicted of a "violent" or "serious" felony (as defined in the Penal Code) if he was already on probation for a previous felony conviction when he committed the new felony offense.[8] The reader might wonder what kind of judge would place a defendant on probation for committing a serious or violent felony when he was already on probation for committing a felony. It happened often enough that I believed legislation was required to prevent it from ever happening again. It was not easy going, because several liberal Democrat legislators were opposed to any mandatory sentencing law (in this case, the mandatory denial of probation) no matter how serious the crime or how lengthy the defendant's record. Jim Rogan was the driving force behind these two bills getting legislative approval.

With Governor Pete Wilson's signature, both of these bills that I wrote and helped lobby through the legislature became the law in California. When I was working on the assembly line at General Motors or delivering liquor on the Sunset Strip, I could not have imagined that one day I would write a bill that would become law.

Jim soon had his eye on Washington. In 1996, he ran and won a seat in Congress, thus, becoming my congressman. I once went to a $100 per seat Rogan fund raiser. I waited in a receiving line to shake his hand. Once I reached him, he asked me whether, when I was mentoring him in the DA's office, I ever thought I would pay $100 to hear him speak and wait in line to shake his hand. I replied, "Hell no"—but I lied.

Although Jim was re-elected to Congress in 1998, he was targeted by the Hollywood liberal establishment and defeated in 2000, the result of his very active role in the impeachment trial of President Clinton, as well as the fact that the demographics in his congressional district had shifted in favor of the Democrats.

In October 2006, Governor Schwarzenegger appointed Jim to a superior court judgeship in Orange County, California. One month later, President Bush nominated Jim to a federal judgeship in Los Angeles, and at this writing he is awaiting Senate confirmation.

73

MY FIRST MURDER TRIAL— THE HAND

I have already discussed the first murder case that was assigned to me: the case of the real estate agent who killed her husband. That case never went to a jury trial. My first murder case I tried before a jury was quite macabre. A woman was walking her dog near some railroad tracks. When she returned home, she noticed that her dog had what appeared to be a big clump of dirt in its mouth. The woman tried to get the dog to drop the clump, but the dog crawled under a car and wouldn't come out. Finally, the woman was able to grab hold of the dog's collar and pull him from under the car. The woman, with some effort, removed the clump of dirt from her dog's grip and began to break it apart. The first thing she saw was a ring. She brushed more dirt away and realized the ring was on the finger of a partially decomposed hand. Startled, she called the police.

The woman led the police on the same route she took when she had walked her dog. The police found a partially decomposed female body in a shallow grave near the railroad tracks. It was wrapped in a large piece of pale-green plastic.

It was 1971. My supervisor came into my 6th floor cubbyhole of an office in the old Hall of Justice—a year before the Criminal Courts Building was built across the street. He put a file on my desk. He said he was assigning the case to me and left. I saw that it was a murder case. I opened the file and read that J. Miller Leavy, my supervisor's supervisor and a legendary trial attorney, had approved seeking the death penalty. I realized that the assignment of this case to me had to be a mistake, because I had never tried a murder case. Deputy DAs try many murder cases before being assigned a death penalty case. I took the case back to my supervisor and told him there must be a mistake. I told him I had never tried a murder case, and Mr. Leavy had approved the death penalty. With a sweep of his hand, my supervisor dismissed me and said, "Go on, you can handle it."

I took the file back to my office. I was looking for the date the trial was set. I could not find it anywhere. This was long before computers. With great reluctance, because of my fear of looking like a dolt, I went back to my supervisor and asked him when the case was set for trial. With exasperation in his voice he said, "I told you, the jury is there now." Any obsequiousness I might have displayed earlier was now gone. I said, "You *are* kidding, of course. Is this some kind of ritualistic test to see how I will react? I don't know the first thing about trying a death penalty case. I haven't had time to read the file. I don't know who my witnesses are, and I'm supposed to ask the jury to kill this guy?" During my career as a DA, I never heard of a hand-off of a death penalty case.

My supervisor assured me that if I told the judge that I had just been assigned the case, he would give me a short continuance. I couldn't believe this was happening. I didn't know how to voir dire jurors in a death penalty case. Voir dire, as discussed earlier, is the process of jury selection. The purpose is to ask the prospective jurors probing questions designed to reveal biases that would prevent the prospective juror from giving both sides a fair trial. But in a death penalty case, the voir dire is also designed to weed out those jurors who could never, under any circumstances, vote for the death penalty, or those jurors who would always vote in favor of the death penalty—regardless of the evidence presented in the penalty phase of the trial. Of course, we do not reach a penalty phase unless the jury finds the defendant guilty of first-degree murder.

Before I left for court, I told my office mate what was happening and what court I was going to. He told me, "Too bad, the PD owns that courtroom." That means the PD and the judge are close, and the PD dominated the courtroom.

I went to the courtroom which was in the same building. I saw the prospective jurors who filled every seat in the spectator section. Everyone had been waiting for the prosecutor to show up. I did not want to tell the judge in front of the prospective jurors that I knew nothing about the case, so I asked the judge if we could discuss a matter of importance in chambers. When the PD, the judge, and I went into chambers, I told him of my plight and asked for a continuance. The PD objected, and the judge denied my request for a continuance. He ordered me to be ready the next morning for jury selection.

I was up nearly all night, reading my file and learning about death penalty voir dire, listing my witnesses and exhibits to introduce into evidence, and doing all the necessary things a DA must do to prepare for trial.

The defendant, the victim's boyfriend, had murdered her and buried her in the shallow grave near the railroad tracks. I had several witnesses who heard the defendant tell his girlfriend on several occasions that he would kill her if she tried to leave him. I also had several witnesses who identified the green, plastic material the body was wrapped in as resembling the cover that had been on the defendant's couch for years, but was no longer seen on his couch after his girlfriend disappeared. The victim had been missing for a few months before the woman's dog exhumed her hand.

The defendant had given a tape-recorded statement that was inconsistent with some physical evidence. The defendant did not take the stand, and there was no explanation for his missing couch cover. The victim's mother testified that her daughter was afraid of the defendant and had tried to leave him at the time she disappeared.

It was important to bring the green couch cover into the courtroom so the witnesses could identify it in front of the jury. The smell was indescribably bad. The PD had tried to keep it out, (i.e. prevent the jury from seeing the real thing, in lieu of a photo) but the judge ruled in my favor. Several jurors, as well as the witnesses on the witness stand, had to cover their noses with their handkerchiefs to avoid gagging.

Every DA should interview his witnesses prior to trial, but in this case there was no time for that. So each day, after the trial was adjourned for that day, I had to drive to witnesses' homes to interview them. One late afternoon after work, a colleague and I drove to the home of the victim's mother to interview her. Before we got out of my car, several black, teenage males surrounded my car pounding on it and chanting, "Piggy, piggy, piggy," a favorite epithet directed towards police in the 1960s and 1970s.

Here we were, dressed in business suits, driving my own car—and they had us pegged as connected to law enforcement. How could they know? We didn't feel it would be smart to get out of the car so we drove to the nearby LAPD Newton Division police station. We told the watch sergeant our situation and he laughed. He said to us, "Don't you know you can't just drive to that neighborhood and get out of your car. Where do you think you are? Are you crazy?" The cops had a good laugh at our expense. The watch sergeant dispatched a patrol car to follow us back to the mother's house. The police car sat behind my car the entire time it took me to interview the murder victim's mother.

After all witnesses had testified, I felt I had proved beyond a reasonable doubt that the defendant had committed first-degree murder on the theory that the murder was willful, deliberate and premeditated. It is customary, at least in Los Angeles County, for the DA to submit to the judge all the jury instructions the judge will read to the jury. The jury instructions contain the law that applies in that case. It is also customary for the DA, the defense attorney, and the judge to review the proposed jury instructions in the judge's chambers prior to the closing arguments in order to give the defense attorney the opportunity to object to any particular jury instruction the DA is submitting.

As the judge was going through the instructions, I noticed he was making two piles of them. I asked him the reason for the two piles. He said he didn't believe the jury should be instructed on first-degree murder, and he was removing all first-degree murder instructions. I couldn't believe it. The judge was not going to allow the jury to even consider finding the defendant guilty of first-degree murder! He said he would only give second-degree murder and manslaughter instructions. He said there was insufficient evidence of "deliberation" and "premeditation" (each has its own definition) for the jury to find the defendant guilty of first-degree murder.

I protested passionately. I told the judge there was over-whelming evidence of deliberation and premeditation, and that there were numerous appellate court cases affirming first-degree murder convictions with *less* evidence of these two elements than I had presented. The PD just sat there. He knew he didn't have to enter the fray. It occurred to me that the judge's motive in refusing to instruct the jury on first-degree murder was that it would allow him to avoid the issue of the death penalty. As mentioned, the death penalty can only be imposed on a defendant convicted of first-degree murder. In 1971, there was no such thing as a "special circumstance" allegation. That was not required until 1978 after Prop 7 passed.

The judge said that if I could show him one appellate case supporting my position, he would consider instructing the jury on first-degree murder. But he told me I only had the lunch hour to find that case. Needless to say, I worked through lunch.

I've always been a good researcher. In fact, I have always believed that I've won most of my cases in the law library. For many years, I counseled new deputy DAs that one of their main functions as DAs was to lock the judge into the law by citing (showing) the judge an appellate case in our favor that binds the judge, under the legal doctrine of *stare decicis*, to apply the *holding* of that case to the present case. This often requires a good deal of research to find that case. I've never researched the law by using a computer. To this day, I don't know how.

I got lucky. I found a case *on all fours*, a legal expression meaning the facts are nearly identical. The case involved a boyfriend/girlfriend situation in which the boyfriend had threatened repeatedly to kill her if she left him. She tried to leave him and he killed her. The appellate court discussed the sufficiency of the "deliberation" and "premeditation" evidence, which was less than in my case, and affirmed (upheld) the first-degree murder conviction. I submitted the case to the judge after lunch. I told him this case was controlling authority that required him to instruct the jury on first-degree murder. The judge read the case and, being an honorable man, he had no choice but to agree. The doctrine of stare decicis says the judge is bound to apply the holding in the appellate case if the facts in the present case cannot be distinguished from the facts in the appellate case.

It was checkmate. The judge instructed the jury on the law of first-degree murder (as well as second-degree murder and manslaughter) and the jury convicted the defendant of first-degree murder. We then entered into a separate phase of the trial called the penalty phase. The same jury that heard the evidence in the guilt phase would now hear the penalty-phase evidence. In the penalty phase, evidence is admissible that the jury would not be allowed to hear in the guilt phase, such as prior acts of violence and prior felony convictions. Before 1978, the jury in the penalty phase had two choices: life or death. There was no L-WOP for first-degree murder until 1978. The jury deliberated for $1^1/_2$ days and finally returned with a sentence of "life." A "life" sentence in 1971, as well as in 2007, means that the defendant is eligible for parole in seven years. However, prior to Prop 7 in 1978, a defendant convicted in California of first-degree murder and sentenced to "life" served, on average, approximately 139 months or 11 $^1/_2$ years in prison.

74

DEATH PENALTY CASES— PRIOR MURDER EVIDENCE

As mentioned earlier, it was not uncommon in the 1970s for a defendant, convicted of murder, to have a prior murder conviction of which the jury did not become aware until the penalty phase of a death penalty case. I remember one jury that became upset with the DA after learning for the first time in the penalty phase that the defendant had a prior murder conviction.

The defense attorney and the DA talked to the jurors after they rendered their penalty verdict. The jury explained how they had agonized in the guilt phase in arriving at a first-degree murder verdict. They complained that if they had known the defendant had been convicted of another murder several years before, they would not have had such a difficult time convicting him of the current murder. The defense attorney and the DA tried to explain to the jurors that that is the very reason the law prohibits the jury from learning about the prior murder conviction in the guilt phase— unless the defendant testifies. Convicting someone of murder, or of any crime, is not supposed to be easy. And, convincing all twelve jurors beyond a reasonable doubt is not easy. That is the reason DAs reject so many cases that the police believe are good, solid cases.

I have mentioned the dark humor that permeates the DA's office. The truth is that it is widespread within the Criminal Justice Club. For a period of time in the 1970s, we had a weekly, doubles tennis game in the evening after work. One of the players was a PD. On one of our tennis nights, the PD showed up nearly an hour late. As this was long before cell phones, he was unable to call us. When he finally did arrive, he looked dejected. We were all very eager to know what happened. The PD apologized but explained that he was in a death penalty case, and his penalty-phase jury returned late in the day with a death verdict for his client. We asked what the penalty-phase evidence was. He said it was a prior murder conviction. I said, "What did you expect? Your jury just found out for the first time in the penalty phase that your client had murdered before." The PD looked very somber and said, "I don't know, I'm getting to think that whenever the public defender's office decides it wants a guy snuffed, they assign me the case."

We laughed, forgave him for being late and played tennis. Sound hardhearted not to feel sympathy for this two-time convicted murderer? We could all laugh because we knew justice had been achieved. The defendant's death sentence was later reduced to life when the death penalty in California was declared unconstitutional. As mentioned, the death penalty statute was later rewritten and reinstated by a vote of the people in 1978 when they passed Proposition 7.

The reason we rarely see defendants today with prior murder convictions is that Proposition 7 sets sentences at 25 years-to-life and 15 years-to-life for first- and second-degree murder, respectively. That ended the practice of releasing second-degree murderers after serving less than five years and first-degree murderers who typically served under twelve years.

7 5

THE CHARLENE HARTSOUGH
MURDER CASE

For twelve years of my DA career, 1985-1997, I was assigned to the Pasadena Branch Office, located about a mile from the Rose Bowl. One of my unforgettable cases occurred in Pasadena. The murder victim's name was Charlene Hartsough. Her husband, Chris, was employed as an engineer at the Jet Propulsion Laboratory (JPL), a part of NASA.

On April 23, 1986, Chris left home for work about 7 a.m. Charlene was taking a morning class at a nearby junior college. Her class was over at 11a.m. Charlene usually came home for lunch. Chris had lunch at a restaurant that day with some colleagues. He called home and received no answer. Concerned, he went home after lunch, arriving about 1 p.m. Upon entering the house, he called out for Charlene. No answer. Upon entering the den, he saw a scene he would never forget. Chris knew immediately Charlene was dead. Her body was spread over the couch. The telephone cord was wrapped around her neck. There was a large, heavy, broken lamp nearby. There was blood splattered on the wall. Her face was covered with blood. The coroner later determined that nearly every bone in her head had been broken.

Chris knew he had to call the police, but fainted before he could reach the phone. When he regained consciousness, he called 911 and reported his wife had been murdered. When the Pasadena police officers arrived, they saw that a window screen had been pulled away from the window, which had been broken out. Outside the broken window, they saw what appeared to be a tennis shoe print in the dirt. The house had been ransacked and Chris noticed his VCR was missing.

Before noon that same morning, Anthony Trotter, age 24, walked into the Pasadena police station. He told the officer at the desk he thought there was a warrant out for his arrest for DUI. Trotter said he wanted to turn himself in on the warrant. He gave the officer his name and date of birth, and the officer found the warrant. As he began to book Trotter into the jail, he noticed blood spatter on both of his shoes and a small amount of blood on his left arm. The officer asked Trotter how he got blood on his shoes. Trotter looked at his shoes and for a moment he looked incredulous. Then he explained that en route to the police station he kicked a dog that was trying to bite him.

The police at this time were not aware there had been a murder. Nevertheless, the booking officer notified a detective that Anthony Trotter, known to the police as an active residential burglar, had surrendered on a DUI warrant and had blood on his shoes. But it was not until about 1:30 p.m., after the police had responded to the murder scene, that the detectives thought there might be a connection between Trotter and the murder. They rushed back to the jail, but it was too late. Trotter had been able to wash every bit of blood out of his tennis shoes by using the sink in his cell. He had also washed the blood off his arm. The detectives noticed both of his pant legs were wet. The detectives asked Trotter why his pant legs were wet. Trotter said he had stepped in a puddle. The detectives took Trotter's shoes and all of his clothes for evidence.

The shoes were taken to the murder scene to be compared with the shoeprint outside the broken window. The pattern looked similar. Photos were taken, and a plaster cast was made of the shoeprint. Trotter's shoes, the photos of the shoeprint, and the plaster cast were all sent to the sheriff's crime lab for analysis. The crime lab criminalist made the comparison and wrote a report that said Trotter's shoe "probably" made the shoeprint in the dirt, but he could not make a positive identification.

Trotter's parents lived only $1^1/2$ blocks from the home of Chris and Charlene. The police, knowing that Trotter was an active residential burglar, suspected that Trotter turned himself in on the warrant in an attempt to give himself an alibi for the murder.

Several hours after Trotter surrendered on the warrant, detectives advised him of his Miranda rights. Trotter gave up his right to remain silent and to have an attorney present and agreed to speak to the detectives. Trotter told the detectives he knew nothing about a murder in Pasadena that morning. When the detectives said they did not believe him, Trotter told them he would not talk to them any more without a lawyer. The detectives left.

The next day the detectives received word that Trotter wanted to speak to them. The detectives reminded Trotter of his constitutional rights, but Trotter told them he would only speak to them "off the record." As mentioned earlier, an off-the-record statement means that the suspect wants to make a statement, but he does not want his statement used against him in court. An off-the-record statement cannot be used in court because the suspect has not waived (given up) his Miranda rights to remain silent and to have an attorney present. Off-the-record confessions to the police by career criminals are not uncommon. Naturally, the police would rather have a suspect waive his Miranda rights and make an incriminating statement which can be used in court, but absent that, they welcome off-the-record confessions because it allows them to "clear" unsolved crimes.

When detectives clear unsolved crimes as a result of off-the-record confessions, they take the case to the DA's office and request a reject based on insufficiency of the evidence. In 1986, Trotter confessed, off the record, to 24 residential burglaries. There was no other evidence, other than his unusable confessions, to connect him to the burglaries. Consequently, all 24 burglary cases were rejected by the Pasadena DA's office.

When Trotter told the homicide detectives he would only speak off the record, the detectives had no alternative but to agree if they wanted to learn what happened. The detectives agreed to hear Trotter's statement with the understanding it would be off the record. They asked Trotter if he objected to the statement being tape-recorded. Trotter said he had no objection. Trotter told the detectives in the recorded statement that he broke into the house by breaking the window. He said while he was going through the house looking for things to take, a lady came home. Trotter said the lady was holding a knife on him. Trotter said that when the lady picked up the phone to call the police he attacked her. He first choked her with his hands. Then he wrapped the telephone cord around her neck and strangled her until blood started gurgling from her mouth, and she fell into unconsciousness. He then picked up the lamp and hit her in the head two or three times. He took a VCR and some jewelry. He traded the VCR for some cocaine, and he and two friends then smoked the coke. He then went to another area and traded the jewelry for more cocaine. It was then that he got the idea of surrendering on the DUI warrant. Trotter said that while he was being booked, it was called to his attention that he had blood on his shoes. He washed the blood out in the sink in his cell. He told the detectives that he supported his $200-per-day coke habit by committing burglaries. Trotter told the detectives he had committed about 40 burglaries in the previous two months.

When Trotter finished his confession, one of the detectives asked him if he wanted to go back on the record. Trotter said he wanted his lunch. Trotter said that after lunch he would repeat his confession on the record. But after Trotter had lunch, he told the detectives he had thought it over and decided it would not be in his best interest to say any more.

At this point, although we had a tape-recorded confession, we had insufficient evidence to file a murder charge against Trotter, because we could not use the confession in court. The law says that once a suspect invokes his Miranda right to remain silent, the interrogation must cease. The officers could not again approach Trotter to ask him to talk. However, the law also says that if the suspect, who had invoked his Miranda right to remain silent, changes his mind and asks to speak to a detective, the detective may speak with him.

The challenge for the Pasadena detectives was to help Trotter change his mind without asking him if he changed his mind. They got a bright idea. They were aware that a female police officer, Mary Goldie, had known Trotter and his parents for many years. Officer Goldie had been a juvenile officer and had counseled Trotter when he was a juvenile. The plan was to give two of the jailers a script to read loudly within earshot of Trotter. Here is how it went: Jailer # 1:"Is Mary Goldie working today?" Jailer #2: "Yeah, I think I saw her out back earlier." Jailer #1: "The guy in cell# F2 (not Trotter) wants to speak with her." Jailer #1: "Well, you'd better call her. The last time somebody asked for her and I didn't call, she got real mad."

Trotter overheard this exchange and yelled to the jailers, "Tell her I want to talk to her too." The ploy worked! Officer Goldie was waiting a short distance away with a tape recorder hidden in her clothes. Officer Goldie said, "Hi, Anthony." The first thing Trotter said was to request that their conversation be off the record. He told Officer Goldie that he was not ready to speak on the record. Trotter then went on to give Officer Goldie a lengthy tape-recorded confession to murdering Charlene Hartsough. Many times during their conversation Officer Goldie told Trotter she had always considered him to be very smart. Trotter told Officer Goldie that this was the first time he had killed anyone. Trotter told Officer Goldie, "I want to get to court, get my time and get it over with, then start a new life." Trotter then asked her, "So, once I do get out, it will be pretty difficult for me to find employment, right?" In another part of the statement, Trotter asked Officer Goldie, "The type of violent crime that I did, is there a possibility that I might perhaps get five years?"

This was not an unreasonable question. This was not the first time, as a deputy DA, that I had heard a murder suspect express his belief to detectives that he would start a new life after he completed his sentence for murder. Remember, up until 1978, second-degree murderers typically served under five years and first-degree murderers served under twelve. In the 1970s and 1980s, the people who lived in the criminal subculture often knew people who were on the street after having completed their sentences for murder. These people often knew approximately how much time one really served for murder. Only the law-abiding citizens were kept in the dark.

If a person who is living in the criminal subculture knows, worst case scenario, that convicted murderers only serve five or twelve years, arguably he would less likely be deterred from committing murder than if he knew that murderers served twenty-five or thirty years or a true life sentence in prison. Although many criminals would probably not be deterred by lengthier sentences (see Chapter 31), logic and my experience tell me that some criminals would.

So here we had two off-the-record, detailed, tape-recorded confessions to a brutal murder of an innocent housewife, neither of which we could use in court. We had a shoeprint that our criminalist would testify was "probably," but not "positively," made by Trotter's shoe. And we had what appeared to be blood on Trotter's arm and shoes—later washed away. That was it. We needed a miracle to avoid rejecting the case and allowing Trotter to walk out of jail. And we got it.

I received a phone call from Chris Hartsough. I had read his name in the police reports, but I had not spoken to him. He asked me if I was the DA on the case. I said I was. He asked if I would have any objection if he visited Trotter's parents. I asked him why he would want to do that. He said he felt very bad for Trotter's parents, and he wanted to tell them how sorry he was that their son was in jail for murdering his wife. I was stunned by this magnanimous gesture. Here was a man whose wife was viciously murdered, and he was expressing sympathy for the killer's parents!

Chris Hartsough had somehow heard that Trotter had confessed. What he did not know was that no jury would ever hear the confession. I did not want to tell Chris that we had no case against Trotter. Then it came to me. I called my investigating officer (I/O) and told him about Chris Hartsough's plan to visit Trotter's parents. My I/O met with Chris and asked him if he would agree to wear a wire when he visited Trotter's parents. Chris agreed. The I/O asked Chris to ask Trotter's parents why they thought their son would do a thing like this to his wife. Incidentally, for the readers who may be wondering, yes, surreptitiously tape-recording Trotter's parents by the police or Chris Hartsough, under these circumstances, is legal.

Although Chris' initial motive in wanting to visit Trotter's parents was simply to express his sympathy, his visit cemented our case against Trotter. Here is what happened: Chris visited the parents and expressed his condolences. He then asked them if they had talked to their son. Both said they had visited their son in the county jail where he had been transferred from the Pasadena jail. Both parents said he had admitted killing the lady because she wouldn't let him out of the house.

Even non-Club members realize that it is not necessary for parents (or anybody else, other than police officers) to "Mirandize" (read the Miranda rights to) a suspect before speaking with him. I now had a confession to murder from the defendant to his parents—the two people who are the least likely people on the planet to lie about receiving a confession. Of course, I expected the parents, when called to the witness stand, to deny what they told Chris. But the entire conversation was tape-recorded.

Yes, OK, I felt bad about having to use Trotter's parents to convict their son of murder and put him in prison, possibly for the rest of his life. But the alternative was to let him go and hope he didn't kill again in a future burglary. That, of course, was not a realistic alternative. I called both parents as witnesses at the prelim.

As mentioned, in every felony case in California there is a preliminary hearing—unless the grand jury indicts the defendant. In contrast to the federal system, an indictment is relatively rare in state court. Full discovery does not usually occur before the preliminary hearing. Trotter's defense attorney was not aware, prior to the preliminary hearing, that his client's parents' conversation with Chris Hartsough was tape-recorded. If he had been aware of the tape recording, I doubt that I would have been able to locate the parents to call them as witnesses at the prelim; and the rules of evidence would not have permitted me to simply play the tape in court without putting the parents on the witness stand—or at least have them in court to be identified by Chris.

When Trotter's mother took the stand, she denied that her son had confessed the murder to her. I then played the taped conversation between herself, her husband, and Chris. At the point she is heard on the tape saying that her son told her the lady wouldn't let him out of the house, she testified it was not her voice on the tape. It was really very sad, this seemingly nice lady fighting to save her son. Finally, though, she admitted that the only three people in the conversation were herself, her husband, and Chris Hartsough. She also finally admitted on the witness stand that what she told Chris was true, that her son admitted killing the lady when she caught him burglarizing her house. Trotter's father was also called as a witness and also reluctantly related his son's confession.

That was it. The case was effectively over. Even if the parents later disappeared and could not be located for the trial, the law permits the DA to read the parents' prelim testimony into the record at the trial, and the jury would have heard about Trotter's confession to his parents.

Trotter had no options left but to plead guilty to first-degree murder. He admitted two special circumstance allegations, i.e., that the murder was committed while he was engaged in the crimes of robbery (because he took property by force or fear in Charlene's presence) and burglary—entering Charlene's house to commit theft. He was sentenced to life in prison without the possibility of parole.

Naturally, my goal as a prosecutor was always to build the strongest case I could against a defendant. I always had a long "to do" list for my investigating officers. The cases I tried were *never* even close to being ready for trial when they were filed. There was always more to do to build a stronger case: witnesses to find or to interview, additional scientific tests to perform, legal research to do, loose ends to tie up, etc. It was like the proverbial iceberg, two-thirds below the surface, one-third above. In my cases, it seemed more like 90% preparation whereas the jury saw only the top 10%.

I thought of my criminal trials like a chess game in terms of trying to anticipate the defense strategy, and then planning to counter it. I frequently prepared for defense moves that were never made. My greatest fear was being caught by surprise by a defense story or tactic I had not anticipated, but I cannot remember it ever happening. I was almost always overprepared except in the early days when I was given hand-offs and there was no time to prepare. My goal was always to prepare my cases so well that the defendant would not risk a jury trial but, instead, would have no realistic alternative to pleading guilty. I recall a case where the defendant pled guilty after hearing my opening statement to the jury. A plea of guilty is the best kind of conviction, because it is difficult to appeal from a guilty plea.

76

THE ACLU "DEBATE"

In the late 1970s, when I was Deputy in Charge of the Glendale Area Office, I received a call from one of the top supervisors in the office. He asked me to represent the DA's office in a debate with a *Los Angeles Times* columnist, the late Phil Kirby. The debate was to be held at a chapter of the ACLU. I asked what the debate topic was. He said I was to debate the question whether police should ever be able to search a newspaper office—even with a search warrant. I jokingly asked if I were being punished for something. I told my supervisor that debating this subject in front of an audience of ACLU members was a no-win proposition for a deputy DA. But I had no choice. This was a command invitation.

I spent much of the following weekend in the Los Angeles County Law Library. While I was poring over U.S. Supreme Court decisions dealing with the First Amendment and freedom of the press issues, my debate strategy came to me. If the police could not search a newsroom, even with a search warrant signed by a judge, this would place newspapers above the law. It had only been a few years since President Nixon had been ordered by the U.S. Supreme Court to produce the Watergate tapes, proving that even the president is not above the law in this country.

Presumably, Phil Kirby was going to take the position that freedom of the press is so precious, so sacrosanct, that under no circumstances should a newspaper office ever be subjected to police searches. On the surface, this view has some appeal. I could envision Gestapo-type tactics—police marching into a newspaper office, searching the files and smashing the presses. I deeply believe that no democracy can long endure in the absence of a free press. And it is frightening to imagine a system that would permit a newspaper that, for example, has been critical of the politicians currently in power, to be the target of harassment from those politicians who use the police power of the state to attempt to intimidate that newspaper. That would be intolerable. But having said that, we should also not place any person or institution, including the press, beyond the reach of the law.

Of course, when we hear the word "newspaper," we probably think of a paper of the stature of the *New York Times* or *Los Angeles Times*. But in this country anybody can start a newspaper. There are very big and very small newspapers. And the same law regarding searches of newspapers would apply equally regardless of the size or the stature of the newspaper.

The debate was held in a private home in Westwood, a very affluent neighborhood. At the start of the debate, I was permitted to go first. Here is the scenario I presented: I asked the ACLU audience (largely Jewish), to assume that the PLO (Palestine Liberation Organization) had an underground cell in Los Angeles that prints a newspaper and distributes anti-Semitic literature. This PLO cell sends a message to the B'nai B'rith, a Jewish organization, threatening to blow up certain synagogues in Southern California, unless $10,000,000 is paid within a specified time at a designated drop point. The B'nai B'rith reports the threat to the police. The police learn that there is an FBI agent who has infiltrated this local PLO cell. The police contact this undercover FBI agent and inform him of the PLO threat to bomb synagogues. The FBI agent tells the police he will find out what he can. The FBI agent learns that the notes containing the names of the leaders of the plot, the locations of the synagogues, and the times they are to be blown up are located in the safe within the PLO newspaper office. The police go to a judge to seek a search warrant to seize that evidence. I told the audience that if Phil Kirby had his way, the judge would not be authorized to issue the search warrant because the place to be searched was in a newspaper office. Either the B'nai B'rith would have to pay the $10,000,000 or the synagogues would be blown up.

The debate moderator asked Mr. Kirby for his response to my scenario. He replied that my scenario could never happen. The moderator asked, "But what if it did?" Again, Mr. Kirby said the scenario could never happen. And that was the end of the so-called debate. We then stood around talking and indulging in coffee and cookies. Some of the ACLU members told me in lowered voices afterwards that they realized how dangerous it would be to place any person or any institution above the law, no matter how highly revered the person or institution.

77

BEING TESTED BY THE
L.A. TIMES TEST

I tried a murder case late in my career that is worthy of note. The murder occurred in June 1995. A fifty-nine-year-old woman living in a nice neighborhood in Pasadena failed to show up at work on June 6. A colleague called her home all day, but there was no answer. Finally, the next day, when she again failed to show up at work, the colleague called the police and asked them to check her house. When a police officer arrived at the house on June 7, he rang the doorbell. No response. The officer walked around the house, but saw no evidence of forced entry into the house. The officer entered the house through an unlocked window. Upon entry, the officer smelled natural gas. He went to the kitchen and saw that one of the gas burners on the stove was on and lit. Another gas burner was on but was not lit. The officer looked through the house and discovered the victim's burnt body in a bedroom. She was lying on her back on the floor, rolled up in blankets. The fire had smoldered and had burned a hole in the floor directly under the body. It appeared the victim had suffered two blows to her head. The crime scene investigators lifted a very detailed tennis shoe print left on the hardwood floor in the dining room.

The victim's adult daughter told the police that her mother had a Visa card. It was not found. But what was found, hidden under a sewing machine, was $2,000 in cash. A police detective checked with Visa the next day. Visa told the detective that the victim's Visa card had been used in a Las Vegas casino on June 6. The detective contacted the casino. The manager of the casino remembered the Visa transaction and told the detective that the man who used the victim's credit card was a regular customer of the casino. The detective told the casino manager to call him next time the man entered the casino. The next day, the man returned to the casino and was arrested by the Las Vegas police who had been alerted by the Pasadena police.

The suspect, age 34, turned out to be a former boyfriend of the victim's daughter. He and the daughter had lived in the victim's home for a short time. Neither the victim nor the victim's daughter had seen him for about two years—ever since he was arrested for assaulting the daughter and using the victim's credit card without her permission. The victim had ordered him to leave her house. He now lived with his new girlfriend in Las Vegas.

The Pasadena detectives flew to Las Vegas and obtained a search warrant for the suspect's apartment. During the search, the police found several items that had been taken from the victim's home, including her driver's license, MasterCard, and some of her jewelry which was identified by the victim's daughter.

I filed the case and charged the suspect with murder, residential burglary, robbery and arson. I also charged two special circumstance allegations: that the murder was committed during the commission of a burglary and a robbery. Either of these special circumstance allegations, if found to be true by the jury, made the defendant eligible for either the death penalty or L-WOP. The defendant had no prior criminal record. We did not seek the death penalty. The defendant waived extradition, meaning that he gave up his right to a formal extradition hearing and agreed to accompany the Pasadena police detectives back to Los Angeles.

Months later, when I was preparing this case for the preliminary hearing, I could not find any mention in the police reports that the detectives had booked (listed as evidence and preserved) the defendant's shoes. His shoes could be important because of the shoeprint lifted at the crime scene. I called the detective. He told me that in all the rush of obtaining the search warrant in Las Vegas and finding and inventorying the victim's property, they simply forgot to take and book the defendant's shoes. I thought I had surely lost this important evidence, but nevertheless I obtained a court order directing the sheriff to go to the defendant's jail cell and remove and book the shoes he was wearing. This was done. I then requested the sheriff's crime lab to compare the soles of the defendant's shoes to the shoeprint lifted from the crime scene.

The criminalist testified that no shoe, other than the defendant's left shoe, could have made the shoeprint at the crime scene. The reason the criminalist could be so positive is that it is not just the pattern on the sole that is compared to the shoeprint. The soles of tennis shoes have little cuts, gouges and wear patterns. The print they leave can be as distinctive as fingerprints. Just to be sure, the criminalist asked his supervisor to perform her own independent comparison. She arrived at the same conclusion. I got very lucky; lucky that the defendant was still wearing the same shoes when he was arrested that he wore when he murdered the victim; and lucky that he had not yet read the police reports. If he had read the police reports while in his jail cell, he would have seen that a shoeprint lift was made at the crime scene. If he had known that, I doubt that he would still have been wearing the same shoes while sitting in his cell. Somehow, he would have gotten rid of them, for example, by trading shoes with another inmate.

In selecting the jury, I decided to leave on the jury a woman who was attractive, articulate, and intelligent. Her answers on her jury questionnaire indicated that she was affiliated with various liberal causes, which admittedly gave me pause. But her sister was a Los Angeles County deputy DA, and I believed that may have had a neutralizing effect. During jury selection, the PD and I had a soft drink in the court cafeteria during a court recess. We discussed which one of us was going to bump (excuse) this prospective juror. He said I should bump her because of her liberal affiliations. I told him he should bump her because her sister was a deputy DA. Whichever side bumped her must use one of the valuable peremptory challenges that each side is given. Neither one of us bumped her.

The county medical examiner who performed the autopsy testified the victim died from two blows to the head—not from the fire. The defendant's new girlfriend testified that she and the defendant were both heavy gamblers, and they did not have the money to pay their rent in Las Vegas. She testified the defendant left for Los Angeles on June 5, allegedly to borrow the rent money from his brother. She also testified that on June 6, the defendant returned to Las Vegas. He had with him the victim's driver's license, jewelry, etc. She identified an envelope recovered during the search of the defendant's apartment. On the envelope, the victim's purported signature had been written repeatedly. The girlfriend testified that she was instructed by the defendant to practice signing the victim's name on the envelope, which she did. She also testified that when the defendant returned from Los Angeles, he had a big scratch on his chest which he did not have when he left.

The jury found the defendant guilty of all counts and found the two special circumstance allegations to be true. The jury was excused. The case was set for sentencing (P&S) in three weeks as is customary in felony cases. I had an Alaskan fishing trip planned in the interim.

After the jury convicted the defendant, I received an invitation from the woman juror whose sister was a deputy DA. The juror and her husband were having a party at their house. I attended the party. I saw *the* Public Defender of Los Angeles County at the party. It was the night before I was scheduled to leave for Alaska. While talking to this former juror about what she did for a living, she mentioned that more than ten years before, she had worked in the Los Angeles County DA's Office, but only in an administrative capacity inasmuch as she was not an attorney. She explained that one of her duties was to establish an affirmative action program in the office. I was stunned by this information. I asked her why she did not include this information on her juror questionnaire. She said the questionnaire only requested employment for the last ten years, and it had been more than ten years since she had worked for the DA's office.

Even though this juror was technically correct, I knew I had to reveal this information to the defense attorney. And even though I was not aware of any statute or case law directly on point, the failure to reveal it would not have passed the L.A.Times test discussed earlier. But the next day was Saturday and I would be on a plane to Alaska. This information weighed on me the entire trip, because I knew when I told the PD that the juror whom we had debated excusing had worked in my office, he would have to make a motion (i.e., a formal written request of the judge) for a new trial.

After returning from my Alaskan vacation, I called the PD and told him. He was not happy. He knew his duty as a defense attorney required him to request a new trial based upon what he would label juror misconduct. The PD made his motion and I responded, citing the applicable law on the issue. We argued our respective positions, and the judge denied the defendant's motion for a new trial.

The victim's daughter described her mother to the probation officer as a very vibrant, outgoing, strong woman. Until this case, I had never heard of a probation officer urging in his sentencing recommendation to the judge that the defendant be executed—when the DA's office was not seeking the death penalty. He obviously felt strongly about this case. In his report to the judge, he said, "The defendant murdered a woman because he wanted her property. She had never done him any harm and had only treated him with courtesy and respect, but that did not stop him from snuffing out her life. In order to have true justice in this case, the defendant's life has to be ended, because it is not just or right for him to continue to live when he deprived an innocent woman of her right to live." The judge sentenced the defendant to life in prison without the possibility of parole. The defendant appealed, and the conviction, including the judge's denial of the defendant's motion for new trial, was affirmed by the Court of Appeal.

78

CRIME SCENE SCREW-UP— MURDERER WALKS

As the above case illustrates, whether or not a murderer is held accountable for his crime often depends on the competency of the crime scene technicians. In the case discussed above, the technician who lifted the shoeprint from the crime scene was competent and was able to collect such detail in the defendant's shoeprint that a positive match could later be made with defendant's left shoe, which placed the defendant at the crime scene. If I had been unable to place the defendant inside the victim's house through his shoeprint, his defense would likely have been that he had purchased the victim's credit cards, jewelry, and driver's license from the real killer, somebody he would claim he had earlier talked to about the victim and revealed that she always hid money in her house. One might think this would be a pretty weak defense, but it might be just enough to give one or two jurors a reasonable doubt, which would result in an 11-1 or 10-2 hung jury. Remember, next to an acquittal, this is the defense attorney's goal—to hang the jury.

A good deal of strategy goes into the defendant's objective to get that one juror who is thought most likely to hang the jury. For example, it is not uncommon for defendants charged with the most heinous crimes to wear crosses around their necks and to carry a Bible when they come to court. If the ploy results in just one juror not being able to vote for guilt, the defendant will not be convicted—regardless of the evidence.

I lost a murder case because technicians who lifted a shoeprint from a murder scene did a poor job. But I didn't lose it at trial, because the case never got to a jury trial. It was dismissed at the preliminary hearing. The case was the familiar triangle: two people in love with the same person, in this case a man and a woman both in love with another woman. The male defendant lay in wait in the bushes at night for the victim to arrive home. When she came home, he emerged from his hiding place and shot her in the face. She died that night. The defendant then ran several miles to where the object of his (and the murder victim's) affections lived. But the police were waiting for him in the wee hours of the morning and arrested him. His pants and shirt were filthy, and he had grease on the back of his shirt, as if he had been hiding under a car. He was out of breath and soaked from perspiration from running so far. I had an eyewitness who saw him running from the murder scene, but he could not be one hundred percent positive of his identification. The defendant had a strong motive for the killing. The female love object of both the defendant and the victim was in the process of dumping the defendant in favor of the female victim. There had been a recent violent confrontation between the victim and the defendant.

When the defendant was arrested, the police booked his boots into evidence. The sole of the boots had a chevron pattern. The crime scene technicians from the relatively small city police department took a photo of a shoeprint in the dirt at the murder scene. This shoeprint also had a chevron pattern. The police department had run out of plaster of Paris to make a mold of the shoeprint, so no plaster cast of the shoeprint was made. It was later discovered that the photo taken of the shoeprint did not afford the crime lab sufficient detail to enable the criminalist to make a positive match with the defendant's boot, notwithstanding the same size chevron pattern on each.

After the crime scene technician took the photo of the shoeprint in the dirt, he returned to the police station. He then decided he should take more and better photos of the shoeprint. He returned to the crime scene, but discovered that someone had walked over the shoeprint, preventing him from getting more photos.

This was a case where it was essential to place the defendant at the murder scene, which I was not able to do. After the case was dismissed at the preliminary hearing, I refiled the case—which the law permits the DA to do one time in felony cases. I went before another judge. The result was the same. If the investigating police agency had called the Los Angeles County Sheriff's crime scene techs to make a mold of the shoeprint, I have little doubt the defendant would now be serving a prison sentence for the victim's murder.

Cases like this can be quite frustrating. But as mentioned previously, in about one-half of all murders in Los Angeles County no arrest is ever made. It would be too painful to be other than "philosophical" in cases like this—where justice has failed.

Preservation of crime scenes is often crucial to a successful murder prosecution, but it is not always achieved. I once attended a police training seminar put on by the LAPD. The main speaker was a very funny LAPD police lieutenant. His premise was that you can always win money by betting that at least one police officer will, in some manner, contaminate a murder scene. He gave as an example a typical murder that occurs inside a house. He explained that very often, immediately after the murder, the killer is nervous and excited and has the urge to use the toilet. By habit, the killer flushes the toilet. The lieutenant explained that the little chrome toilet flusher is one of the best surfaces to hold fingerprints, and that many murder cases have been solved by lifting the suspect's print from the chrome flusher. The lieutenant told his audience that unless a police officer is assigned to stand guard at the bathroom door, some cop will use the bathroom, flush the toilet, and smudge the murderer's fingerprint. This seminar was given early in my career. Police officers are better trained in crime scene preservation today.

79

COULD THERE BE AN UPSIDE TO THE L.A.TIMES' LIBERAL BIAS?

Throughout this book, I have criticized the media, and particularly the *Los Angeles Times*, for their bias against the police, prosecutors, and crime victims and the lengths they will go to mislead their readers when trying to defeat criminal justice initiatives they oppose. But, I have found a possible upside to this liberal bias. As a deputy DA, I never felt pressured by anyone to do something I believed was wrong, unethical or inappropriate. I have learned that this is not always the case in other DA's offices.

Many years ago, one of our deputy DAs quit the office, because he wanted to raise his family in a more rural environment. He became a deputy DA in a small northern California county. I visited him in his new country digs, and he told me a story I would not forget. He said the police chief and the editor of the local newspaper were close friends. He told me that anytime a deputy DA rejected the filing of a case brought to them by one of the local police officers, the officer would report the rejection to the police chief who, in turn, would call his editor friend to complain about the DA's office.

The next day's newspaper would invariably criticize the DA's office and charge the elected DA with being soft on crime. My friend told me that the criticism became so frequent that DAs were filing charges in cases that should not have been filed. He was careful to say that DAs were not charging people who they thought might be innocent, but that because of the pressure from the local press, they were filing cases that ordinarily they would have rejected for lack of sufficient evidence. My friend told me that oftentimes these cases would later be dismissed by the judge at the preliminary hearing when the judge could see that the DA was less than enthusiastic about his prospects of winning the case before a jury. By shifting the onus for the dismissal to the judge, the DA avoided the bad press.

I cannot imagine having to work as a DA in such an oppressive environment. Also, I cannot imagine the Los Angeles Times accusing the DA's office of being soft on crime simply because a deputy DA exercised his or her judgment and rejected a case for legally sound, ethical reasons—even if the rejected case was a high-profile murder case. When my friend told me this story, I told him that I never thought I would ever appreciate the Los Angeles Times. However, don't misunderstand; my appreciation is very limited.

8 0

POTPOURRI

I have included in this catchall chapter some of my thoughts and experiences which have moved me, impressed me, or from which I learned something that affected my general outlook. We are all products of our genetic code, our experiences, and how we react to our experiences. Some of my experiences mentioned in this chapter have little to do with the criminal justice system, but they all contributed, in some degree, to who I am.

The Disabled Black War Vet

In the early 1960s, when I was still in law school, I saw a story on TV about a disabled, black veteran who was refused service in a restaurant in the Deep South. This was against the backdrop of southern racism, as exemplified by Bull Connor and the beatings his officers administered to nonviolent civil rights marchers led by Martin Luther King Jr. I was very moved, angered and energized by the thought of this veteran, who had sustained serious injuries fighting for his country, being refused service in a public restaurant because of his skin color. This, and other civil rights injustices, were among the reasons that compelled me to write, print, and distribute 10,000 pamphlets in 1964 pointing out Barry Goldwater's views on race and other issues. (See "More About the Author," pages 403-405.)

The East Berlin Restaurant

In the 1970s, I had a supervisor in the DA's office, Bob, who told me a story that made an impression on me. Bob told me that while on a trip with his family to Europe during the Cold War, he took his wife and two children through the Berlin wall for a one-day visit from West Berlin to communist East Berlin. Bob had a friend at the American Consulate in West Berlin. The friend recommended a restaurant on the communist side. Bob took his family to the restaurant which was open but empty. Bob asked the maitre d' for a table for four. The maitre d' told Bob that all the tables were reserved. Bob pointed out that the restaurant was empty. The maitre d' repeated that all the tables were reserved. Bob and his family left the restaurant assuming the maitre d' was a communist who disliked Americans.

The following day, Bob visited his consulate friend and told him the story of the anti-American maitre d'. The consulate official told Bob that he was not refused a table because the maitre d' was anti-American, but because there was no reason to give him a table. Bob was confused by this answer and asked for clarification. Bob's consulate friend explained that because Bob was not an important communist party official, or a high-ranking East German military officer, there was no reason to serve him. There was no profit to be gained from serving Bob and his family, because the government owned the restaurant. Bob's friend explained that the chef and waiters were probably in the kitchen having a good time socializing and drinking vodka. He told Bob there was no reason for them to stop having fun and start working when there was nothing in it for them. They all made the same money whether or not they served customers. And besides, the maitre d' knew there was nobody to whom Bob could complain.

My life's experience has taught me that man's greatest motivating force is self-interest and the opportunity for himself and his family to prosper. The communist system places severe limitations on what the ordinary person can accomplish. The communist system, in limiting one's freedom, frustrates the individual's ambitions and stifles his dreams.

The reason our capitalist system has produced the greatest economic engine the world has ever seen is that it rewards education, effort, self-discipline, tenacity, creativity and risk-taking. Our system allows the average person the opportunity to realize his or her dreams. Our system energizes those who realize that we have nearly unlimited opportunity in this country; yes, even for minorities, the poor and the great, great grandchildren of slaves— despite some of the liberal naysayers who symbolize what some have called "the soft bigotry of low expectations."

No matter how hard that maitre d' worked in the government-owned restaurant in East Berlin, he had no hope of someday owning his own restaurant or even his own home. And that is the reason the communist system is a dream killer and is destined to fail everywhere—sooner or later. Rock legend Frank Zappa said it all in one short sentence: "Communism doesn't work because people like to own stuff."

Don't misunderstand. Totally unregulated capitalism has resulted in young children working in factories twelve hours or more a day, as was the case before child labor laws. It has resulted in cars built that were too dangerous to safely drive, in air that was too unhealthy to safely breathe, food too contaminated to eat, and rivers too polluted for fish to live. And the struggle for a clean environment is far from over. Our fight for clean air, for example, seems to be a never-ending battle against those interests who want to weaken our clean-air laws. Raw, laissez-faire capitalism must be restrained to some extent by our elected representatives in the interests of basic justice and public health and safety. Despite the claims of the pure free-market folks, who rail against *any* regulation, we cannot realistically expect boards of directors and CEOs of corporations, whose allegiance is to the shareholders, to voluntarily sacrifice profit for the greater public good—even though in the long run it may be the wisest course.

Two of my more poignant experiences which further eroded my naiveté were a couple of *60 Minutes* segments I saw many years ago. Each story involved a major American auto maker. One story told about a car model that had a tendency to explode into flames when rear-ended. Several people had been killed as a result of the gas tank being positioned too close to the rear bumper. The *60 Minutes* story showed company documents which revealed that top executives in the car company had decided it was more economical for the company to pay the projected future wrongful-death settlements or judgments for the people who would burn to death than to spend the money for brackets to move the gas tanks forward a few inches.

The next story involved two retired auto company metallurgists. They told the *60 Minutes* interviewer that they had been assigned by company executives to weaken the metal in a narrow line across the hood and both fenders of their company's cars so that when the car was involved in a very low-speed, front-end collision, the hood and both fenders would buckle across the built-in weak area, which would require the car owner to purchase a new hood and fenders.

These two *60 Minutes* stories had an effect on me and provided additional evidence that mankind's alleged essential goodness, in which I was raised to believe, was a myth. But the decision makers in these two stories seemed more evil than most. The difference was that these immoral decisions were not made by street thugs but by highly educated, top executives in one of America's largest and wealthiest industries.

Although this book has been more critical of liberal Democrats than conservative Republicans, I have no doubt we would be worse off without both parties competing against one another for the public's trust. The advantage of this competition is that each party attacks the problems the other party tends to ignore or downplay. In addition, it is likely that in a one-party system, the ruling party would abuse its power—to the detriment of the public. In our present two-party system, the party out of power can be relied upon to point out every failing of the party in power—all to the benefit of the public. Thus, the watchdog role of the party out of power tends to deter the party in power from abusing its power.

Corporations have done many unethical and indefensible things in the name of self-interest. They should be held accountable by a watchful public through their elected representatives, a free press and the judicial system. But we must also be watchful of those who, purportedly acting on behalf of the general public, would strangle our free enterprise system with so many regulations that investors would not risk their money in new ventures. In the end, this hurts all of us.

We must acknowledge, for example, that new lifesaving drugs are discovered mainly because of self-interest, the hope of making big profits, with only a smidgen of altruism. Those who want to limit these profits must realize that investors would have less incentive to invest in the high-risk business of new drug development, with the tragic consequence that fewer lifesaving drugs would be developed.

Capitalism works because it appeals to and excites our desire for prosperity. It teaches us that with some talent, self-discipline, tenacity, sacrifice, and hard work, our dreams really can come true. There are many in this country who cannot abide the reality that in our free enterprise system, some people are wealthy while others are poor. Churchill said, "The inherent vice of capitalism is the unequal sharing of blessings; the inherent vice of socialism is the equal sharing of miseries."

Look at Him, Isn't He Cute. He Has a Temper Just Like His Father.

I have little doubt that when a little boy throws a temper tantrum or hits his sibling, and the boy's mother or grandmother smiles and makes a comment like the above, thereby giving the child approval and positive reinforcement for the display of an out-of-control temper, it tends to set the child on a negative course. Most boys want to be like their dads. And if the little boy's temper tantrum, or violent acts, instead of provoking condemnation, elicits a positive comparison with his father, this can result in lasting and serious damage. He will reasonably believe that a display of temper is masculine and good and is what is expected of a real boy—and later, a real man.

Most Murders in Los Angeles Are Not Reported in the Press

We filed murder cases nearly every day in the DA's office. One of the many things that surprised me when I became a deputy DA was discovering that very few murders are reported in the press—unless the suspect or the victim was a celebrity, wealthy or very good-looking. That always struck me as unfair—a kind of discrimination against the ordinary person, the poor and the plain. It seems to me that if the *L.A. Times* were really concerned about the poor and minorities, their violent end at the hands of a murderer would deserve at least a small mention.

Home on Probation

How cruel it is for juvenile courts to allow juveniles to believe they can continue to commit serious crimes repeatedly and each time be immediately released "home on probation" to the parent (usually the mother) without any sanction. The child will necessarily get the message that the crime he committed is no big deal if he suffers no penalty. It might seem compassionate, but it is cruel in the long run.

It's like allowing a pet to continue wetting on the carpet, never scolding the pet, and then when the pet wets on the carpet the eighth time to beat him severely. Wouldn't that be unfair? Why can't we see that our continued tolerance of felonious acts by juveniles is not in the best interests of the juvenile or society? Don't misunderstand; I am not suggesting that the juvenile be imprisoned for a year on his first residential burglary offense. But I do believe he should serve a few days in a juvenile facility instead of being released immediately to his parents after his arrest.

This is the point where we should expend resources to try to rehabilitate the youthful offender. One of the greatest challenges facing the system is this: How do we convince the young criminal, often a "gang banger" who has grown up without a father in the home, that getting a good education and doing homework every night, can free him from poverty and ignorance, give him hope and enable him to have choices? How do we separate this kid from the influence of his gang and convince him there is a better way?

The juvenile must receive an unambiguous message, even on his first offense, that the crime he committed will not be tolerated. The juvenile who is released immediately and repeatedly to his parents after each felony offense will not get this message. Such juveniles, who receive no penalty, crime after crime, can easily slide into becoming a second or third striker as a young adult. A few days in jail on the juvenile's first felony offense, with follow-up counseling, might be that ounce of prevention he needs to avoid a prison term a few years later as an adult.

But the allegedly "compassionate liberal" will surely oppose *any* incarceration by arguing that the juvenile will only learn to be a better criminal if he is in jail with other, more experienced criminals. I say he has already learned how to be a criminal—*before* going to jail. That is the reason he is in jail. If he is taught by the courts that there is no price to be paid for his criminal conduct, he is more likely to commit more crimes and be back in jail.

The liberal's answer to this logic would surely go something like this: "It is an oversimplification of the problem. Everything isn't so black and white. The answers are far more complicated, so complicated that only the academics can really understand the motivating causes and supply the solutions for juvenile and adult crime. Give the juvenile job training, build more parks, make him pay back his burglary victims or pay his injured victim's hospital bills. We have to get to the root causes of crime instead of simply treating the symptoms," they say. I've heard all these standard liberal responses countless times since I was a teenager. And, for many years, I repeated them myself. What do you do if he doesn't respond to job training because he prefers not to work, making $10 per hour, or less, instead of $2,000 per week selling drugs? What if he says he has no money to pay back his crime victims? What if he does have the money but refuses to pay? What if he just likes his lifestyle of gangs, crime and drugs?—which is the most common reason he continues doing what he is doing.

I agree with the liberals that for most criminals the root causes are the real culprits, but I differ with the liberals on how to attack the root causes. The liberals believe that expensive government social programs administered by uncaring bureaucrats can penetrate the juvenile's psyche, reach the root causes of his antisocial behavior and effect a cure. I have not seen much evidence of this—especially when the juvenile is already a violent or career criminal.

We may find one day that one of the root causes of criminal behavior is genetic. I have no doubt at least one major root cause of juvenile and adult criminal behavior can be traced back to having no father in the home to act as a positive role model and boundary setter for the child and adolescent. The liberals offer no remedy for this unfortunate reality, because they realize there is nothing the *government* can do to force fathers to remain home, live principled lives, and be positive role models for their children. Also, they do not feel comfortable talking about this root cause because it could be interpreted as a racial attack, and thus fail the political correctness (PC) test. And besides, liberals have an affinity for government programs—whether they work or not. Starting a big government program makes them *feel* as if something is being accomplished— like the billions of dollars spent on President Johnson's War on Poverty in the 1960s. It makes them *feel* good! The fact that nothing, or very little, is accomplished doesn't seem to bother them too much. When was the last time a liberal legislator admitted that a so-called rehabilitation program he supported had failed and urged its funding be cancelled? I can recall only one time: the MDSO program—and then only because the psychiatrists themselves confessed failure.

The Sheriff Lost My Jacket

Early in my DA career, I took a guilty plea from a defendant charged with very serious offenses including kidnapping for robbery, which called for a sentence of life in prison. At the time of sentencing, the judge asked the defendant if he wanted to say anything before he was sentenced. The defendant appeared very angry. He told the judge that for the last few months, ever since his arrest, he had been angry. The judge asked why he was so angry. The defendant told the judge that the sheriff deputies who arrested him had lost his jacket. The loss of his jacket, he said, had consumed his thoughts. I had a difficult time understanding this. How could the number one concern of a person about to be imprisoned for life be the loss of a jacket? This incident was one of many that highlighted for me the differences in our values. But this was just the beginning. There was much more to come—such as the following story.

You Promised to Get Me Coffee—Bang!

The elderly wife sent her elderly husband to the store to get some coffee. Instead, he bought a bottle of liquor. When he returned home with the liquor instead of the coffee, an argument erupted. The elderly wife shot her elderly husband. He survived. It was just another case we handled in a few minutes in the short-cause court where the elderly wife pleaded guilty to assault with a deadly weapon (ADW), received probation, and was released from jail at the urging of her elderly husband. It was no big deal for anyone—including the defendant and the victim. This case also occurred early in my career, and I was slowly, but reluctantly, accepting the fact that the values of the people I knew and the people I prosecuted were galaxies apart.

My Eleven-Year-Old Murder Witness

In the 1980s, I prosecuted a defendant for a murder that occurred in a high-crime area. One of my eyewitnesses was an eleven-year-old gang member. I had to interview this witness in preparation for the preliminary hearing. But this kid was in a juvenile detention facility awaiting his own case to come to court. My I/O and I visited him in the juvenile facility. We had with us a large aerial photo of his neighborhood which showed the murder scene. He seemed transfixed by the big blowup photo. He had never seen an aerial photo. He began identifying familiar places: "Oh look, that's the house where they killed the old lady. And look, here's the alley where they shot my brother." He was very excited. Places of violence and murder were his frames of reference. During the murder prelim, when this kid was being cross-examined by the defense attorney, this eleven-year-old threatened to kill the defense attorney. I felt this kid would probably not live though his teens.

Sociopaths

We know that sociopaths are not capable of feeling remorse. They can steal, maim or kill with no pangs of conscience. We know that many are charming but also arrogant. But there is another consistent character trait I have noticed in sociopaths. They are unrealistically optimistic. No matter how much evidence exists to prove their guilt, they believe to the end they will be acquitted. They cannot imagine twelve jurors rejecting them. And then, after they are convicted, they are optimistic about their chances on appeal—no matter how dim their chances. I do not believe they are putting on an act. They really believe it when they brag, "I'm gonna beat this case." Sometimes they do.

My 99-Stab-Wound Case

There was hardly a day in my 32-year career as a deputy DA that I did not learn something new—usually many things. I was filing a murder charge when a veteran LAPD homicide detective stuck his head in my office to say hi. He asked me what kind of case I was filing. I told him it was a murder case. He asked what kind of a murder case. I told him the defendant stabbed the victim 99 times breaking two butcher knives in the process. The seasoned detective said, "Oh, a sex case, eh?" I replied that the case had nothing to do with sex. He said, "Yes it does." I asked if he was familiar with this case. He said he was not, but he had no doubt this murder had something to do with sex. I insisted that it did not. I told him the homicide report (which we call the "murder book"—usually about three or four inches thick) said nothing about sex. He laughed and said, "You'll see. Call me and tell me when you receive the defendant's rap sheet."

In the 1970s, before computers and faxes, we often did not receive the defendant's rap sheet until after the case was filed. It had to be sent by mail from Sacramento. Somehow I ended up trying this murder case. I say *somehow,* because the DA who files the charges is generally not the DA who tries the case. When I received the defendant's rap sheet, it had a couple of entries indicating he had prior commitments as a sexual psychopath. I called the old homicide detective and told him what the rap sheet revealed. I asked how he could know that sex was involved in this case merely from the number of stab wounds. He said that in his experience, numerous stab wounds indicates extreme rage, which has been characteristic of crimes dealing in some way with sex—often jealousy or rejection. I learned later that the defendant and the victim were homosexuals, and the victim was making a move on the defendant's boyfriend. Like I said, I learned something new nearly every day of my career.

Rap and the Media

Does the media believe that the pro-violence, anti-woman, anti-police, and anti-white lyrics in rap music is a positive influence for our kids? If not, it is a shame the liberal media does not have the courage to criticize it. The reluctance of the media to criticize such negative messages in rap music is more evidence that we are all reluctant to even discuss a subject with racial implications because of our fear of being labeled with the dreaded "R" word. I have a suggestion to the liberal media: If you believe the lyrics in some rap music are damaging some young kids, criticize it. It is the right thing to do. If you are called "racist" by the predictable racial rabble-rousers, few will believe it. To paraphrase Franklin Roosevelt, you have nothing to lose but your fear of violating your self-imposed political correctness.

Violent Videos

I have no doubt young kids who frequently watch ultraviolent video games, showing heads and arms chopped off or blown off and blood spattering everywhere, become desensitized to violence. Some of those who defend allowing young kids to watch these games say, "I watched violent video games when I was a kid and I turned out OK." But these people are missing the point. A kid who grows up in a relatively stable home, with a working, law-abiding parent, or parents, may have enough stability in his life to withstand the negative influence of these games. But a kid who is already on the edge, a kid who lacks the influence of a strong, principled, male role model at home (most of my defendants), and who is exposed to a steady diet of such extreme violence, can be seriously damaged. I have come to this conclusion after reading many probation reports for convicted violent offenders that say the defendant has watched these types of video games since he was a small boy.

I realize the companies who distribute these games to kids make a great deal of money and claim the First Amendment protects them. Perhaps. But I have no doubt these games contribute to an attitude among young kids that extreme violence is just a part of life. It is tragic that the media and the politicians are reluctant to criticize such video games that continue to influence and damage countless impressionable children already on the edge. The video games I am talking about are far more violent than anything seen on TV or at the movies.

My Public Defender Friend, Dave

I learned a good deal about human nature during my years as a deputy DA. In the 1970s, I came to know a public defender named Dave. He was a nice guy and a good lawyer. One day I came to work and discovered that Dave had been murdered the night before during a robbery of bar patrons in Hollywood. I wanted to know the facts of the case. I was able to get a copy of the police report. The bar had been filled with people. The robbers entered displaying guns and ordered everyone to lie on the floor. Everyone complied immediately except Dave. He only delayed for a moment and attempted to reason with the robbers. One of the robbers shot and killed him. None of the other customers in the bar was injured.

I thought I understood what had happened. Dave had been dealing with robbers and murderers for years. He was not intimidated by them. In his dealings with dangerous criminals, as their lawyer, he had always been in control as the authority figure, and the criminals always had to listen to him. When Dave was sitting at the bar, and heard the order shouted by the robbers to get on the floor, Dave was unable to assess the situation quickly enough to realize that this time he was not in control. The robbers were in control. His attempt to reason with them cost him his life.

The Killers and Their Ladies

Every murder trial I had was different. But there was one thread that ran through nearly all of them: The cooperation of the defendant's present or former girlfriend or wife. She was a key factor in arresting or convicting the great majority of all murderers I ever prosecuted. The motives of these women and the kinds of assistance they gave us varied, but I have no doubt there would be far fewer murderers in prison if we had not been assisted by their ladies.

Johnnie Cochran and O.J. Simpson

Ever since the O.J. case, I have met people who were still angry at Johnnie Cochran for getting O.J. off. But what Johnnie Cochran did in the O.J. case is what competent defense attorneys do in criminal cases every day. Their object, as stated previously, is to get their clients off, and they have few legal or ethical limitations. What Johnnie Cochran did in the O.J. case was simply good lawyering.

I had known Johnnie Cochran since the 1960s. For awhile in the late 1970s, he was the Assistant District Attorney, the number three DA in the office—recruited by DA John Van de Kamp. He was more than a competent lawyer. Johnnie Cochran was a *great* trial lawyer. Jurors loved him.

If a defense lawyer believes "playing the race card" will work, I expect him to play the race card. I have seen it many times. The fact that Cochran was able to convince twelve jurors to acquit O.J., despite a mountain of evidence saying he murdered two people, is not uncommon in the criminal courts. But many people were upset because they had never seen it before. They think the O.J. acquittal was an aberration.

As every Club member knows, and as the statistics reveal, jury acquittals of felony defendants, even in very strong cases, are not uncommon. As mentioned, in 2005, of the 1,613 felony defendants who had jury trials in Los Angeles County, our DAs convicted 1,094 or 68%. Remember, DAs refuse to file charges against 30% to 40% of the suspects the police have asked us to charge. And, as mentioned earlier, DAs agree with the police that in nearly all of these rejected cases, the suspects are most likely guilty. In addition, the police do not arrest many suspects they believe have committed felonies if they anticipate a DA rejection. Thus, they avoid needlessly completing the paperwork documenting the arrest, and then more paperwork required for releasing the suspect after the DA rejects the case.

Don't blame Johnnie Cochran for O.J.'s acquittal. He was just very good at what he did—and what the most honorable defense attorney is supposed to do. Inside the Criminal Justice Club, I never met anyone who knew Johnnie Cochran who did not like him and respect him. Having said that, I cannot imagine that Johnnie could have looked me in the eye, held a straight face, and told me he thought O.J. was innocent. After all, Johnnie Cochran was a veteran Club member.

81

"JUSTICE WILL ONLY BE ACHIEVED WHEN THOSE WHO ARE NOT INJURED BY CRIME FEEL AS INDIGNANT AS THOSE WHO ARE."

This is the caption of a poster I had on my DA office wall since the mid-1970s. The poster, painted by Kirwan, shows a dumpster filled with throw-away crime victims labeled with the crimes of rape, robbery, murder, etc. Of course, it is unrealistic to expect those not injured by crime will ever feel as indignant as those who are. Francois La Rochefoucauld, the French author and moralist said, "We all have strength enough to endure the misfortunes of others."

However, if we ever decided that we would no longer tolerate the thousands of murders and other crimes that occur annually, I have no doubt, if we made our voices heard, we could reduce the crime rate substantially. Reducing the crime rate is not just numbers. It must be seen as sparing the suffering and heartache of thousands of victims and their families.

I also have no doubt, if we were serious about fighting crime, and we accorded public safety the high priority it deserves, we could greatly reduce crime without sacrificing fairness and due process for defendants.

If we were really serious about solving rape cases, for example, no police department would have destroyed 1,100 DNA samples in unsolved rape cases without first calling the DA's office to make certain there was no objection.

If we were really serious about fighting crime, we would not have had a backlog of DNA samples from 20,000 unsolved rape cases in California that had not been compared to the statewide DNA database, and a backlog of 287,00 unprocessed DNA samples taken from convicted felons, because of not hiring enough lab techs.

If we were really serious about bringing murderers to justice, we would not tolerate having fingerprints from 6,000 unsolved homicide cases sitting in file drawers which had not been compared with the fingerprints in the national database—simply because LAPD assigned too few clerks to the job.

If we were really serious about solving murders in one of LAPD's highest murder areas, LAPD would not have neglected to include an interrogation room in their newly renovated Southeast police station.

If we were really serious about crime, the Los Angeles Police Department would not hire convicted criminals with multiple felony arrests to become police officers. There are more acceptable alternatives to achieve diversity.

If we were serious about fighting crime, we would not tolerate convicted felons serving only 10%, or less, of the jail sentences pronounced by judges in Los Angeles County.

If we accorded public safety the priority it deserves, our politicians would provide the funds necessary to construct the necessary jails and prisons and adequately staff our police and sheriff departments, especially the homicide units, in Los Angeles city and county. Currently, this is not the case. Public safety should be government's highest priority, as the *Los Angeles Times* told the *Mexican* government; and, it should be nonpartisan.

If we were really serious about fighting crime, we would not tolerate the Los Angeles County Sheriff's unwritten policy of not reporting to the DA incriminating statements made by inmates in the county jail.

If we were serious about fighting crime, we would not tolerate losing the estimated $51 billion (or $85 billion, depending on which estimate is more accurate) to fraudulent medical claims in

2003. We would insist that more medical fraud investigators be hired, and we would launch an all out war on medical fraud. Our governments, both state and federal, and the purchasers of medical insurance, could use these billions of dollars that are now going into the pockets of the crooked lawyers, doctors and chiropractors.

If we were serious about fighting crime, we would not tolerate losing $57 billion dollars in 2005 alone, over $1 billion each week, to identity thieves, and then watch and do nothing as the Democrats in the California legislature kill a bill to strengthen the law against identity theft.

If we were really serious about fighting crime, we could substantially reduce our insurance premiums by adequately funding the fraud-fighting unit of the California Department of Insurance.

If we were serious about curbing fraud in the federal food stamp program, random checks of applications for food stamps could be made. I have no doubt that a significant amount of taxpayers' dollars are helping people buy food who are financially capable of buying their own food.

If we were really serious about fighting crime, our politicians would not have remained silent as illegal aliens, convicted of child molesting and other serious crimes, were released back into the community after serving their sentences, instead of being deported; and, if we were serious about crime, we would tighten our borders and thus avoid booking over six hundred thousand illegal aliens into our nation's jails and prisons each year. Immigration officials told the *L.A. Times* (June 23, 2007) that 632,189 fugitive illegal aliens with criminal records who were arrested, ordered deported, and then released, have ignored the deportation order and remain in this country. How could this happen? Where is the outrage?

If we were really serious about bringing murderers to justice, our government would not have tolerated, for many years, Mexico's refusal to return the estimated three thousand murder suspects who have fled to Mexico. As mentioned, Mexico has refused to return murder suspects to the U.S. to stand trial if the murderer could be sentenced to *either* death *or life in prison*. This Mexican government policy, in which our federal government has acquiesced, has protected all those who have murdered in this country and fled to Mexico. In 2005, the Mexican Supreme Court voted to modify that policy. However, given Mexico's historical reluctance to permit the U.S. to extradite suspected murderers, we can only wait and see whether our DAs will have the full cooperation of the Mexican government. History teaches us that our government must exert continuing pressure on Mexico.

Has the *Los Angeles Times*, in any editorial, ever expressed outrage, or even opposition, to the refusal of Mexico to return suspected murderers to this country for trial? If not, why not? Such an editorial would seem appropriate, given the *Times* editorial telling the Mexican government that public safety should be their highest priority.

The *Los Angeles Times*, on their editorial page, constantly laments gang violence and the ongoing killings and assaults upon innocent victims. But what solutions do they offer? Job training— for career criminals who have no interest in jobs; court orders to defendants to make restitution to the victims for their injuries or their property loss—which, in reality, are unenforceable and will rarely be paid; counseling—which the violent and career criminals consider a joke, and more parks—where gangs can meet and claim the park as their territory. The naiveté of the liberal community seems to know no bounds. They are so mired in the trenches of their liberal philosophy, they refuse to even consider the mountain of evidence showing that such measures will not make our streets safer, but will instead create many more victims by allowing violent and career criminals to remain on the street. Albert Einstein said, "The world is a dangerous place to live, not because of the people who are evil, but because of the people who don't do anything about it."

82

ARE THERE ANY ANSWERS?

Perhaps. With great humility, I offer a few suggestions which are simple in concept but difficult in the follow-through. One is a massive public relations campaign to criticize and hopefully stigmatize fathers who abandon their children. If fathers would remain with their kids, serve as good role models and help to raise them to be responsible, educated, principled adolescents and adults, I have no doubt crime would eventually plummet. However, given the mainstream press' reverence for political correctness and fear of offending, I am not optimistic such a campaign could ever become a reality.

So how do we achieve this grand objective of raising kids to become responsible, educated, principled adolescents and adults? The question reminds me of historian Will Durant's response when asked to define wisdom. He said, "I feel like a droplet of spray, which, proudly poised for a moment on the crest of a wave, undertakes to analyze the sea." Having said that, I offer the following: we need a multi-pronged approach, including more investigation into the role of genetics in the various causes of crime.

We often criticize law-abiding Muslim groups and clerics for not speaking out more forcefully against radical Muslim terrorists. The same could be said about the law-abiding, successful blacks in this country. It would be helpful if there were more successful blacks like Bill Cosby who have the courage to speak out against black crime and emphasize the value of education. Cosby deserves kudos. But what he got was criticism from some blacks and the liberal press. It is understandable why other successful blacks would be reluctant to get involved.

We have an important but simple rule parents can use and reinforce often. It is the Golden Rule. I know, to some it sounds corny and old hat. But the Golden Rule is truly wonderful in its simplicity and so large for its principle: "Treat others the way you would like others to treat you." The best way to teach our kids the concepts of justice and fairness is to teach them again and again and again from near infancy, the Golden Rule. Kids should hear their parents say, "Turn it around" throughout their childhood. "Turn it around," meaning, "Would you like what you are doing to be done to you?" This is a rule that any kid (other than a sociopath) can readily understand and apply in virtually every situation.

The big challenge is to get the parents to practice the rule themselves. Their example speaks a great deal louder to their children than their words. I am under no illusion that the constant references to the Golden Rule and the parent's admonishments to the child to "Turn it around" will have any effect on the true child sociopath. But logic compels the conclusion that it will have a positive influence on some children.

Of course, I expect this suggestion for parents to repeatedly impress the Golden Rule upon their children to be criticized by the liberals and academics as being far too simple a solution for a very, very complicated problem that only the academics can fathom—although they haven't fathomed it yet. I feel strongly that if we started teaching, applying and reinforcing the Golden Rule early enough, first by parents and then by teachers starting in preschool, we would see positive results.

Finally, a March 2005 Rand Corporation study found that universal, quality preschool for 4-year-olds would result in reduced school dropout rates and crime. The study concluded that California would receive back $2.62 for every dollar invested.[9] A follow-up Rand Corp. study, released in December 2005, is more specific. This later study concluded that Los Angeles County would have 3,245 fewer high school dropouts annually and 9,560 fewer criminal cases against juveniles filed each year—a 26% decline.[10] The key is to hire high quality, caring, and enthusiastic teachers. If enough inner-city kids could be reached, this could help break the cycle of basic educational deprivation and counter other negative influences impacting many inner-city kids in their highly impressionable, formative years.

These, of course, are long-term solutions. In the short term, we must look realistically at the recidivism rates and protect the public by keeping violent and career criminals in prison.

83

WHAT I MISS THE MOST— THE CAMARADERIE

The prospect of retirement was difficult because I enjoyed my work. But what I miss most was the camaraderie among the DAs, PDs, private defense attorneys, and the judges. As a calendar deputy representing the People in an assigned courtroom, I worked daily with the same group of two or three PDs from several months up to a year or more.

Late in my career, I tried a three-defendant murder case. The case had been assigned to a courtroom in the city of Pomona, about thirty miles east of Los Angeles, but still in Los Angeles County. The defendants were all charged with robbing and murdering the owner of a jewelry store in the city of Burbank. One of the three defense attorneys was a PD, Paul Enright, later appointed a superior court commissioner. Paul and I had worked together every day in the Pasadena court.

One day, near the end of the trial, I had to drive to Pomona in a blinding downpour. When I arrived at the courthouse parking lot in Pomona, the wind was blowing so hard that it turned my umbrella inside out. When I reached the courthouse I was soaked, but worse than that, while standing in the lobby waiting for the elevator, I discovered that I had left my reading glasses at home. I was lost without them. Just then Paul blew in the door. He was also soaked. I told him I had left my glasses at home. Without hesitation, he headed back through the door into the deluge yelling that he had a pair of glasses in his car that might work. When he returned with the glasses, he was dripping wet. We were set to argue our case before the jury. I was very touched by this act of kindness—from an attorney whose client I was trying to send to prison for life. The glasses worked.

84

THE NEW MEDIA COMPETITION

Our form of government, with its checks and balances, is a product of the founders' understanding of human nature. Each of the three branches of government is designed to have checks on the other two to prevent any one branch from becoming too powerful. And, in California, when the legislative branch has failed to correct injustice by reforming the justice system, the people fortunately have had the final word through the initiative process.

There is only one institution in this country which, up until recently, had no discernable checks: the media. Who is in the position to expose *their* bias and hold *them* accountable for their misleading statements? Again, I cherish freedom of the press, and

I do not want to see it diluted. This book is simply a plea for the media to take the high road and to resist the powerful temptation to use its power to mislead its audience to achieve its objectives. It is a plea to the media, both newspapers and television, to present both sides of important public issues and to present them fairly. Self-restraint exercised by the powerful is elegant. Am I being naïve and unrealistic to even make such a plea in these times when the country is so divided, when half of the country is so angry at the other half and when the great majority of media people are liberal Democrats? The truth is that up until fairly recently, if the media did not police itself, there was no other route to media accountability. But it seems things are changing, and that is one reason I am optimistic

For the first time in my memory, one of the traditional three large broadcast networks, CBS, and its former top news anchor, Dan Rather, were held accountable for recklessly claiming that four memos about President George W. Bush's service in the National Guard were authentic. Mr. Rather was forced to make a public apology. They were held accountable only because of the existence of an expanded media: cable, the internet, and talk radio. The National Guard story was so juicy, so tempting for CBS and Dan Rather, so corroborative of their own bias, that CBS and Rather did not do their homework and ignored early warnings that the memos might be fraudulent. Just a few years back, there would have been little outrage expressed over CBS's false assurances that the allegedly forged memos were authentic, because there was then no outlet for the outrage. Today, cable, the internet, and talk radio are the new channels for giving voice to the people's outrage.

Competition is an essential ingredient in what makes this country work—politically, economically and now, more recently, in the media. The American people are now exposed to a greater variety of ideas and are thus better informed today because of the expanded media and for having more television news choices than just the three large, traditional networks, ABC, CBS, NBC, and also CNN, all of which have a similar political bias: liberal.

85

CLOSING THOUGHTS

I have shown the reader just a glimpse into how often the media mislead us about the criminal justice system. So much false information has been written in newspapers and depicted in movies and television that for many years I've believed someone should debunk the misinformation and tell the people how the system really works. I never thought it would be me. I believe we are sufficiently sophisticated to handle the truth—to paraphrase Jack Nicholson's memorable line in *"A Few Good Men."*

The truth is, at least in Los Angeles County, the criminal justice system is not an unjust, racist system. In my thirty-four years as a prosecutor (as a deputy city attorney and deputy DA), I have never seen a defendant treated more harshly by the DA's office or the courts because of his or her gender or skin color. When I first became a prosecutor, I expected to see racism in our courts and in the prosecutor's office, because I had been taught for many years by my mother, my liberal friends, the ACLU, and the media to believe this.

The findings of a five-year study by the Rand Corporation titled "Predicting Criminal Justice Outcomes: What Matters?" were published in the *Los Angeles Daily Journal*, May 9, 1991. The Rand study concluded, "Neither race nor ethnicity played a role in the conviction and incarceration rates for criminal defendants." But Ramona Ripston, the executive director of the ACLU of Southern California, criticized the conclusions of the Rand study. She said discrimination begins when the charges are filed which, she said, wasn't examined in the Rand study. Ms. Ripston said, "Anyone with practical experience knows that there is discrimination in the criminal justice system."

I once participated in a panel discussion in Santa Monica, California. The subject was the criminal justice system in Los Angeles. I was representing the DA's office. A very hostile, young, liberal defense attorney on the panel told the audience that if an LAPD detective came to the DA's office to file armed robbery charges, whether or not the filing deputy DA alleged the use of the gun, which, at that time, added two years to the sentence, depended upon whether the robber was black or white. It was such an outrageous lie that I could not believe anyone could say this with a straight face. But I had learned as a deputy DA that if the lie is really a whopper, like the cross-dressing defense in the burglary case (see chapter 59), some people might believe it. It is difficult to defend against the big lie.

Of course, I told the audience that the defense attorney was not telling them the truth. But that did not seem a sufficient rebuttal. So I did something that was a bit out of the ordinary. I gave the audience my office number and told them they were all invited to tour our DA Complaint Division and to sit with the many deputy DAs who file felony charges all day. I told the audience they were welcome to talk to the DAs and watch them work with the police detectives. They could then see for themselves how we operate. A few actually called me and I gave them the tour.

People like this angry attorney and Ramona Ripston have a great deal of emotion invested in their charge of racism in the criminal justice system—specifically the DA's office, where they both charged that deputy DAs discriminate in the filing of charges on the basis of race. They seem to have a need to believe it. Putting others down by charging them with racism makes *them* feel superior and special—regardless of the truth of the charge. But do these people *really* believe that DAs in Los Angeles County file more serious charges or sentence enhancements against a suspect if the suspect is black, Hispanic or a woman? Do they *really* believe, even when the evidence of guilt is very strong, that Los Angeles

County DAs would not charge the suspect with a crime or a sentence enhancement if he were a white male?

These charges of racial or gender discrimination in the filing of criminal cases are reckless, ugly, irresponsible and untrue. These false charges do a disservice to the hundreds of quality, ethical attorneys in the Los Angeles County DA's Office, most of whom now are women, about one-third minorities, and about one-third white males. Most of the DAs I know are prosecutors because they get a good deal of satisfaction from representing the People of the State of California and being on the side of crime victims—a great many of whom are also women and minorities.

This is my story. I have never lost my idealism. I have always hated injustice. I detest bullies. As prosecutors, we are guardians of the public trust and, because we are part of a powerful institution, we must guard against any tendency to become arrogant or to become bullies ourselves. On the other hand, we must be aggressive, but always fair, in our pursuit of justice. This may sound corny to some, but I believe it to my core.

I am most fortunate; a high school dropout who became an attorney, and as a deputy DA, never told a jury something I did not really believe. What a rare luxury for a lawyer! Being a Deputy District Attorney for thirty-two years was most honorable and gratifying. The job description of a deputy DA in Los Angeles County is to do the right thing. Who could ask for more from any profession?

MORE ABOUT THE AUTHOR

I was brought up in a politically liberal household. I had no siblings. In the 1930s my father, Marty Lewis, worked as an editor for *Radio Guide Magazine* in Chicago, my birthplace. We moved to New York where we lived for about four years. In the early 1940s, when I was about five, we moved to Hollywood, California. Dad worked at Paramount Pictures as a publicity executive for about ten years. In the early 1950s, he accepted an offer from his old boss at *Radio Guide*, Walter Annenberg, for a position as West Coast representative for a new magazine to be called *TV Guide*. Dad worked for *TV Guide* for over 30 years. Except for the ten years Dad was at Paramount, he worked for Walter Annenberg for nearly his entire working life. Annenberg had been the Ambassador to Great Britain under President Nixon. Dad was so fond of Walter Annenberg that he named me after him. Dad died in 2003, just short of his 99th birthday.

My parents divorced when I was ten. I was raised in part by my maternal grandmother, in part by my maternal uncle and in part by my mother, Ruth Lewis, who was a tall, very beautiful blonde of Scandinavian descent. She was also quite talented. Although she could not read music and never had piano lessons, she was able to play any melody she heard. She was also a terrific dancer and had a fine singing voice. In the 1930s, she was a model. In the 1940s she was an actress under contract with 20th Century Fox. However, she only had small speaking and showgirl parts. For awhile, she was a Hollywood theatrical agent. For a time in the 1950s, she wrote a daily Hollywood gossip column for the now defunct *Los Angeles Daily News*—not the current newspaper with the same name. My mother was fluent in French and Spanish. I inherited neither her musical talent nor her gift for quickly learning languages. At various times in the 1960s and 1970s, she owned several boutique dress shops in Westwood, Beverly Hills, Santa Monica and West Los Angeles. My mom died in 2000, just short of her 85th birthday.

Although my father was rather apolitical, my mother had a good deal of emotion invested in her liberal beliefs. She taught me to believe that everyone is basically good—with the possible exceptions of conservative Republicans, Hitler and Bull Connor— the Birmingham Alabama Commissioner of Public Safety who, in 1963, turned his police dogs loose and firehosed peaceful civil rights demonstrators led by Martin Luther King Jr.

For the most part I attended public schools in Hollywood: one elementary school, Van Ness Avenue; one junior high school, Le Conte; and two high schools, Hollywood and Fairfax. However, for the first and second grades I attended a public school in Harvey, Illinois. At that time, I was living with my mother's parents. My mother lived in Hollywood.

When I was in the eighth grade my mother moved to Paris, France for a couple of years. I was placed in a Seventh-day Adventist boarding school, Newbury Park Academy, about forty miles west of Los Angeles. The teachers, staff, and the kids I met there, were the nicest bunch of people I had ever met. My mother's parents had been lifelong Seventh-day Adventists. Strict Adventists do not believe in eating meat. It is rare to find any Adventist who eats pork. There was no meat served at Newbury Park Academy. I liked eating meat, having grown up eating hamburgers like most kids. So, I would often go AWOL for a few hours and hitchhike into nearby towns to eat a hamburger. Camarillo, about ten miles away, was the closest town.

The first time I ran away from the Academy to eat a hamburger, I hitched a ride into Camarillo. It was 1950. I was 14. There were no fast-food places in those days—only drug store lunch counters. I hadn't had a hamburger since arriving at the

Academy several weeks before. As soon as I got on the stool and ordered a hamburger and a malt, the old man behind the counter said he had not seen me before. He asked if I had run away from Newbury Park Academy. I admitted this was true—but only to eat a hamburger. It was the best hamburger I had ever eaten.

By the time I finished, it was getting dark and it was not as easy hitching a ride back to the school. When I got back it was completely dark. I lived on the second floor of the boys' dorm—which meant I had to walk by the apartment of the boys' dean which was at the foot of the stairs. Upon entering the dorm, I saw that the door to the dean's apartment was open a bit. As I approached, I smelled the unmistakable aroma of cooking lamb coming from his apartment—a big no no! As I started to climb the stairs, as quietly as possible, the boys' dean emerged from his apartment, opening his door wide. "How did you enjoy the hamburger and the malt in Camarillo?" he asked. I couldn't believe it. I was snitched off by that old man behind the counter! "Fine," I replied, "How are you enjoying your lamb?" He just stared at me and I at him. It was checkmate. "Don't let it happen again," he said, as he hurriedly closed his door. I had a lot of hamburgers after that.

My dad would sometimes come to visit me at the Academy. Dad loved beautiful women. On one of his visits, he brought with him his then current girlfriend, movie star Rhonda Fleming. We took a ride in his black Cadillac convertible. All three of us were sitting in the front seat. I was closest to the passenger door. It was a beautiful day, and Dad had the top down. Ms. Fleming had a wonderful singing voice. She was singing along with a song playing on the radio. While I was watching her sing, her long, red hair blowing in the wind, I remember thinking this was the most gorgeous creature I had ever seen. Even at age 14, I had a real appreciation for female beauty. I remember wondering how my dad managed to attract such a woman. He was not what I would call handsome, but he was very charming and had a good sense of humor and a quick wit. He also had an impressive studio position before joining *TV Guide*.

Although Newbury Park Academy was co-ed, there was a no-touching rule. Our one co-ed activity was roller skating once each week in the gym. But there was always a member of the faculty present to enforce the no-touching rule.

All of the students worked in the fields each day after school and on Sundays picking lettuce, celery and other vegetables which the students and faculty ate. We also had a few dairy cows. For Adventists, Sabbath begins at sundown on Friday night and ends at sundown on Saturday. We made 35 cents an hour working in the fields, but we didn't see the money. It was credited against our tuition.

We all did a lot of praying at the school. I remember one sermon where the pastor told us the streets of heaven would be paved with gold. It puzzled me why gold would be valuable in heaven just because we all agreed it was valuable here on earth.

I was scheduled to be baptized, but I couldn't go through with it. Here is what happened: My maternal grandmother had a lady friend going back about 40 years from Harvey, Illinois named Sarah. Sarah was a religious Jew who worked as a waitress at a Jewish delicatessen in Hollywood. I had known her for as long as I can remember. Sarah felt sorry for me being sent to a religious boarding school while my mother lived in Paris. Sarah was then in her 50s and was not in good health. Yet, several times on her days off she visited me at the boarding school. She had to walk about a quarter of a mile from the bus stop to the school. She carried two shopping bags filled with Jewish food she had made the night before. Her Jewish accent was so thick I could sometimes barely understand her. When she arrived at the school the first time, she asked me whether this was some kind of "kettle wrench." It took me a moment to realize she was asking whether this was a cattle ranch. Sarah was my Mother Teresa, cooking for me and sacrificing her one day off to visit me, riding a bus for about 80 miles round trip from her home—and she was not even a blood relative.

In one of the sermons given at the school, the pastor said no person could get into heaven unless he accepted Jesus Christ as his personal Savior and the son of God. I knew Sarah was Jewish and did not believe Jesus was the son of God. I spoke to the pastor about this. I told him about my friend Sarah. I asked him if that meant Sarah had to go to hell. He said if she did not accept Jesus Christ as her personal Savior and the son of God, she would not be allowed to enter the kingdom of heaven and could not be saved.

It had only been five years since the end of World War II. Hitler was still in our thoughts as the embodiment of evil. I asked the pastor, if Hitler had prayed to God and said he was sorry for what he had done, and was sincere in asking God to forgive his sins, and accepted Jesus as his personal Savior and the son of God, whether he could get into heaven. The pastor said if Hitler was really sincere, and God would know this, and asked God to forgive him, and he accepted Jesus Christ as his Savior, Hitler could get into heaven. After the pastor left, I kept thinking of Sarah burning up in hell while Hitler entered the gates of heaven. It continued to bother me. My scheduled baptismal ceremony was approaching.

On the day several of us were to be baptized, we were waiting in line to be dunked in the water. We were all wearing baptismal gowns. As I was moving forward in the line, I became increasingly agitated and conflicted: Sarah goes to hell. Hitler, the murderer of millions, could go to heaven. I got out of line and walked back to the dorm in my gown and got dressed. It seemed so unjust. I could not be a part of it.

After I left the Adventist school, I lived with my uncle Harold, my mother's brother, and his wife and daughter. I attended Louis

Pasteur Junior High in the southwestern part of Los Angeles. I worked in my uncle's gas station every day after school, pumping gas, washing windshields, lubing cars, and doing oil changes. He often took me deep-sea fishing and stream fishing in the High Sierras, and he taught me to drive in his Model A Ford. I owe a lot to my uncle Harold. He had a very earthy sense of humor, was a man's man, and the main adult, male influence in my youth. When my mother returned from Paris, I moved back to Hollywood.

Between my mother's and my father's connections, I met many movie stars. Paramount Pictures was within walking distance of our house in Hollywood. My dad had the run of the studio and would often take me on the movie sets to watch movies being made and introduce me to the stars. My mother also knew many movie people. Perhaps my most memorable, star-studded afternoon occurred when my mother's boyfriend at the time, Sy Bartlett, a Hollywood writer/producer who had just written *12 O'clock High* starring Gregory Peck, took me to Bing Crosby's house, Lana Turner's house, and horseback riding with my all-time favorite, Gregory Peck, and his sons—all in one afternoon. I was about twelve. The only thing I recall from meeting Lana Turner was when her then husband, Bob Topping, walked down from the house to the swimming pool, where we were all sitting, and announced to his wife, "We finally decided. We are going to call them Bon Bons and they will only be sold in movie theaters." Funny the things kids remember.

I have worked since I was about eleven or twelve. I had, at various times, delivered several afternoon newspapers: the *Mirror News*, the *Hollywood Citizen News*, the *Daily News* (not the *Los Angeles Daily News* in business today), and the *Herald Express*—all now defunct. In those days we had to go door to door at the end of the month to collect from each subscriber. That was the worst part of the job. I learned some people don't like to pay what they owe. I also sold newspapers at a Hollywood intersection, Melrose and

Vine—until I was hit by a car. I was knocked down, but was not seriously injured. Nevertheless, my grandmother, who was again caring for me at that time, made me quit.

At various times, I worked as a box boy for two Hollywood markets, delivered horse meat for a pet shop, and worked at two gas stations, a Shell station at the corner of Larchmont and Beverly near my home in Hollywood, and my Uncle Harold's Signal station on West Adams Boulevard. I recently found a little flyer I had distributed throughout my Hollywood neighborhood when I was very young. It said Walter Lewis will mow lawns, run errands, baby-sit, and do odd jobs, and gave my phone number. For several years, through much of high school and into the second year of college, I delivered liquor on the Sunset Strip in West Hollywood at a store called, "The Liquor Locker." I made the minimum wage, $1.10 per hour, plus tips. I delivered liquor to many stars of that era including, Paul Newman (beer only), Boris Karloff, Carol Channing, Art Carney, Marlon Brando and many more. I cannot remember not having a job.

I was a Cub Scout and a Boy Scout. I joined the Air Scouts and took flying lessons. Although I first soloed an airplane at age seventeen, I started and stopped flying lessons so many times, over so many years, that I did not get my pilot's license until 1997.

I attended Hollywood High School but I was often truant and was expelled along with two friends. The three of us then transferred to Fairfax High School a few miles away. After one semester, I quit in my senior year. I was now a high school dropout—a disappointment and an embarrassment for my father. I got a job on the assembly line at a General Motors plant in South Gate, California, a suburb of Los Angeles, where Buicks, Pontiacs and Oldsmobiles were assembled. I worked the night shift, 5:30 p.m. to 2:00 a.m. I rode my motorcycle to work. After about six months of this, I decided I did not want to assemble cars for the rest of my life. I moved from my mother's house into my own very small apartment located directly behind the Grauman's Chinese theater in Hollywood. My rent was $65 per month. I enrolled in the Hollywood High School adult, night-school program where I finally received my high school diploma in June 1956 at age nineteen.

After graduating from high school, I attended Los Angeles City College (LACC). Before being admitted to this two-year junior college, I was required to meet with the school's academic counselor. He looked at my high school transcripts then at me and suggested I go to work instead of school. He told me that, based upon my academic history, there was little chance I would succeed in college. That was the first time anybody had ever told me I couldn't make it. It shook me up quite a bit. I could see he was serious. That is, he wasn't playing a psych game with me. I decided right then that succeeding in college would be akin to a life and death challenge for me. I just could not fail. When I wasn't working on the Sunset Strip delivering liquor, eating, sleeping or in class, I was studying. I remember an occasion when friends came to my door, and I wouldn't open it. I yelled to them that I was studying. I knew if I opened the door, my studying would be over for the night.

I found I could not study at home. I would get hungry or sleepy or the phone would ring, or I would want to watch *just one* TV show. I declared war against all these weaknesses and temptations. I was determined that nothing was going to distract me. I took sandwiches and a thermos of coffee to the college library. But at the library, I was distracted by the attractive girls. I found a place in the library where I could face the wall which prevented me from seeing the girls. At the end of the first semester at LACC, I had a B+ grade average—by far the best grades I had ever achieved. It did not come easy, but in this one semester, I broke a lifelong habit of screwing up in school.

My biggest breakthrough came when I took a speech class at LACC. I had never spoken in front of any group. We had to write our own speeches. I wrote a speech about the First Amendment's guarantee of freedom of expression. It was around this time that I joined the ACLU. I was so nervous when I first got up in class to give the speech I nearly fainted. Everything went blurry, my knees buckled, and I had to hold on to the lectern to keep from falling. But the applause I received at the end of this speech was sweet. My speech professor entered me into the All School Speech Contest. I competed against the top students in other speech classes. I gave this same First Amendment speech again and again and kept placing first. Finally, I made the finals. There were judges from UCLA and USC. I placed second. I still have the trophy—which symbolizes the turning point in my life. After two years at LACC, I transferred to USC and majored in English. I attended Southwestern Law School. Throughout law school, I worked in the afternoons at a one-man, general practice law firm in down-town Los Angeles.

For about six years in the late 1950s and early 1960s my exclusive girlfriend was Terry Karger. Terry's parents had been divorced. Terry's mother, Patti Karger, was a very attractive, smart and tough attorney. Her dad, Freddie Karger, was a successful song writer. His biggest hit was "From Here to Eternity" made popular by Frank Sinatra. My mother had dated Freddie, a very classy, handsome and debonair gentleman. Freddie married Academy Award-winning actress Jane Wyman—twice. He also had had a long-standing relationship with Marilyn Monroe. Terry and Marilyn were close years before Marilyn became a megastar. Marilyn would take Terry, then a preteen, to the beach and would often visit Freddie's mother, Anne, with whom Marilyn developed a very close and enduring relationship.

During the years Terry and I dated, Terry would often talk about Marilyn. I kept telling Terry I wanted to meet her. Terry's grandmother, Anne, lived near Sunset Boulevard and Crescent Heights in West Hollywood, about one block from the Liquor

Locker. One night, while I was working at the store, Terry called in an order to be delivered to her grandmother's apartment. When I arrived at the apartment, Terry opened the door. She said she had a surprise for me. As I walked in with the bag containing the order, Marilyn Monroe walked out of the kitchen where Terry had her hiding.

The three of us sat on the couch and talked for about fifteen minutes. Although Marilyn was gorgeous, my dominant impression of her was her sweetness and vulnerability. I remember very little of what we said, but I do remember this: Marilyn told me there was something she had never told Terry, and she thought this would be a good time to tell her. Marilyn said she had always been a little envious of Terry's legs. Pointing to Terry, but looking at Marilyn, I replied, "*You* are envious of *her* legs?" Terry hit me in the upper arm with her fist. Marilyn was the opposite of the kind of woman who had always attracted Freddie: strong, assertive women like Patti Karger, Jane Wyman and my mother, Ruth Lewis.

I'm sure my attitude toward gays was largely influenced by my mother's liberalism, the fact that I lived in Hollywood, and that so many people in the entertainment industry are gay. Because my mom had been a Hollywood gossip columnist, I learned which stars were gay long before most of the public. Few people "came out" and declared themselves to be gay in those days. But the biggest influence that helped determine my early acceptance of gays as a fact of life was my exposure to so many gays to whom I delivered liquor around the Sunset Strip in the 1950s.

It was then a felony in California for two consenting adults of the same sex to have sex. When I was about 17, I remember delivering wine regularly to two middle-aged lesbians who had lived together for many years. They took a liking to me and wouldn't let me leave until I ate some homemade cookies or other pastries. They also encouraged me to read and would even lend me books and made me promise to read them. They were always very kind to me, and I thought of them the same as I would any other older, married couple.

I recall discussing these two women with my mom. I remember her saying they were breaking the law and could be sent to prison for what they were doing. Her objective, of course, was to persuade me how unjust the law was that would send two nice women to prison, women who loved each other and were hurting nobody. I decided then that the government should have no say in what these two women, or any consenting adults, do in the privacy of their bedrooms. It amazes me that it took the U.S. Supreme Court about 50 more years before they came to the same conclusion.

I took the California Bar Exam in August 1964. I didn't learn I passed until late November, the month Americans were to make a choice for President between Barry Goldwater and Lyndon Johnson. I was so concerned about the possibility Barry Goldwater might win that, while waiting for bar results, I wrote an eleven-page pamphlet titled *What is Barry Goldwater Really Like*? The pamphlet was a compilation of Senator Goldwater's voting record and his verified quotes on the issues of the day.

In 1964, President Johnson pushed through Congress the most far-reaching civil rights bill in our history. The bill passed by a large margin in the U.S. Senate with 67 percent of Democrats and 75 percent of Republicans supporting the bill. Goldwater voted against it.

Goldwater's quoted remarks were often quite radical and irresponsible. On October 25, 1963, he told the *Washington Post* that "NATO commanders should be authorized to use tactical nuclear weapons on their own initiative."

On the issue of Social Security, Goldwater, on January 22, 1964, while campaigning in Keene, New Hampshire, stated, "I think we would be better off with Social Security as a voluntary setup. Many people can buy better policies today in private companies than the government can provide."

With respect to the issue of school integration, Goldwater wrote in his book, *Conscience of a Conservative*, "I am not impressed by the claim that the Supreme Court's decision on school integration [*Brown v Bd. of Education, 1954*] is the law of the land."

In July 1963, Goldwater told the *U.S. News and World Report* that "It may be just or wise or expedient for Negro children to attend the same schools as white children, but they do not have a civil right to do so which is protected by the federal Constitution or which is enforceable by the federal government."

I recall two bumper stickers from the Johnson/Goldwater campaigns. The Goldwater bumper sticker read, "In your heart you know he's right." The Democrats responded with, "In your guts you know he's nuts."

I was so alarmed by the thought of Goldwater becoming President that I begged and borrowed enough money to print and distribute 10,000 of my pamphlets. I mailed them only to Republicans in and around what was then a very conservative area, Glendale, California. I received a good deal of hate mail.

On October 4, 1964, the *Los Angeles Times* endorsed Barry Goldwater for President. The *Times* stated in its editorial that "We...strongly recommend the election of the Republican Party's candidate for President, Barry Goldwater." The *Times* concluded its editorial by saying, "The *Times* believes Barry Goldwater deserves the support and the votes of all moderates and all conservatives of both parties."

The *Times'* editorial in support of Goldwater was not the only editorial in the November 1964 election that angered and energized me. On October 18, 1964, the *Los Angeles Times* endorsed Proposition 14, an initiative designed to repeal the recently enacted Rumford Fair Housing Act, which had outlawed discrimination in the sale or rental of housing in California. Prop 14 would permit a property owner to refuse to rent or sell to a person *solely* because of the person's skin color. Prop 14 passed by a vote of almost 2 to 1, but was later declared unconstitutional by both the California and the U.S. Supreme Courts.

I have no doubt the *Times* would not endorse Barry Goldwater or Prop 14 today. I only mention these endorsements because it marked the start of my differences with the *Los Angeles Times*. Also, it was these two issues, the prospect of a Goldwater presidency, and Prop 14's attempt to legalize racial discrimination in California housing, that infused fire into my liberalism.

Reflecting back on my youth and my commitment to liberalism, my movement towards conservatism was slow and sometimes uncomfortable, because I had so much emotion invested in my liberal philosophy. It was like a religion. I *knew* I was right. But my conversion was forced by having to face the truth, at least with respect to the criminal justice system. And the truth was that my beliefs, which I thought were "progressive" and "compassionate," resulted in a good deal of pain and heartache for crime victims. It was inevitable that, as a career deputy DA, my former beliefs in the media-created myths would give way to reality in light of my experiences. Thomas Sowell (see Chapter 22) said, "Despite the warm glow of self-satisfaction that the liberal vision confers on liberals, ugly facts keep intruding to undermine that vision. Some liberals eventually jump ship and defect to conservatism when the facts keep piling up too high to ignore."[11]

My vision and my plea is for a more honest, fair and unbiased media; for fathers to stop abandoning their children and become good role models for them; for parents to teach and reinforce in their children the Golden Rule, starting when the child is first able to understand the concept of "turn it around" (see Chapter 82); and for the voters to demand that violent and career criminals, including so-called nonviolent, white-collar criminals who make their living committing fraud, not be released repeatedly after short periods of incarceration. If this vision were to become reality, not only would we save billions of dollars now going into the pockets of criminals, but large numbers of people would be spared becoming crime victims.

ACKNOWLEDGMENTS

Many people have permitted me to use excerpts from their writings, for which I am grateful. In particular, I thank Professor Joseph Bessette, former Acting Director of the United States Bureau of Justice Statistics, and currently professor of government and ethics at Claremont McKenna College. Professor Bessette permitted me to use excerpts from his 1992 *Los Angeles Times* op-ed piece titled "Crime, Maybe a Little Punishment." He also gave generously of his time to update criminal justice statistics that appeared in that op-ed piece.

I thank Los Angeles County District Attorney Steve Cooley for making available DA statistics and for the cooperation of his deputies, Sharon Matsumoto, Carolyn Nakaki and Pricilla Musso. I also thank USC Law School Professor Susan Estrich for permitting me to use excerpts from her 1994 *Los Angeles Times* op-ed piece titled "Defense Lawyers and Truth: Just Where Do They Meet." My thanks also go to psychology Professor Roy F. Baumeister for permitting me to use excerpts from his 2005 op-ed piece in the *Los Angeles Times* titled "The Lowdown on High Self-Esteem"; to author Jan Golab for permitting me to use excerpts from his 2005 piece published in the *American Enterprise* magazine titled "How Racial P.C. Corrupted the LAPD"; to psychologist Paul Berg, Ph.D. for permitting me to publish his views on crime victims who feel the need to befriend their victimizers, published in a *Los Angeles Times Magazine* story titled "The Ultimate Forgiveness" April 2004; to Professor John Lott Jr. Ph.D. for permitting me to use excerpts from his 2004 speech to the National Leadership Seminar titled "A Case Study in Bias"; to Thomas Sowell, Ph.D., for permitting me to use excerpts from a May 2005 *Townhall.com* article he authored titled "Liberals, Race and History." Thanks also to author Shelby Steele for permitting me to use excerpts from his 1999 essay in *Harpers* magazine titled "The Age of White Guilt and the Disappearance of the Black Individual."

Many people have read my manuscript and offered valuable editing suggestions, including my wife Barbara, my daughter Jennifer, my cousin Preston, retired Los Angeles County Deputy DA George Palmer, Geraldine Glidden, Aaron Van Etten, Carolyn Porter, Alan Gadney, Ernie Weckbaugh and Penny Alfonso.

Thanks also to Karen Ross who designed both the cover and the interior of the book, and to Todd Meisler who helped me prepare the manuscript and the cover for the printer.

I am very grateful and I thank you all for your help in getting this book edited and published.

APPENDIX

Notes from chapters 1 through 12

1. "Serial Killings Suspect in La. Found Guilty," *L.A. Times*, August 11, 2004

2. *United States v Wade* (1966) 388 U.S. 218, 256

3. "Defense Lawyers and Truth: Just Where Do They Meet?" *L.A. Times*, August 7, 1994

4. *U.S v Swanson 943 F.2nd 1070* (9th Cir.1991)

5. "In Rape Cases, Who's on Trial?," *L.A. Times*, July 6, 2004

6. "Punishing Start for the Freed," *L.A.Times*, August 16, 2004

7. "L.A. Attorneys Divided on Ashcroft Directive," *L.A. Times*, October 17, 2003

8. *Associated Press Stylebook and Libel Manual* (1992 edition)

9. "Talking To Police Limits Defense, Experts Say," *L.A. Times*, June 23, 1994

10. "4 Plead Not Guilty in Slaying of West Hills Boy," *L.A. Times*, August 26, 2000

11. "Youth No Protection From Bloodshed in 2000," *L.A. Times*, January 1, 2001

12. "Jurist Decries Death Row Backlog," *L.A. Times*, May 1, 2006

13. "Judge Hands Out the Max," *Glendale News-Press*, September 4-5, 2004

14. *California Penal Code*, section 193 (b)

15. "Media Bias Against Guns," speech delivered May 25, 2004, reprinted in September 2004 edition of *Imprimis*

16. *California Penal Code*, section 4019

17. "County Let 119,577 Out of Jail Early," *L.A. Times*, November 25, 2004

18. "Suspect in 3 Deaths Left Jail Early," *L.A. Times*,
    January 17, 2005

19. *California Penal Code*, section 1192.7(c)

20. *California Penal Code*, section 667.5 (c)

21. "Three Strikes Law Hits Target," *L.A. Times*,
    September 28, 2004

22. "Life on a New Track Could be Derailed by Sentencing
    Dispute," *L.A. Times*, March 31, 2004

Notes from chapters 13 through 24

1. Professor Bessette's statistical sources: The 1988 data are from
   BJS, *Felony Sentences in State Courts, 1988*. The 2002 data are
   from the same report for 2002;
   http://www.ojp.usdoj.gov/bjs/abstract/fssc02.htm
   Additional data for prison inmates released in 1988 and 2001
   are from *BJS National Corrections Reporting Program*, for 1988
   and 2001. Both the 1991 and 1997 data are from *BJS,
   Correctional Populations in the United States*, 1997, Table 4-10, at
   http://www.ojp.usdoj.gov/bjspub/pdf/cpus9704

2. California Research Bureau; "The Changing Role of Probation
   in California's Criminal Justice System"; also, "California's
   New Probation Subsidy," by Gerald W. Smith, *Journal of the
   California Probation, Parole and Correctional Assoc.*

3. L.A. County District Attorney's Office statistics—1976

4. "Probation Subsidy Repeal Effort Fails," *L.A. Times*,
   August 5, 1976

5. "The Changing Role of Probation in California's Criminal
   Justice System," by Marcus Nieto, May 1996, California
   Research Bureau, California State Library

6. *People v Zimmerman* (1984) 36 Cal.3d 154

7. "Despite Gains, Prosecution of Rape Still a Tough Task,"
   L.A. Times, July 23, 2004

8. "The DNA Sexual Assault Justice Act of 2002," *Senate Report* 107-334

9. "Taking the Initiative on '04 Ballots," *L.A. Times*, January 11, 2004

10. "Death Penalty: No on 7," *L.A. Times*, October 16, 1978

11. *California Penal Code*, section 190.2

12. "Three-Strikes Law Hits Its Target," *L.A. Times*, September 28, 2004

13. Florida Department of Law Enforcement, State DNA Database Statistics, Tallahassee, Florida

14. "DNA in "Minor" Crimes Yields Major Benefits in Public Safety," U.S. Department of Justice, Office of Justice Programs, National Institute of Justice, November 2004

15. "Prison Life, Parole Touch High Level of Young Blacks," *L.A. Times*, November 2, 1990

16. AP story by Karyn Hunt, February 13, 1996, reporting a study by the Center on Juvenile and Criminal Justice

17. *California Penal Code*, section 1203.065

18. *California Welfare and Institutions Code*, section 6300, Sec 4

19. *California Penal Code*, section 136.1

Notes from chapters 25 through 36.

1. "State Prisons' Revolving Door—A Siege Against Success," *L.A. Times* Editorial, November 23, 2003; 2005 CDC&R statistics; Report of Little Hoover Commission, titled "Back to the Community: Safe and Sound Parole Reforms," press release November 13, 2003

2. Ibid, Report of Little Hoover Commission

3. "Inmates Losing Space as Prisons Add Bunks," *L.A. Times*, July 28, 2004

4. "More Killers Gaining Parole," *L.A. Times*, September 18, 2004

5. "Panel to Probe Prison System," *L.A. Times*, March 6, 2004

6. *California Health and Safety Code*, section 1210.1

7. "Evaluation of the Substance Abuse and Crime Prevention Act," 2003 Report, Chapter 7: Treatment, Completion and Duration, by UCLA; issued September 23, 2004

8. "Horrors Should Remain Horrific," *L.A. Times*, January 11, 2004

Notes from chapters 37 through 48

1. "Study Urges Harder Line Early in Criminal's Career," *Los Angeles Daily Journal*, September 6, 1977

2. "The Stanford Prison Experiment: A Simulation Study of the Psychology of Imprisonment," http://www.prisonexp.org

3. "D.A. John Van de Kamp, Guest Lecturer," printed in the *Barrister*, February 14, 1978

4. "Fingerprints Unchecked in 6,000 Death," *L.A. Times*, February 10, 2003

5. "Detective's Diligence Pays Off," *L.A. Times*, October 26, 2004

6. "Mortal Wounds: Getting Away With Murder in South L.A.'s Killing Zone; Unsolved Homicide Cases Stack Up Relentlessly Throughout The City's Urban Core," *L.A. Times*, January 1, 2004

7. AP story by Vickie Smith, September 6, 2003

8. *Sourcebook of Criminal Justice Statistics Online*; also, www.abmc.gov and www.infoplease.com

Notes from chapters 49 through 60

1. "Man Sentenced in Mexico for 2 U.S. Killings," *L.A. Times*, January 10, 2003

2. Ibid

3. "Marchers Want Changes in U.S.-Mexico Extradition Pact," *L.A. Times*, May 9, 2004

4. "Sanctuary Laws Stand in Justice's Way," *L.A. Times*, January 19, 2004

5. Ibid

Notes from chapters 61 through 85

1. "Death Upheld for Crips Founder," *L.A. Times*, September 11, 2002

2. Los Angeles County District Attorney's Office, Auto Insurance Fraud Division statistics

3. Ibid

4. California Department of Insurance statistics

5. National Health Care Anti-Fraud Association

6. *Los Angeles Times*, March 12, 2005

7. *California Penal Code*, section 992

8. *California Penal Code*, section 1203 (k)

9. *Rand/The Costs and Benefits of Universal Preschool in California*, March 2005 www.rand.org/publications

10. "Report Touts Advantages of Preschool," *L. A. Times*, December 15, 2005

11. "Preserving a Vision: Part IV," www.Townhall.com, June 5, 2006

INDEX

Additional copies of **The Criminal Justice Club** by Walt Lewis are available from the publisher:

Walbar Books
2029 Verdugo Blvd. #726
Montrose, CA 91020

Email: walbarbooks@earthlink.net
Websites: www.walbarbooks.com, or
www.criminaljusticeclub.net

The Criminal Justice Club (ISBN: 0-9787870-0-5) is $28.95 for hardbound edition, plus $4.95 for shipping and handling, plus applicable sales tax for California orders.

See website for quantity discount schedule.